EXCHANGE *and the* MAIDEN

Marriage in Sophoclean Tragedy

EXCHANGE

and the

MAIDEN

KIRK ORMAND

UNIVERSITY OF TEXAS PRESS

Austin

An earlier version of Chapter 5 was published as "Silent by Convention? Sophocles' Tekmessa," *American Journal of Philology* 117 (1996): 37–46.

LIBRARY OF CONGRESS
CATALOGING-IN-PUBLICATION DATA

Ormand, Kirk, 1962–
    Exchange and the maiden : marriage in Sophoclean tragedy / Kirk Ormand. — 1st ed.
        p.   cm.
    Includes bibliographical references and indexes.
    ISBN 0-292-76051-5 (alk. paper). — ISBN 0-292-76052-3 (pbk. : alk. paper)
        1. Sophocles — Political and social views.   2. Literature and society — Greece — Athens — History.   3. Domestic drama, Greek — History and criticism.   4. Women and literature — Greece — Athens — History.   5. Sophocles — Characters — Women.   6. Marriage in literature.   7. Tragedy.   I. Title.
PA4417.O65   1999
882'.01 — dc21   98-41684

For GAYLE *and* KEVIN

CONTENTS

ACKNOWLEDGMENTS   *ix*

JOURNALS AND THEIR ABBREVIATIONS   *xi*

Introduction   MARRIAGE AND TRAGEDY   *1*

Chapter 1   THE SEMANTICS OF GREEK MARRIAGE   *9*

Chapter 2   MALE HOMOSOCIAL DESIRE IN THE *Trachiniae*   *36*

Chapter 3   ELECTRA, NEVER A BRIDE   *60*

Chapter 4   FAMILY MATTERS IN THE *Antigone*   *79*

Chapter 5   THE *Ajax*, OR MARRIAGE BY DEFAULT   *104*

Chapter 6   NATURE AND ITS DISCONTENTS IN THE *Oedipus tyrannus*   *124*

Epilogue   EXIT TO SILENCE   *153*

NOTES   *163*

BIBLIOGRAPHY   *195*

GENERAL INDEX   *207*

INDEX OF PASSAGES CITED   *217*

ACKNOWLEDGMENTS

A work like this one necessarily has a long history. The current volume began life as a doctoral dissertation nearly ten years ago, and since then has been through countless changes of state. Along the way, numerous people have contributed to whatever good and useful is included here.

My thanks, then, to my dissertation committee, Marsh McCall, David Konstan, and Rush Rehm, for their patience, tact, helpful comments, sound criticisms, and words of encouragement.

Georgia Nugent, David Halperin, Helene Foley, Karen Bassi, Page duBois, Darice Birge, and Brian Lavelle read early drafts of chapters and provided many useful suggestions. Paul Rehak deserves special mention for going out of his way to help me with the manuscript and with my career in general—an ideal colleague in every way.

Nancy Sorkin Rabinowitz read the full manuscript in a much earlier state, and her suggestions are responsible for innumerable improvements. Laura Slatkin and Peter Rose read the full manuscript in its penultimate form, and provided sharp observations, inspiring comments, and kind encouragement. Two anonymous referees for Oxford University Press and Cornell University Press also contributed considerably to the book's current form (though I suspect they will still disagree heartily with what is printed here).

Victoria Wohl and Laurel Bowman were very kind in allowing me to read their excellent works previous to publication, and in providing me with encouragement and comments at a crucial point in the history of the manuscript.

My editor at the University of Texas Press, Jim Burr, has kept me from making numerous errors, and has been a delight to work with. Special thanks must also go to the copyeditor, Sherry Wert, for tirelessly cleaning up my prose and improving the manuscript in ways that I never imagined.

As always, I must emphatically state that the people named above cannot be held responsible for the errors that are contained in what follows. On countless occasions, people who knew better tried hard to keep me out of trouble, and I refused to listen.

Acknowledgment must also go to institutions: my thanks to The Johns Hopkins University Press for allowing me to reprint, in somewhat revised form, my article on the *Ajax* as Chapter Five. This article (and the chapter that appears here) was funded in part by a summer research leave from Loyola University–Chicago. Epic Systems (a medical software company) has provided me with a means to earn a living for the past year. At the same time, the Institute for Research in the Humanities at the University of Wisconsin–Madison has generously provided me with facilities and library access to continue my research.

Most importantly, my love and thanks go to my partner, Gayle Boyer, and my son, Kevin. They have suffered far too long with this work, and I can offer little in repayment for their patience, understanding, and support.

LIST OF JOURNALS AND
THEIR ABBREVIATIONS

AJAH	American Journal of Ancient History
AJP	American Journal of Philology
BICS	Bulletin of the Institute of Classical Studies
C&M	Classica et Mediaevalia
CJ	Classical Journal
Cl. Ant.	Classical Antiquity
CPhil.	Classical Philology
CQ	Classical Quarterly
GRBS	Greek, Roman, and Byzantine Studies
ICS	Illinois Classical Studies
JHS	Journal of Hellenic Studies
JRS	Journal of Roman Studies
LCM	Liverpool Classical Monthly
PCPS	Proceedings of the Cambridge Philological Society
Rev. Ét. Grec.	Revue des études grecques
TAPA	Transactions of the American Philological Association
UCPCP	University of California Publications in Classical Philology
YclS	Yale Classical Studies
ZPE	Zeitschrift für Papyrologie und Epigraphik

Introduction MARRIAGE AND TRAGEDY

> *In Morris Zapp's view, the root of all critical error was a naïve*
> *confusion of literature with life. Life was transparent, litera-*
> *ture opaque. Life was an open, literature a closed system.*
> *Life was composed of things, literature of words. Life was what*
> *it appeared to be about:* . . . *if you were trying to get a girl*
> *into bed it was about sex. Literature was never about what it*
> *appeared to be about, though in the case of the novel consider-*
> *able ingenuity and perception were needed to crack the code*
> *of realistic illusion* . . . *it was surprising how many people*
> *thought that Jane Austen's novels were about finding Mr. Right.*

> DAVID LODGE, *Changing Places*

Marriage is not natural. It is an ideology, in the Marxist sense of the word.[1] That is, marriage operates as a normative structure of society (in Althusser's term, as an "ideological state apparatus") and ensures the continuation of that society. Like all ideology, it "interpellates," or "hails" individuals as "subjects"; that is, it defines roles for individuals at the same time that it validates those roles as real, important, and natural. Althusser explains the idea of interpellating the subject with the analogy of hailing an individual on the street: "The hailed individual will turn round. By this mere one-hundred-and-eighty-degree physical conversion, he becomes a *subject*. Why? Because he has recognized that the hail was 'really' addressed to him, and that 'it was really him who was hailed' (and not someone else)."[2] In this formulation, the creation of subjects is curiously both active and passive, a concept that Althusser explains through his punning use of the word "subject." The individual is clearly "subject to" a variety of social forces that "hail" him or her to diverse subject positions. He or she is constructed by the act of hailing. At the same time, however, the "subject" is active in that he or she turns around by him/herself, must actively recognize that "the hail was 'really' addressed to him." This is the ultimate goal, then, of ideology: to create subjects that act "all by themselves."[3]

Marriage can also "hail" an individual, who then recognizes that he/she "really is" the person who was called. Take, for example, the following literary act of identification from Sophocles' *Trachiniae*:

Αγ.	οὗτος, βλέφ' ὧδε. πρὸς τίν' ἐννέπειν δοκεῖς; ...
Λι.	πρὸς τὴν κρατοῦσαν Δηάνειραν, Οἰνέως
	κόρην, δάμαρτά θ' Ἡρακλέους, εἰ μὴ κυρῶ
	λεύσσων μάταια, δεσπότιν τε τὴν ἐμήν.

Messenger:	You, look here. To whom do you think you are speaking? . . .
Lichas:	I speak to Deianeira, who holds power, the daughter
	of Oineus and wife of Heracles. Unless I am not seeing
	straight, [I speak to] my mistress.[4] (402–7)

Deianeira's identity, as well as the fact that she partakes of a certain authority, is expressed and determined by her marriage to Heracles. In Althusser's terms, her marriage "represents the imaginary relation of an individual to his [or her] real conditions of existence."[5] To say that she is Heracles' wife (and Oineus's daughter) is a way of representing her social status as well as her relations to particular families. As other sections of the drama demonstrate, her marriage also creates and validates a social status for her son, Hyllus. As her legitimate male offspring, he will inherit Heracles' social standing and property. To say that marriage is ideology is not, therefore, to imply that it is not real. Deianeira really is the wife of Heracles, and she really is the *despotis*. Rather, marriage is ideology because there is nothing about Deianeira that makes her intrinsically the wife of Heracles, and *despotis* of Lichas. Her marriage, to borrow Zizek's formulation of ideology, is "an 'illusion' which structures [her] effective, real social relations and thereby masks some insupportable, real, impossible kernel."[6]

It is particularly useful to speak of marriage in ancient Greece as ideology, moreover, because it exists specifically in practice.[7] As we shall see, it is surprisingly difficult at times to determine whether or not two Athenians are married. Evidence brought up in legal cases usually involves hearsay references to various material practices: wedding banquets, the introduction of the new wife to the phratry, the presentation of children as legitimate, etc.[8] Being married in fifth-century Athens, it turns out, depended primarily on acting as if one were married. While this is still true in most modern Western societies (e.g., our notion of "common-law" marriages), we tend to think of marriage as a state of being that is supportable by legal documents. In Athens, or at least in the imagination of Athenian jurists, the boundary between married and not married was much more fluid, and dependent specifically on the couple behaving in the appropriate manner in a variety of social contexts.[9] This book explores the way that Sophocles uses and represents these legal and social definitions in his dramas.

One of the great problems of cultural studies, of course, has been the difficulty of showing exactly what relation artistic productions bear to the material conditions that they represent.[10] This difficulty is especially keen in dealing with Greek tragedy: it has long been recognized that the women of fifth-century Athenian drama play a more active and public role than did their "real" counterparts.[11] In part this is due to the fact that tragedy typically takes the private affairs of individual households and makes them public, putting them onstage. But why should the family be the favored site of tragedy? Aristotle (*Poetics* 1453b) suggests that conflict between enemies or between people with no link between them will not create a sensation of pity.[12] Only conflicts between family members fulfill this requirement of the genre. While his pronouncement may be correct, it takes for granted the structure of kin-relations as a background for the problems of the plays. Aristotle does not suggest that those relations might actually *be* the problem.

Recent feminist scholars have gone a step farther by discussing the ways in which tragedy uses the hierarchy of gender in ancient Greece as a literary device. They productively suggest that the gender conflict in ancient tragedy stands in for various other conflicts in the Athenian state: humans versus gods, private versus public, past versus present, etc.[13] Though under no illusions about the constructed nature of gender roles, these readings ultimately analyze male-female relations in tragedy only to displace their meaning elsewhere. Because of the apparently natural asymmetry of power in gender relations, gender seems an obvious analogue for other such asymmetries. Woman becomes a code for social inferiority.

While I am sympathetic to this last approach (and indeed make considerable use of it), I also wish to take a more literal stance. I do not suggest that the picture of women in the tragedies is an undistorted mirror of real life. Indeed, it has been argued that the marriages in tragedy have little to do with Athenian marriages. After all, most tragedy does not take place in Athens, and Sophocles is most famous for the perverted marriages of the notorious Theban house of Laius. As Zeitlin has argued, Thebes in these plays is an "other" of Athens,[14] and Seaford points out that the destruction of the aristocratic family, which these plays represent, is necessary for the establishment of a *polis* cult (an Athenian concern).[15] If Thebes is a distorted reflection of Athens, however, it is important to emphasize the reflection as well as the distortion. Taken as pure morality tales set in distant locales, Sophocles' dramas provide us with fairly banal teachings about marriage: "Do not kill your husband, exile his son, and marry his enemy. Do not get too attached to your brother. Do not, under any circumstances, marry your mother." More interesting is to note that these plays are engaging social and legal tensions that existed in Athens at the time of their production. In the institution of the *epiklēros*, for example, Athenian marriage law demonstrates a tension between the practices of endogamy (marriage within a social group) and exogamy (marriage outside a social group), arguably the same tension dramatized in the *Antigone*.[16]

In fact, we know that marriage as an institution underwent important changes at this time. In 451/50, Pericles persuaded the Athenian assembly to pass legislation to the effect that only children of two citizens would be citizens.[17] Patterson has argued that Pericles' legislation essentially made civic membership analogous to family membership.[18] Obviously this carries important ramifications in the political arena. But it also creates new requirements for family life. By the fourth century, an Athenian man could get into serious difficulty for marrying a foreign woman, if a neighbor thought he was passing her or her offspring off as Athenian.[19] This made citizen women more valuable, as the potential producers of citizen children, and we expect to see a corresponding rise in concern over the sexual accessibility of women. As it turns out, both legal and literary texts demonstrate considerable anxiety over the issue of women's fidelity.[20] In civic terms, marriage became a way to define citizen status — it hailed individuals, in other words, as citizens. It should perhaps not surprise us, then, that so many dramas deal with crises within marriage. These are exactly the crises that became important as marriage became a defining factor of Athenians' most treasured subject-status.

We find exploration of familial crisis in various artistic media. Sutton has extensively studied the male-female interaction on red-figure vases, and he finds an important trend throughout the fifth century: later pots seem to show a greater degree of mutual feeling, of what we might call romance.[21] Husbands frequently turn backward to look at their (possibly frightened) brides in a gesture of concern. Simply put, this evidence suggests that some portion of Athenian society was becomingly increasingly interested in the notion of reciprocal feeling in marriage. We know that marriages were often arranged, and that the bride's feelings might not have been of prime concern in creating a match. But Sutton's findings suggest that mutual attraction and consideration were increasing in social value.[22]

In the fifth century we also see a shift in metaphors that literary texts used to describe women's role in marriage. DuBois has studied a series of such metaphors, and she finds that in sixth-century lyric, the typical image associated with woman is the uncultivated field. Fertilized by rain in an entirely natural process, such a field spontaneously grows food for humankind.[23] In the fifth century, however, and especially in tragedy, we see a marked increase in the use of the image of the ploughed furrow. Women, it seems, must now be cultivated, do not produce spontaneously.[24] Such a finding is entirely consistent with the notion that *citizen* brides were becoming more valuable as objects of social exchange. In the fifth century, marriage needed to take on the aspect of producing culture, and so reproduction within marriage is increasingly depicted as a civilizing act.

Seen in this light, tragedy itself also functions as ideology, not in the sense of crude propaganda, but in the sense stated above: as a material practice that represents and performs Athenians' "imaginary relation to the real conditions of their existence." That is, tragedy formulates marriage (among other structures) in terms that make it a necessary and natural component of the *polis*, and in terms that create appropriate subjectivities for the men and women involved in the marriage transaction. Particularly fruitful for discussions of gender roles, moreover, tragedy is a specialized form of ideology, in that it performs its work not only through representation (as do all ideologies), but also through the representation of other ideological structures (marriage, funerals, class, etc.)—that is, through representing other representations. In so doing, it may distort those other structures in keeping with the tragic mode. Requirements of genre affect the depiction of characters and situations, as does the fact that individual poets were engaged in a public competition. Apparent valorization of unacceptable principles could result in a poor showing for the poet.[25] We cannot, therefore, assume that the sort of marriage that takes place in tragedy corresponds to a real marriage in any given particular. Indeed, Seaford has shown that tragic weddings tend to emphasize the "negative element" of whatever image is used to describe the event.[26]

These difficulties notwithstanding, it is useful to analyze the way that tragedy portrays marriage, because tragedy and marriage are, in important ways, analogous ideological structures. Cultural representations of marriage (including the wedding ceremony itself) typically focus on the bride's supposed experience: texts emphasize the bride's feelings as she occupies a new social position, and as she becomes part of another *oikos*. We hear that she must establish her relationships within this new household, and establish power relations between herself and her husband. At the same time, the structure of the wedding ritual suggests that the woman adopts a new identity, and the language that describes her status changes. In short, our texts present the wedding as the woman's "rite of passage" into the adult world.[27] The ritual appears to focus on the woman's subjectivity.

In a similar way, tragedy, and especially Sophoclean tragedy, purports to show the personal experience of women, even as it gives them unusual privilege: female characters act and speak out of doors without escort in a way that would be unacceptable in normal Athenian practice. These two ideologies are exactly parallel, moreover, in the way that this momentary subjecthood is circumscribed. As we shall see, marriage contains female desire and the shifting female subject in a structure of economic transfer between two men. Women's desire, though posited as necessary, becomes a reflection of masculine culture and values. In a similar way, the "women" in tragedy who speak and act so boldly cannot be taken as real women. Rather, these "women" (who were played by men) represent an idea of femininity created by and for the male citizen-subject; ultimately they demonstrate nothing so much as what men fear and desire, paradoxical as the representation may be. As a result, these "women's" actions are contained by the male characters in the drama just as the drama itself contains these dangerous or wrong-headed women within the ritual space of the Athenian dramatic festival.[28]

Nevertheless, such attempts at depicting female subjectivity clearly reveal something about the imagination of the Athenian (male) public and the way that Athens used myth to create and justify its mode of social organization. Specifically, Sophocles' tragedies often have difficulty expressing women's experience of desire, and in some rare cases emphasize this very difficulty. We can look to those difficulties, those gaps in meaning, to understand Athens's concern and anxiety over what women experienced and thought. Such issues often come to light most clearly, as one would expect, when Sophocles represents marriage; for it is in marriage that female subjectivity is most explicitly constituted, in real life and in drama.

A full-scale study of marriage in the fifth century would need to take into account all three major tragedians, plus a host of other literary and nonliterary texts. I focus on Sophocles for several reasons. First, Sophocles has somehow maintained a transcendent status, standing apart from those politicized theoretical approaches that would link him too closely to the real world. (We may recall here that Sophocles does not partake in the poetic contest staged in Aristophanes' *Frogs*.) When Hexter and Selden set out to put together a volume of modern critical approaches to the classics, they found that, "Greek was obviously still sexier than Latin, and Attic tragedy was particularly hot. Within this rich area of study, moreover, it is indicative that we received multiple proposals for papers on Aeschylus and Euripides, but nothing on Sophocles."[29] Second, good work has already been done on the issue of marriage in Aeschylus and Euripides.[30] Sophocles' texts deserve similar scrutiny, as several of his seven extant plays bring marriage up as a central issue.[31] Finally, I see Sophocles treating the representation of marriage in ways that are different from his two fellow tragedians. A much larger study than the present work would be necessary to confirm these differences, but I offer the following illustration.

DuBois points out that the fifth century shows a shift in the representation of women. They are less frequently compared to uncultivated, spontaneously producing fields, and increasingly described by the image of the ploughed furrow. In Aeschylus, the former image occurs several times, often at key moments.[32] Though the idea of man as cultivator is also present, Aeschylus demonstrates an anxiety over woman's apparently spontaneous fertility, and the necessity of integrating that power into society. Sophocles, on the other hand, emphasizes the image of the furrow.[33] His concern, then, is more with marriage as a process of cultivation and civilization. For Sophocles, marriage (and its pitfalls) is bound up with the production of culture. This may be the result of a chronological shift: our last secure date for Aeschylus is the *Oresteia* in 458, while most scholars put our earliest extant play of Sophocles (generally believed to be the *Ajax*) in the 440s. Between these two dates, as I have mentioned, falls Pericles' legislation concerning marriage and citizenship.

Euripides' plays show a similar concern with production of culture, of course, and in many ways Sophocles seems closer to Euripides than to Aeschylus. But here again I see an important difference. Sophocles takes familiar images of women in marriage and explores the contradictions that are inherent in them. Euripides, by contrast, writes about women who create problems by actively manipulating those same images. For now, one example will suffice. As duBois points out, another common metaphor for woman is the inscribed tablet.[34] When Euripides uses this image in the *Hippolytus*, Phaedra is sexually false — that is, she lusts after her stepson, and tries to cheat on her husband. When she fails to seduce Hippolytus, however, she writes a deliberately untrue story on a tablet, saying that he raped her.[35] She duplicates her sexual falseness, then, by inscribing it on the tablet, and this deception leads to Hippolytus's death. In Sophocles' *Trachiniae*, the same metaphor receives different treatment: Deianeira follows the directions of the centaur Nessus, which she has remembered as if they were written on a tablet (682–83). Those instructions prove to be fatal to her husband. The deception, however, lies within the words on the tablet themselves, and in Deianeira's inability to interpret them. Deianeira had no intent to deceive — the medium of writing itself proves to be at fault.[36] I see this pattern consistently in Sophocles. He positions his heroines so that they are not the root cause of difficulties; rather, the idea of marriage itself and the female subjectivity that it constitutes create a paradox that leads to crisis.

In the chapters that follow, therefore, I will treat the representation of marriage in five plays of Sophocles: the *Trachiniae*, the *Electra*, the *Antigone*, the *Ajax*, and the *Oedipus tyrannus*.[37] My aim is twofold. First, by pointing out how one of the central and celebrated authors of the fifth century dealt with the theme, I intend to shed some light on the issues surrounding marriage in classical Athens. At the same time, I hope that my treatment will contribute to our understanding of Sophocles' poetics. I should add that I do not analyze these plays according to any one theory, or with an eye to proving a single point about, or chronological progression of, Sophocles' views of marriage. Though Marxist and feminist theory underlie my understanding of marriage as cultural ideology throughout, I focus on different aspects of matrimony in each play, and use different critical theories as they seem most productive. I hope that what I have lost in coherence by this procedure I have gained in interest.

Before turning to Sophocles, however, I wish to articulate a variety of Athenian views of marriage, in order to provide legal and social context for my study of Sophocles' particular portrayals. In Chapter 1 I look at a variety of sources — legal, literary, and archaeological — and explain the variety of meanings that these sources posit. I focus in particular on the ways that these sources portray women's experience.

I need to be clear about a few important points. First, all of the sources I cite are public, and by definition, therefore, male. We must bear in mind that the women in these texts are the fictional creations of men, and reflect more on the culture of men than on the experiences of women.[38] Second, my aim in this chapter is to see where myth and law concur, where both types of source point to a similar construction of marriage and gender. As a result, I do not distinguish my sources by treating them differently; I view both law and poetry as representations of Athens by Athenian society, with a vested interest in propagating that society. Obviously, these different types of text served different purposes, and we must make allowances for the influence of context on content.[39] Given that allowance, however, it is fair to treat various sources as comparable representatives of (male) Athenian ways of thinking. Finally, at the end of the first chapter I note several places in which tragedy significantly differs from other sources specifically in its treatment of the position of married women; these differences, I hope, will point to some of the specific ideological roles adopted by tragedy as a representation of the *polis*. I avoid for the most part discussion of Sophocles in this chapter, since the marriages in his plays will receive full treatment in the chapters that follow.

Chapter 1   THE SEMANTICS OF GREEK MARRIAGE

This is matrimony: when a man begets children and presents his sons to his phratry and deme, and gives his daughters, as being his own, in marriage to their husbands.

[DEMOSTHENES] *Against Neaira*

MARRIAGE AND CULTURE

The bare bones of fifth-century Athenian weddings are as follows: possibly long before the marriage, the bride's father promised her to the groom. This betrothal, or *engyēsis*, was a legally recognized act, and it is often referred to in court cases to establish the legitimacy of a marriage. Before the bride was actually handed over to the groom (*ekdosis*), she underwent ritual purifications. She took a special bath (*loutra*) with her friends, traditionally in the spring Callirhoe, dedicated toys to Artemis, and cut her hair. In the ceremony proper (*gamos*), the bride and groom processed to their new home, accompanied by friends and relatives. The mothers of each acted as torchbearers. Upon entering their new *oikos*, the couple was showered with dates or other food symbolizing fertility. They shared a meal of sesame cake, at which time the bride probably removed her veil (*anakaluptēria*), though some sources suggest that this took place during the procession. The groom's mother then led them into their marital chamber (*thalamos*). The wedding party remained outside and sang wedding songs (*epithalamia*). Some guests may have stayed through till morning. This first night was known as "camping out" (*epaulia*). On the next day, the bride's parents sent her gifts (*phernē*), which seem to have consisted of combs, mirrors, and other beautifying objects. After these rituals were completed, the groom might have introduced his bride to his phratry at the ceremony called the *apatouria*. The phratry might also have held a *gamēlia*, or wedding banquet, in honor of the marriage. These rituals completed, bride and groom began the business of "sharing a house" (*sunoikein*) that socially, if not legally, defined marriage.[1] At the same time, the groom adopted the position of legal guardian (*kurios*) of the bride, a role that her father or closest male relative had filled up to this point.[2]

So much describes the ritual that marked a woman's transition from unmarried girl, *parthenos* or *korē*, to *gunē*, a term that can mean woman or wife. Though symbolically suggestive in a variety of ways, the ritual itself tells us little about the function of marriage in the Athenian state. That function, necessarily, will have had a large effect on how women experienced marriage. To start describing a variety of ways of thinking of marriage in the Athenian state, therefore, I turn to some of the legal uses of marriage in ancient Athens. My purpose here is to show the ambivalence of women's positions in both state and household, an ambivalence that exists as well in our literary texts. That is, women are an integral part of the Athenian household and, by analogy, the Athenian city-state, and yet they are consistently figured as outsiders to those institutions.

In the middle of the fifth century, near the beginning of Sophocles' career, marriage underwent a significant legal, if not necessarily social, redefinition.[3] Under the Periclean citizenship law of 451/50, a citizen could only be produced by the union of two *astoi* (a general term for "citizens"). This law, Patterson argues, explicitly borrows from the language of family membership, so that it "established a legitimacy requirement for the polis itself, and can be seen as part of the way in which the Classical Athenian polis structured itself on the model of the family."[4] The new legislation discouraged Athenian men from marrying noncitizen women, though it appears that it was not until some time later — possibly the beginning of the fourth century — that a law was passed that specifically made marrying a foreign woman and passing her off as an Athenian illegal.[5] It also created a new legal problem within the Athenian court system: how to establish the legitimate citizenship of women, who played a severely curtailed role in the public sphere.

In the middle of the fourth century, a man named Apollodorus attacked a certain Stephanus for *xenia* — that is, for living with a noncitizen woman, Neaira, as if she were his legal Athenian wife. If convicted, Stephanus stood to be sold as a slave (59.16).[6] Apollodorus's courtroom speech has been preserved as [Demosthenes] 59. Apollodorus's charge, which rests on somewhat dubious ground, depends entirely on his ability to prove that Neaira is not a citizen. To this end, he argues that Stephanus gave away Neaira's daughter fraudulently, claiming that she was his own daughter from a previous marriage to an unnamed woman (59.51). The unsuspecting bridegroom, Apollodorus says, became incensed when he learned "that she was not the daughter of Stephanus, but of Neaira" (59.51), and he returned his bride to her parents. Thus the speaker presents this bridegroom as fearing his own marriage to a noncitizen, which his new wife would be if one of her parents were not of citizen status. For Apollodorus, the bridegroom's rejection of his wife's parentage amounts to a public assertion that "Neaira is not herself a citizen-woman" (59.64).[7]

The bridegroom's actions (and the law that may have motivated them) reveal the role that marriage played in ensuring citizenship. They also reveal the surprisingly slippery nature of such evidence: regardless of the facts of the case, Neaira's citizenship or noncitizenship (and consequently her daughter's) is largely a matter of hearsay—Apollodorus bases his argument only on the implicit belief of an unfortunate bridegroom, and not on any material evidence.[8] Apollodorus further suggests that he is genuinely worried that Neaira will infiltrate the citizenry as a result of this illegal marriage, passing her children off as legitimate Athenians, and living as legal wife with an Athenian man. If she succeeds, he argues, she will usurp power from the Athenian assembly (which jealously granted citizenship only rarely, 59.89ff.) and, perhaps more importantly, will compromise the position of all the listeners' wives and daughters: if prostitutes can be wives and produce citizen children, then wives will be looked on as no better than prostitutes (59.114).

Neaira threatens the specific privilege of citizen wives in Athens: the right to produce legitimate citizens both for the family and for the state. However we view the public role (or lack of it) of Athenian women, and despite the continual Athenian male fantasy of reproduction without women, women played an important and well-guarded role in the reproduction of the household, by bearing legitimate children.[9] Nor was this merely a private issue; as Patterson has argued, this status was transferred to the civic sphere with Pericles' citizenship law. By implication, the properly married woman became the cornerstone for both family membership and civic membership, and her identity and person had to be carefully established and protected.

At the same time, the speech against Neaira indicates how women, so constructed, endanger that culture. Aided by sensual charms, a foreign woman threatens to usurp the role of proper Athenian wife and the result, if she succeeds, is to put legal marriage (in two separate generations) and citizenship itself at risk: ἐξουσία ἔσται ταῖς πόρναις συνοικεῖν οἷς ἂν βούλωνται, καὶ τοὺς παῖδας φάσκειν οὗ ἂν τύχωσιν εἶναι ("Prostitutes will be allowed to live with/marry [sunoikein] whomever they wish, and to say that their children are fathered by whomever they happen to be with," 59.112). Neaira can pose this sort of threat specifically because women's status within the *polis* was not defined by public structures. Unlike male children, female children were not enlisted in the phratries.[10] They did take part in cults, their primary civic role, but as *Against Neaira* shows elsewhere, unqualified women might also usurp this role (59.73ff.).[11] As Sealey observes, "Their citizenship was latent; it consisted in the capacity to bear children who would be citizens."[12] This is not to say that women's citizenship did not exist—Patterson argues cogently that women are viewed as having a "concrete, non-abstract relationship with the Athenian land and family."[13] But because women lacked visibility in the public sphere, their identity is difficult to establish in public terms. Women are crucial to the survival of the *polis*, but the *polis* defines them with a vagueness that makes them potential fakes, intruders in the civic order.

In other words, women like Neaira pose a threat to society because legitimate wives' status as citizens, like Neaira's status, could only be established (or disproved) through witnesses who claim to know of their birth or formal marriage (involving perhaps *engyēsis, apatouria, gamēlia,* and introduction of children to the phratry) to another citizen. Indeed, as Scafuro has shown, a woman's status as *astē* depended entirely on her ability to produce such witnesses.[14] Among the more famous examples of women whose citizenship is attested in exactly this way are Phile in Isaeus 3,[15] and Plangon in Demosthenes 40. The evidence in such cases is necessarily questionable.[16] We find that trials concerning inheritance (in which a woman's civic identity might be questioned) or *xenia* (the accusation that a foreign woman is posing as Athenian) provoke a large number of charges of false witnessing.[17]

This tenuous process of recognition, however, should not lead us to assume that Athens regarded women as nonpersons, having identity only through their male relatives.[18] Rather, their position as citizens was problematic because they were not normally subject to the sort of public, civic scrutiny that men were (e.g., *dokimasia, koureion,* etc.). As long as a foreign woman did not get involved in an inheritance dispute, she might succeed in impersonating a citizen, and thus sneak into "the distinctively Athenian system whose first principle was the integrity and continuity of individual Athenian *oikoi.*"[19] One of Apollodorus's most threatening arguments, then, is that Neaira's success will put even legitimate wives and daughters at risk, that the men in the audience will be unable to distinguish citizens from daughters of foreign *hetairai.* As a result, any Athenian wife or daughter might, like Neaira, be an impostor. Any of the listeners might, at any time, find himself in the position of the angry bridegroom who had married Neaira's daughter.

Women's identity within the institution of marriage is, therefore, suspect because of its susceptibility to mimesis, imitation of the real article.[20] Apollodorus's speech represents one attempt to limit this sort of potentially subversive subjectivity, drawing on a large range of circumstantial evidence to create a weight of probability against Neaira's citizen status. In his discussion of Hestia and Hermes, Vernant argues that Athenian myth also represents an attempt to control women's powers of potentially indiscriminate reproduction in marriage.[21] The goddess of the hearth, Hestia, represents the "female" element in the *oikos*, with all its positive traits. She is fertile, stable, deep in the interior of the house, and cannot be transferred to another *oikos*.[22] The wife, whose duties are largely within the house, and who is particularly responsible for raising the children, becomes associated with these same qualities. As a result, marriage is constructed as endogamy: "Through the goddess of the hearth, the function of fertility . . . can appear as the indefinite prolongation of the paternal line through the daughter, without a 'foreign' woman being necessary for procreation."[23] Such ideology figures infiltration as impossible.

At the same time, however, this construction places the "real" wife in an ambiguous position. The wife is always only a surrogate for Hestia. During the marriage ceremony, she has changed households, and this mobility makes her an outsider in her husband's home, and suspect because of her ability to change allegiances. As Vernant points out, Hestia is a virgin goddess, because "for Hestia, the wedded state would be the *negation of the values* that she represents at the heart of the house: values of fixity, permanence, seclusion."[24] As her surrogate and a married woman, the wife must necessarily take on the "negation of [those] values." As in the legal cases, the woman who enters a household is simultaneously the cornerstone of culture, in that she will bear heirs for the *oikos*, and a point of danger — as a surrogate for the goddess Hestia, she constantly assumes the status of an intruder.

In terms of ideology, then, marriage creates a contradictory subject-position for the bride: "Women stand 'outside' society, yet are essential to it (and in particular to its continued, ordered existence)."[25] Women are posited as subjects through marriage, obtaining a civic and familial identity that they will pass on to their children. Indeed, they are absolutely necessary for the continuation of the state. At the same time, however, that subjectivity, especially in the realm of the erotic, is continually suspect. As objects of exchange between men, with no independent existence in public life, their identity becomes unstable.[26] They are feared for their ability to imitate legitimate subjects and, through this shiftiness of identity, they are viewed as a potential threat to the civic order, and to the city's ability to reproduce more citizen subjects. This ambiguity of status would have been felt keenly, especially after the passing of Pericles' law in 451/50.

What has any of this to do with tragedy? Tragic drama after 451/50 is concerned with these issues primarily in mythic terms. Questions of legal Athenian citizenship arise only rarely in the course of a drama (usually set in the distant past, in any case), though such anachronisms are possible.[27] Tragedies are, however, concerned to explore the contradictory place of women in the political setting of the play. Strong women characters such as Antigone and Electra are viewed as potential subverters of a civic order that is defined as masculine, and this subversion is specifically postulated in terms of their marriages or potential for marriage. Heroines who are already married, like Deianeira or Clytemnestra, become points of weakness in the hero's household, of uncertain loyalty, seducible and therefore unstable. In one case, that of Tecmessa in the *Ajax*, the issue is exactly a question of Tecmessa's status, and thus what the citizen status of her son will be. So while legal structures and mythical paradigms (especially that of Hestia) represent attempts to control and limit this female instability, Sophocles' tragedies explore the rifts and fissures in those social systems. This should not, I think, be taken as radical critique; rather, by exploring these rifts within the carefully circumscribed context of tragic performance, these plays function as yet another form of containment. By focusing on the fissures rather than their containment, however, we can come to a better understanding of just what Athenian society found so necessary to curtail, and why.

MALE HOMOSOCIAL DESIRE AND THE *epiklēros*

The discussion above of *Against Neaira* describes a marriage that went sour — that of Neaira's daughter. When her husband learned that she was (possibly) not a citizen woman, he divorced her. It is important to note *how*: he returned her to the man (Stephanus) who gave her to him in marriage. The two men involved — the woman's father and her bridegroom — evidently regarded the betrothal (*engyēsis*) and subsequent marriage as a contract between themselves. When one of the men learns that his bride does not match the terms of the contract, he declares the contract invalid and ends the marriage. The episode demonstrates that these men view marriage as a transaction of merchandise, analogous, though not identical, to any other commercial transaction. As we shall see, the imagery used to describe marriages in both legal and literary texts from ancient Greece consistently supports such an analogy.[28] It is, in fact, reflected in the formula recited at the ceremony, ἐγγυῶ, δίδωμι ἔχειν γνησίων παίδων ἐπ' ἀρότῳ ("I entrust, I give [her to you] to have legitimate [*gnēsios*] children by ploughing").[29] A man gives a piece of merchandise for a specific purpose to another man.

Literary sources also present marriage in the light of a legal transaction, generally between the bride's father and the groom. While tragedy does not usually speak in the formal terms of a wedding contract, the text often implies that the men in question have reached an agreement. It is clear, for example, that the river-monster Achelous negotiated with Oineus for the hand of Deianeira in the *Trachiniae*: μνηστὴρ γὰρ ἦν μοι ποταμός, Ἀχελῷον λέγω, / ὅς μ' ἐν τρισὶν μορφαῖσιν ἐξῄτει πατρός ("For my suitor was a river, I speak of Achelous, / who petitioned my father for me in three forms," 9–10). Heracles apparently engaged in similar negotiations, since Hyllus refers to his marriage as τὸν Οἰνέως γάμον ("the marriage of Oineus," 792).[30] We cannot necessarily see these negotiations as Athenian *engyēsis*, but they are structurally similar. In both, the contract of marriage exists between the men.

The view of marriage as an exchange of women necessarily creates a gendered idea of culture. *Men* exchange women, and in so doing define society as a series of relations between men.[31] In the very moment that they seem about to obtain some sort of subjectivity, then, women in marriage find themselves posited as objects, their desire and voice neatly circumscribed. Theorists have explained this phenomenon as the workings of male homosocial desire.[32] In brief, Sedgwick and others have shown that men in Western societies express their relations to other men *through* women — that is, women become a means of communication as well as of economic and social exchange. The concept is most easily demonstrated in the common literary trope of cuckolding (so often a threat in the dramas of Shakespeare). A man sleeps with another man's wife, not out of hopeless desire for the woman so much as out of a desire to establish superiority over the woman's husband. The husband, in turn, views this act as an attack on himself. The important players in the scene are the men; the woman is little more than a signifier in the homosocial code, and she often fails to understand the larger relation that surrounds her erotic entanglement.[33]

Male homosocial desire also appears to underlie a good deal of the exchange of women in Greek tragedy.[34] Rabinowitz analyzes the relations of Hippolytus and Phaedra in Euripides' *Hippolytus*, for example, and shows that the play serves to validate marriage as a relation between men.[35] In a play that seems to be about Phaedra's passions and their consequences, Rabinowitz points out, Phaedra conveniently disappears before the end. The play concludes, and emphatically so, with a resolution between Theseus and Hippolytus, thus assuring us that the world is again safe for (male) culture. Phaedra briefly disrupts that culture by desiring the wrong man (Hippolytus), and by falsely accusing him of raping her. But her disruption is contained by the final scene between father and son. Her desire, her relation with Hippolytus, is transformed: at the end of the play, we learn that a cult of Hippolytus will be established, in which women who are of marriageable age will dedicate themselves to the hero, thus commemorating Phaedra's passion. What functioned as a disruption of male society in the play, then, is translated into a guarantee of the continuation of normal social reproduction.

Moreover, Phaedra's disruption—her accusation that Hippolytus has raped her—reinscribes the system of male subjectivity that the play ultimately validates. Phaedra commits suicide because of her own unrequited desire, but her suicide note does not express that desire. Rather, she writes that Hippolytus raped her (transferring the act of desire to him), which Theseus immediately understands as a relationship between Hippolytus and himself, and one that endangers his position with other men:

> εἰ γὰρ παθών γέ σου τάδ᾽ ἡσσηθήσομαι,
> οὐ μαρτυρήσει μ᾽ Ἴσθμιος Σίνις ποτὲ
> κτανεῖν ἑαυτὸν ἀλλὰ κομπάζειν μάτην.[36]

> If, suffering these things from you, I am made inferior,
> Isthmian Sinos will no longer bear witness that I
> killed him, but [suggest] that I make empty boasts. (976–78)

The problem of Phaedra's desire no longer exists as a relation between her and Hippolytus—it has been translated into a relation between Hippolytus and Theseus.[37] Her own actions, therefore, tend to reinforce the masculine economy, at the same time that she confirms the masculine view of women as untrustworthy. Phaedra gets revenge on Hippolytus for spurning her, but in the process she literally writes herself out of the position of desiring subject.

One of the inevitable results of this masculine economy is that the women involved become alienated objects. As such, they are usually figured as in some sense strangers to their husbands—they are something foreign brought in from the outside.[38] This position as an outsider allows a woman to threaten her husband or father and the culture they represent when she (within the confines of the text) thinks or desires for herself—e.g., Phaedra, Medea, Deianeira, Electra, Antigone, and especially Clytemnestra. As I have mentioned, this threatening moment of subjectivity takes place more often than not in the context of marriage and/or erotic desire. Here we see, however, an interesting distinction between Euripides' heroines and Sophocles'. Where Euripides' wives either are deceptive (Phaedra) or directly attack their husbands (Medea), Sophocles' heroines pose a threat, paradoxically, through an entirely proper devotion to husband or father (Deianeira, Electra, Antigone). Sophocles seems interested, then, in exploring the structural problems of legitimate relationships.

An important form of such a structural problem in Sophocles is the split identity that a bride experiences, as she finds herself belonging both to her natal family and to her marital one. Here, too, we find an important parallel in fifth-century legal ideology. The transaction of marriage is not exactly analogous to an economic transaction. When a bride is transferred to her husband's home, her allegiance, it seems, does not always shift entirely to her new *oikos*. The verb typically used for the transfer of the woman is *ekdidomi*, and here as in other uses of the word, the person who "gives" the object away does not renounce all ties.[39] The word *ekdidomi* is used of apprenticeships and of loans of property, for example, and in marriage, too, the transfer of *kurieia* is limited. If the marriage came to an end, the wife would return to her original family; in any case, the dowry that her *kurios* sends with his daughter on marriage remains in some senses hers throughout her life. Moreover, a woman's original family continues to regard her as "theirs" in cases of family vengeance.[40] In Wolff's formulation, "The aim of the *engyēsis* was to entrust rather than to alienate the object."[41] The marriage of a woman, therefore, is a potentially unstable transaction, one that could be revoked on short notice.

This is particularly true when we consider the case of the Athenian *epiklēros*.[42] Briefly put, the *epiklēros* was a woman whose father died without male heirs. According to Athenian law, such a woman was required to marry her nearest male relative beginning with her father's side, to whom she would then transfer her father's property.[43] Public disputes could and did arise over who got to marry such a woman, especially if her inheritance was large.[44] More important, however, the law defined a basic patriarchal principle: when no male heirs exist, the woman preserves the paternal line of her original *oikos*.[45] She becomes the real correlative to the idea represented by the myth of Hestia: the paternal line is preserved through the daughter.[46] Obviously the epiklerate guarantees a certain amount of stability for the bride's paternal *oikos*. It makes her position in her marital *oikos*, however, less stable. The married woman lives under a "divided *kurieia*,"[47] and her allegiance to her husband's *oikos* is not fully secure.

This insecurity, in fact, took on a quite literal form: the law concerning *epiklēroi* could force a woman to marry her nearest male relative even if she was already married. Isaeus goes so far as to suggest that many men had lost their wives this way, though this statement is probably rhetorical exaggeration.[48] It is difficult to imagine many Athenian husbands putting up with such an event in fact. Nonetheless, it appears to be a strong possibility in the Athenian imagination. As a result, a woman's transfer to her husband's household could be seen as temporary and revocable, at least in fictional texts, and conceivably in real life.[49]

Very few tragic texts deal directly with the problems of the *epiklēros*.[50] But the idea that the *epiklēros* embodies, that marriage creates a divided loyalty for the bride, underlies the actions of several *parthenoi* in tragedy. Electra and Antigone, for example, remain dedicated to their paternal households, which prevents them from getting married (see especially *Antigone* 904–20). As I argue, their characters are best understood if read with the structure of the epiklerate in mind. Euripides' Electra does get married, but the marriage is never consummated, again in a show of solidarity with Agamemnon and Orestes. Similarly, forty-nine of the fifty Danaids follow their father's orders and kill their husbands on their wedding night. In Aeschylus's version, their resistance to marriage is in part due to their desire to maintain their status in Danaos's household.[51] Particularly when the focus of the tragedy is on unmarried women, the daughter's devotion to the father has the potential to interrupt the marriage transaction, sometimes with disastrous results for the husband or his family. She is fully stable as neither subject nor object, and neither her loyalty nor her identity in the social order is ever completely secure.

Significantly, it is when women are most analogous to objects of *economic* exchange that marriage becomes least stable. It is a basic law of economics, after all, that anything that has been sold can be resold or, worse yet, stolen, and so become the property of someone else again. We need only think of Helen "with all her possessions" to see the paradigm at work. In classical Athens, moreover, it is particularly women who are *epiklēroi*, whose marriage represents significant economic commerce, who are least secure in their married state. This, too, should be seen as an aspect of the male homosocial economy: denied subjectivity, women-as-objects become ciphers, with no discernible loyalty.[52]

MARRIAGE AS ECONOMY

Athens does not just see marriage as a transaction between men. A variety of evidence also draws attention to the idea that the wedding ceremony signifies a personal transformation.[53] This is true for groom as well as bride. As Foxhall points out, "It is not accidental that thirty, the age of full civic maturity for men, was also the normal age of marriage for them. Often this was the time at which the patrimonial property was preliminarily divided and turned over to the sons."[54] Legally, then, marriage seems to establish (or at least is concurrent with) full adulthood for the man. The tragedies, too, suggest that a young man might experience marriage as a *telos*. Haemon, for example, finds his marriage in death (just as many tragic brides do). The messenger announces: κεῖται δὲ νεκρὸς περὶ νεκρῷ, τὰ νυμφικὰ / τέλη λαχὼν δείλαιος ἔν γ᾽ Ἅιδου δόμοις ("The corpse lies on top of corpse, and the wretch / has hit upon his marital rites in the home of Hades," 1240–

41). In fact, Haemon's experience of marriage here is remarkably parallel to his bride's. While Haemon's experience is not typical for men in tragedy, it is clear that Athenian culture could see marriage as a turning point in a man's life.[55]

Athenian men, however, had other rites of passage as well. They underwent, for example, the *koureion*, in which they were introduced into their phratry as official members.[56] As young men they became *ephēbes*, during which time they apparently underwent serious military training.[57] Young men, then, went through a series of initiations into the public world of adult male life. Young women, on the other hand, partook in a variety of rituals (the *arkteia* at Brauron, for example), all of which prepared them for their eventual marriage into a new household.[58] Women's rites of passage culminate in marriage.

Most texts, moreover, portray the woman undergoing the more radical transformation during the wedding. She changes her identity from daughter to wife.[59] The terminology that describes the bride plainly marks this change in status. Before marriage, she is a *parthenos*, or a *korē*. After her wedding, she becomes a *gunē*. She is the "mobile element" in the wedding, even beyond the pedestrian meaning that she moves to a new house (which the groom might also do). She must also enter a new family, take on a new role in relation to the men around her, and exchange the *kurieia* of her father for that of her husband.[60] Not surprisingly, then, women in tragedy seem more concerned with marriage as an institution than men do. Men (e.g., Theseus and Heracles) worry about their wives' fidelity; but women (e.g., Medea and Deianeira) talk about the difficulties of marriage per se.

For the bride, fitting into her new identity and becoming a fully functional member of her husband's household could be a difficult procedure. Marriages in Athens could be arranged, especially among the upper classes.[61] The bride and groom might, therefore, be virtual strangers at the time of the wedding. Literary marriages reflect this situation in a variety of ways: in the *Alcestis*, Admetus plays on the bride's ambiguous position in his house, telling Heracles that the person who died is a "stranger" connected to the household so that Heracles will not leave out of a sense of decorum.[62] In more extreme cases, like that of Medea, the wife is literally a foreigner. We might be tempted to take Medea's position as entirely topical, but when Medea announces her foreign status, she also generalizes it, and describes the difficulty of making the transition to a new home:

> ἐς καινὰ δ᾽ ἤθη καὶ νόμους ἀφιγμένην
> δεῖ μάντιν εἶναι, μὴ μαθοῦσαν οἴκοθεν,
> ὅτῳ μάλιστα χρήσεται ξυνευνέτῃ.

It is necessary for the bride, having arrived among new
  circumstances
and customs, to be a prophet, not having learned these
  things at home,
especially how to handle her bedmate. (238–40)

Medea's experience as a foreigner, then, is more than a fact of the storyline. It is also representative of the bride's typical experience in her husband's *oikos*.[63]

It is especially in the realm of the erotic that women are characterized as foreign, and in need of masculine, cultured control.[64] As I mentioned earlier, one of the more common images of woman's sexuality, particularly before the fifth century, is that of the uncultivated field, fertilized by rain.[65] Women share, it seems, in the spontaneous generation of the earth. Although in many ways this image suggests a peculiarly female power, it has other important effects. First, woman's representative in the formulation, the earth, is a passive element. Stable and receptive of man's seed (as represented by rain), women assure cultural fertility for others. Second, the image naturalizes woman's role as child-bearer. Her reproductive capabilities are aligned with nature (which, incidentally, also places her outside of culture), so that woman's normative role is the production of children.

In the fifth century, moreover, the image of women as uncultivated earth undergoes an important shift. DuBois has shown that increasingly in this period, literary texts represent women as furrows (especially prevalent in Sophocles) or *cultivated* fields.[66] Increasingly, then, Athens understands marriage as a form of civilizing the (by implication) uncivilized women. It is not entirely clear why this ideological shift takes place. DuBois suggests that it results from Athens's increased dependence on nonagricultural production in the fifth century: "Women's bodies, which were once taken for granted as resembling the father's fields, are now seen as cultivated furrows. The anxiety about the citizens' alienation from agriculture may be translated into an anxiety about traditional representations of sexual difference."[67] The sort of large-scale ideological shift that duBois describes may well be at work. I see a more direct cause as well. We know that in 451/50 marriage requirements became more strict with the passage of Pericles' legislation. It appears, therefore, that Athens was growing increasingly anxious about controlling access to its civic body. To maintain that control, it seems, it also had to increase the security of citizen women's bodies, by placing them under more rigorous masculine scrutiny (see the discussion of Neaira, above). The image of women as cultivated fields reinforces the idea of masculine control: women are still stable and fertile, but now must be sown by specific citizen men.

Agriculture, like other elements of culture, places the realm of fertilization under useful, maintained order. It is thus associated with control of promiscuity.[68]

The idea of masculine control over women's transformations is even more evident in another set of images, taken this time from the animal kingdom. As has often been noted, various texts describe *parthenoi* as wild animals, and describe grooms as "taming" or "yoking" them in marriage.[69] The point here, aside from figuring women's sexuality as a threat, is that marriage becomes a mode of civilization, a way of making women productive members of society.[70] As in the metaphor of ploughing a field, this set of images works under an assumption that the woman is a "wild" object that must be cultivated. This is not to say that Athens did not value women's role; but it gives men, as plowers and tamers, the active, acculturating role.[71]

From the husband's point of view, what this change entails seems clear enough: the imagery of taming a dangerous beast or cultivating a wild field implies that the woman must become subject to her husband's rule of the *oikos*.[72] Of course, not all women transfer their allegiance so unquestioningly. Those who do not might betray their husbands by having an affair, often figured as the prime threat to the marriage itself. A case in point is found in Lysias's *On the Murder of Eratosthenes*. If we believe the speaker, his wife had an affair with Eratosthenes. But more to the point, the affair was enabled specifically by the speaker's trust: after she had a child, she moved her sleeping quarters to the downstairs in order (she claimed) to be nearer to the baby. This made it all the easier for her to sneak out at night. Her affair, then, violates the speaker's belief in her allegiance to him and their *oikos* — trust he presents as typical for an Athenian husband.[73] Like the power to bear citizen children, the power to transfer allegiance implies the ability to fake it, the possibility of intrusion by impostors. This shift in a woman's social status, then, is a moment when her subjectivity is particularly threatening.

Whereas an anxiety over infidelity plays an obvious role in several tragedies — for example, Aeschylus's *Agamemnon*, Euripides' *Hippolytus* and *Ion* — in several instances heroes in Sophocles' tragedies express a more vague concern over the transmission of their bloodlines through a woman. This is true even when the text presents no question of the woman's fidelity. For example, in the *Trachiniae*, when his marriage is coming to an untimely end, Heracles suddenly worries that his son is not "really" his. He says to Hyllus: ὦ παῖ, γενοῦ μοι παῖς ἐτήτυμος γεγώς, / καὶ μὴ τὸ μητρὸς ὄνομα πρεσβεύσῃς πλέον ("Son, become my *true* son by birth, / and do not pay more respect to your mother's name [than to mine]," 1064–65).[74] Here Heracles does not, perhaps, suspect Deianeira of having an affair. But he sees his house divided, and no longer believes that Deianeira was acting in the best interest of the family. He expresses this lack of faith in terms that suggest questions of legitimacy: he wants Hyllus to prove himself "truly born *my* child." It sounds as if Heracles wants to have given birth to Hyllus like Zeus to Athena, without the danger of a woman, this particularly treacherous woman, somehow having poisoned the process.[75] Deianeira's sexual actions may strike us as beyond reproach; but for Heracles, the fact that she has acted against him is best understood and expressed in terms of his bloodline.

So far I have discussed a bride's transformation only in the context of her social allegiance to her husband. We must also note that a woman would gain some economic power upon marriage, and recognizing this power is crucial to understanding her new position in society. The traditional view would have it that married women were severely limited in their movements and powers in Athens. Critics have pointed to texts like Lysias 1 to establish the claim that women, on the whole, were kept indoors and allowed only limited social contacts outside their families. Isaeus 10.10 states that women could not perform economic transactions of a value above one *medimnos* of barley, and is often cited as an example of their exclusion from the public sphere. This view suggests that women were economically and socially excluded from the *polis* and led (at best) quiet and respectable lives under the rule of their husbands — though we must again recognize that such seclusion represents an ideal attainable only by the upper class.[76]

This picture, however accurate as a general sketch, has been challenged in a number of ways in recent years. In particular, we should note that tragedy, despite its portrayal of active speaking heroines, denies certain economic powers to women that we see them wielding in historical Athens. Several nonliterary texts, for example, suggest that women did, in some sense, own property. Foxhall points out that ownership is not easily defined: if we mean the power to dispose of goods, then it is true that women did not own property, since they were barred from the public arena where such transactions would take place. But if we define ownership as the ability to use a good, for one's own benefit, then it seems that wives "owned" property in conjunction with their husbands.[77] Significantly, Ischomachus's wife takes exactly this stance in Xenophon's *Oikonomikos* (9.16.9).

With ownership of this kind goes a limited amount of economic power.[78] Foxhall notes that women apparently kept their dowries if they left a marriage, and that this could be an embarrassment to the husband if the dowry was large. The husband might not have that much ready cash on hand; he might have even borrowed money using the dowry as collateral. Foxhall reads, therefore, the famous incident of the attempted divorce of Alcibiades in this light (Plutarch's *Alcibiades* 8ff.): Alcibiades risked significant public disapproval, physically carrying his wife back into his house, perhaps because he could not afford to lose the dowry that she would take with her.[79] As discussed earlier, moreover, a bride's father does not renounce all ties to her when she gets married. The bride could always return to her paternal *oikos*, with her dowry, if the marriage was not going well.[80]

In the tragic texts that deal with women who are already married, by contrast, women generally do not seem to possess these protections. Medea, for example, generalizes about marriage as if hers were a typical Athenian one. So, although she brought no dowry, she talks as if she had, complaining of "buying a husband" (233).[81] In Medea's eyes, however, bringing such a dowry offers no protection; it merely adds to a woman's insult in marriage. For, Medea says, "it is not possible to renounce a husband" (237). Bad enough that she must have a master, let alone that she has had to pay for him. In her speech, then, a dowry becomes proof of her object status, rather than a guarantee of her husband's good behavior. Elsewhere, when women in tragedy speak of the marriage transaction, it is only to complain that they have been "sold."[82]

What is more, an important element of a woman's complaint against marriage in tragedy is that she cannot return to her father's home. Perhaps the strongest statement to this effect comes from Euripides' *Medea* (Medea speaks):

> ἀλλ' οὐ γὰρ αὐτὸς πρὸς σὲ κἄμ' ἥκει λόγος·
> σοὶ μὲν πόλις θ' ἥδ' ἐστὶ καὶ πατρὸς δόμοι
> βίου τ' ὄνησις καὶ φίλων συνουσία,
> ἐγὼ δ' ἔρημος ἄπολις οὖσ' ὑβρίζομαι
> πρὸς ἀνδρός, ἐκ γῆς βαρβάρου λελῃσμένη,
> οὐ μητέρ', οὐκ ἀδελφόν, οὐχὶ συγγενῆ
> μεθορμίσασθαι τῆσδ' ἔχουσα συμφορᾶς.

> But the same situation does not apply to you and me;
> You have a city, and paternal homes,
> the enjoyment of life and the companionship of family.
> But I, alone, cityless, am abused
> by my husband, having been taken from a foreign land,
> and I do not have a mother, or a brother, or a near relative
> with whom to seek shelter from these misfortunes. (252–58)

We must be careful. Obviously, Medea emphasizes that she is *not* like other women — her situation (having killed her father and brother herself) is not typical. We might suppose, therefore, that it is only her unique position that prevents a return home. But interestingly enough, women in less exotic marital situations in tragedy express similar sentiments.[83] An important fragment from Sophocles' *Tereus* reads:

ὅταν δ' ἐς ἥβην ἐξικώμεθ' ἔμφρονες,
ὠθούμεθ' ἔξω καὶ διεμπολώμεθα
θεῶν πατρῴων τῶν τε φυσάντων ἄπο,
αἱ μὲν ξένους πρὸς ἄνδρας. . . .
καὶ ταῦτ', ἐπειδὰν εὐφρόνη ζεύξῃ μία,
χρεὼν ἐπαινεῖν κτλ.

But when, fully sensible, we reach puberty,
we are pushed out, and sold away from
the paternal gods, and from our fathers [literally, from the
    "sowers"],
some to foreign men. . . .
And it is necessary to praise these things,
once a good-minded woman is yoked.[84] (frag. 583)

Here, the anonymous speaker presumably still has a biological father—but she resents her separation from him. Her choice of words is important as well: the verb *diempolaō* does not carry the limited sense of sale that the more legalistic *ekdidōmi* does.[85] It is, in fact, commonly used for the sale of slaves. Similarly, Deianeira in Sophocles' *Trachiniae* spends much of the play reminiscing about her life before she was married; but nowhere does the play suggest that, in the face of her failing marriage, she might go back to her original *oikos*. Medea's case seems, therefore, a literary amplification of the isolation that tragic women typically experience. In tragedy, whether the specific situation of the play prevents such a return or not, the marriage transaction appears irrevocable. This formulation of marriage will figure prominently in my readings of Sophocles.

We need, therefore, to note the elements of difference between these two worlds: first, the irrevocability of marriage present in so many of the literary texts should remind us that this was not the case in fifth-century Athens. The possibility of the woman having an affair, of being an out-and-out impostor, or of instituting a legitimate divorce all pose threats to the stability of individual marriages. And the institution of *epiklēroi* suggests a "divided *kurieia*"—it provided legally for the possibility that one's wife might be forced to remove herself to her father's household again. Second, we must recognize that the Periclean citizenship law of 450/51 strongly discouraged the sort of long-distance importation of a wife so common in literature. As Patterson points out, under the new law in Athens, the children of a citizen and his exotic wife (such as Jason and Medea) could only result in offspring who were *nothoi*.[86] The dramatic texts, then, present a distorted mirror of fifth-century society, but one in which we can see the normative ideology of Athens at work. That is, the tragic texts guarantee the same stability and integrity to the family that Pericles' legislation tried to guarantee for the *polis*. The difference is in method: the tragedies attain this stability via a concept of foreign importation and irrevocability that would have been unacceptable in practice.

TRANSFORMING THE SELF

My analysis thus far has been curiously, if unavoidably, male-centered. Even when describing the "transformation" of the woman into wife, I have primarily summarized descriptions that emphasize her relations with and allegiances to the men in her life. However, there is another large and complex pattern of imagery that focuses on what men thought *the women themselves* experienced in getting married. Here, clearly, is one of our best sources for the informal social structures in which women lived (though again, these representations should not be confused with actual female experience). As Sophoclean tragedy provides us with some of our most important examples of this type of imagery, it will receive full treatment in the chapters that follow; here, however, I outline some implications.[87]

Most important, an abundance of literature compares a woman's experience of marriage to her death, often specifically her sacrificial death.[88] Persephone is in many ways the paradigm for Greek brides. It can hardly be coincidence that her alternative name, Kore, is virtually synonymous with *parthenos*. Persephone's marriage is both marriage and death, since she marries Hades and goes to live with him in the underworld. Similarly, any number of women in tragedies are killed, and their deaths are staged as marriages: Iphigenia,[89] Antigone,[90] Cassandra,[91] and of course Alcestis. The Danaids, a troublesome paradigm for brides, link the two ideas even as they decide between them. They prefer death to marriage, and, once forced to marry, choose to kill their husbands.[92] But even those women who do choose marriage often find that it leads to an early death, and Loraux argues that death, for women in tragedy, is a mode of fulfillment of their (otherwise unsuccessful) marriages: "In the *Antigone*, . . . Eurydice dies *for* her sons but *because* of Creon, and in the *Trachiniae*, . . . Deianeira dies *because* of Hyllos but *for* the love of Heracles. So the death of women . . . reestablishes their connection with marriage and maternity."[93] A bride's death *becomes* her marriage, and vice versa.

We might suppose that this prevalent imagery is merely a function of tragedy, having little to do with real life.[94] On the other hand, *parthenoi* who died before marriage were said (like Persephone) to be married to Hades (or death).[95] And even in the event of real, happy marriages, we find an element of sacrifice in the *proteleia*, in which the animal's ritual death appears to stand in for the bride's.[96] It is surely the case, to borrow Seaford's phrase, that in tragedy "the negative element prevails," but nonetheless the association of marriage and death carries considerable weight in Greek culture generally. As a transformation, then, Athenian ideology constructs marriage as a radical change of self—the person who was a *parthenos* must "die" in order for the *gunē* to come into being. At the same time, the women in myth who are most admirable as wives are those, like Alcestis or Iphigenia, who are willing to undergo *literal* death for their husbands or would-be husbands.[97]

A similar set of metaphors, but one that focuses even more on the (perceived) woman's experience, comes from the natural world. We have already noted that many texts figure marriage as a cultivation of fertile fields. In a related set of images, the woman is, when carried off, explicitly or implicitly compared to a plucked flower. Io, Europa, and of course Persephone are all out in meadows when they are abducted; their experience is the flowers'.[98] Such images express a sense of regret over the young woman's loss of innocence, of her girlhood status. Something of beauty is lost, or perhaps killed, in order to create the (agri)culture that marriage supports.

Scholars have not, in general, gone much beyond pointing out this imagery and its prevalence.[99] I suggest that we can learn much, however, by examining how these ideas figure marriage. Such images represent an attempt on the part of Greek culture to understand a woman's experience. We can begin by noting that insofar as these texts describe marriage as something that the woman *herself* experiences, they depict it as a loss. The bride loses her life, or she loses her girlhood (and simultaneously her connections with her family and homeland). She has been made a subject, the psychological and social focus of the texts in question, only to be disenfranchised.

More important, we have few poetic texts that both describe this transformation *and* describe it as successfully completed.[100] We have women who, like Penelope, have obviously transferred their allegiances to their husbands' *oikoi*. And we have women like Iphigenia, who sacrifices herself in order to preserve marriage in general. But nearly all of our texts show the *parthenos* who gets married not only resisting the marriage in the first place, but trying to undo it after it has been accomplished. Persephone resists her abduction, and Demeter negotiates her partial return to her original home; Thetis resists her marriage to Peleus, and complains from that point on about having been forced to marry a mortal; Deianeira never stops thinking of her transitional moment of marriage, and seems to regret the loss of her girlhood status.[101] What a woman would experience in a successful transformation, in terms of both her social allegiances and her sense of herself, is almost never represented.[102]

Even more telling is that female characters generally see their marriages as unfulfilled. The fragment of Sophocles' *Tereus* discussed above hints at the dissatisfaction that women might feel with their new lot in life. Though the fragment trails off here, after complaining about being sold to her new husband, the speaker continues in a sarcastic vein: καὶ ταῦτ᾽, ἐπειδὰν εὐφρόνη ζεύξῃ μία, / χρεὼν ἐπαινεῖν κτλ. ("And it is necessary to praise these things, / once a good-minded woman is yoked" frag. 583.10–12). The implication seems to be that the speaker is dissatisfied with her new place, but has no choice but to pretend that it is satisfying. More explicit still, as we shall see, is the profoundly unchanged nature of Deianeira's life after marriage.[103] In short, the literary texts that try to describe marriage as a transformation for the woman either portray the transformation as a failure or fail to describe the transformation — or both.[104]

This failure on the part of the poetic texts suggests an inability to imagine a female erotic subjectivity. I do not mean to suggest that women in the poetic texts do not desire. Quite the contrary; women's desires are often portrayed as stronger, and more dangerous, than men's. Two important distinctions remain, however: first, when a woman's desire is explicit, she is often portrayed as subject to her desire, rather than in control of it. Euripides' Phaedra is completely unable to master her eros for her stepson, despite her best efforts.[105] The lustful women of the *Lysistrata* are as helpless in the face of their desire as the men are, and are only held in check by Lysistrata's stern vigilance. Second, and more important, new brides rarely, if ever, occupy the position of one who desires, and they never do so openly. That sort of activity is left to women who have been married for some time, and even then it is figured as dangerous. New brides are not portrayed as full sexual subjects.

Indeed, once the *parthenos* has been figured as both afraid (of her husband and of the marriage in general) and dangerous (insofar as she is sexually desiring), it is impossible to see her as actively seeking marriage. To do so would be to grant her a sexual subjectivity that would threaten the idea of marriage as a system of exchange between men. We see an example of exactly that disruption in Aeschylus's *Agamemnon*. When Clytemnestra vaunts over her husband's dead body, she uses the conventional imagery of a crop penetrated by rain:

> οὕτω τὸν αὑτοῦ θυμὸν ὁρμαίνει πεσὼν
> κἀκφυσιῶν ὀξεῖαν αἵματος σφαγὴν

βάλλει μ' ἐρεμνῆι ψακάδι φοινίας δρόσου,
χαίρουσαν οὐδὲν ἧσσον ἢ διοσδότωι
γάνει σπορητὸς κάλυκος ἐν λοχεύμασιν.[106]

Thus, falling, he gasped out his life,
spouting a sharp splattering of blood
he struck me with a dark rain of bloody dew,
as I rejoiced no less than does the corn,
when it bursts the pod with the god-sent rain. (1387–92)

Clytemnestra's speech, however, alters the normal direction of this imagery. Here the penetrated sheath (of a seed, standing for the crop by metonymy) is Clytemnestra, and she is active; she, in fact, has penetrated Agamemnon with a weapon. Agamemnon, whose representative in the metaphor is the usually penetrating rain, is strangely passive. The result is a perversion of marriage altogether.[107] Woman's control of her own sexual desire in marriage is, therefore, constructed in tragedy as dangerously uncontrollable (Clytemnestra) or dangerous despite her best intentions (Deianeira). In the case of new brides, it seems nonexistent (Electra, Antigone), or is simply put under ellipse. Insofar as the woman does speak about her marriage, it is to regret her wedding and the alienation from her family and former self that it entailed; her subjectivity denies its subject.

SUBJECTIVITY UNDER ELLIPSIS

McManus observes, "Some anthropologists have described the successful strategies devised by modern Greek women to cope with their unequal position in marriage and society . . . we should not assume that Athenian women did not also employ such coping strategies."[108] It is a futile endeavor, however, to search for evidence of such strategies in our male-authored and male-centered texts. We find in such texts obscure references to female relations and female desire. The fact that such references are often hidden, darkly mentioned, or elliptically constructed does not, however, make them any less a product of men's imagination. On the contrary, such ellipses are important specifically because they indicate to us what men found most threatening, dangerous, or unstable about women, so much so that it can only be represented in a manner that half conceals.[109]

First and foremost, we see a number of structures — legal, social, and literary — that obscure the idea that a young bride might actively desire her husband. Of course, the construction of marriage as a transaction between men implies a hierarchy of power: the husband is the active subject, the wife the object of his desires. Should the bride desire in return, let alone first, she might disrupt the paradigm.[110] Nonetheless, anxious suggestions of brides' desires do enter into some of ancient Athens's most masculine structures of marriage.

Arguably the most thoroughly masculine form of marriage is rape, and we should note that legitimate marriages are in some ways indistinguishable from rape. Vases that show legitimate marriage ceremonies, for example, record possibly vestigial marks of an abduction ritual within marriage: the bride is held *cheir' epi karpo* ("hand on wrist") and is lifted by the groom onto the chariot.[111] Sourvinou-Inwood shows that a series of vases portray "erotic pursuits" in which a young man, often armed, chases a young woman (who sometimes carries a flower), and that these "pursuits" represent a typical understanding of marriage.[112] Particularly interesting is one vase that has an "erotic pursuit" on one side and a "legitimate" marriage procession on the other.[113] Keuls describes a similar black-figure vase that shows the same married couple on both sides. In one picture, the man is dressed as a satyr, carrying off his wife, who is in costume as a maenad. On the other side, the couple embraces out of costume.[114] Rape and marriage can literally be two sides of the same vase.

Even those marriages that are fully legal in the literary texts bear the marks of abduction. Perhaps the most frequent way of marking an abduction is something common to marriages in tragedy: the groom carries the bride over a significant body of water. We might see this as a purely symbolic action — carrying the bride over liminal space to mark her personal transformation — but such action also has a practical side to it. The ocean is troublesome to cross if the girl's father (or first husband, in the case of Helen) wishes to retrieve her. Helen and Europa, for example, are carried overseas. But those women whose marriages are legitimately transacted — Deianeira say, or Phaedra — are also carried over a body of water.[115] They, too, are physically removed from their original families, as a guarantee of fidelity to their new ones. Literature, then, marks marriage with the same signs as rape, and this is important. As Jenkins points out, "The abduction ritual was expressive not only of external, social values but also signified the bride's own experience."[116] That is, the bride is figured as a passive object, probably resistant to the marriage, and dominant ideology dictated that she experience herself as such.

It is not only a question of marriage carrying vestiges of abduction, however. In fact, to distinguish between abduction and marriage may be more problematic than we might suppose. Evans-Grubbs has recently shown that overt abduction of the bride was probably a quasi-legal form of marriage throughout Greek and Roman history.[117] Although custom required the family of the bride to put up a struggle, Evans-Grubbs suggests that often the would-be groom had the implicit consent of the bride's family, as it would save them the trouble of putting up a dowry for their daughter. The woman, too, was expected to resist — though often was suspected of going along with her abductor. Her resistance guarantees her status: because she openly struggles against her abductor, she affirms her purity. The fight she puts up simultaneously assures the manhood and dominance of her husband.[118] The paradigm of abduction as marriage, therefore, results in exactly the hierarchy of active/passive, strong/weak, sexual/pure that "legitimate" marriage also sought to create.

More interesting, however, is that in all these representations of rape/marriage, suggestions surface that the bride is *not* reluctant, that in fact she *does* desire both marriage and her groom. Such active desiring on her part would threaten the male homosociality of marriage and would posit the woman as a potential rival to male subjects. Nonetheless, vase paintings, even of abductions, contain elements of consent and of mutual sexual desire: Sutton's large-scale study shows conclusively that fifth-century vases increasingly emphasize "the elements of union over those expressing separation and transition."[119] Even when the groom appears to be pulling his bride along, he usually turns to give the bride a look "of reassurance and love."[120] Moreover, Sutton observes that around 440, *erotes*, small pictures of the god Eros, begin to appear, a clear icon of mutual desire.

Sutton suggests that the intended audience of these scenes was probably female, because they appear most often on *loutraphoroi*, a type of pot used by women in their ritual prewedding bath.[121] McManus agrees, and therefore assumes that these scenes were rather crude propaganda, arguing that "such patently unrealistic portrayals may have been intended to deconstruct the more frightening aspects of marriage and aid in the Athenian girls' socialization."[122] Not all critics, however, assume that real brides would necessarily have been terrified.[123] Redfield points out that, despite a certain expectation of "virginal modesty" on the bride's part, vases often show the bride willingly lifting her own veil, indicating her consent.[124] He suggests throughout that this element of consent was present in real marriages — that it is only the tragic marriage, with its built-in crises, that presents the bride's experience otherwise.

Rather than choose between these alternatives, however, I find it more helpful to assume that the experiences of the bride on these vases (and in real life) were multiple and contradictory. Vases and literature represent young women as both frightened and desiring. Although they appear mutually exclusive, these two representations form an ideological consistency. In the first place, the women's fear is a guarantee of their sexual purity. At the same time, their desire for their husbands is a guarantee that they will not desire anyone else, so that it, too, becomes a guarantee of fidelity. Both elements contribute to the construction of "the desirable bride"—a woman who will be faithful to her husband and no one else—so both elements are pictured. What is more, any given bride might well experience both elements.[125]

In her analysis of abduction marriages, Evans-Grubbs creates a picture that is complementary to that of the vase paintings: ". . . there is always a presumption . . . that the abducted girl was willing to be taken, and even if she puts up resistance and is subjected to violence during the abduction, she is still considered partly responsible."[126] We must be careful here; perhaps this is nothing more than a typical example of a patriarchy blaming victims for its own crimes. But, as Evans-Grubbs points out, the abduction marriage is advantageous for both husband and wife in that the husband's courage is proven, as is the wife's purity; and if one result is that women who do not desire marriage are suspected of desiring it, the abduction also provides useful camouflage of innocence for a woman's (potential) sexual subjectivity. Like the Athenian court cases, the abduction always defines the woman as an object of transaction, but suspects her of being the dangerous subject who might try to sneak into a foreign *oikos*.

In fact, we may have literary evidence for exactly this sort of overdetermined attitude. As has often been noted, Persephone lies to her mother in the *Homeric Hymn to Demeter*.[127] When she is in the underworld, Hades offers her a pomegranate to eat (not telling her the implications of her eating). The third-person "omniscient" narrator does not even narrate Persephone's eating of the seeds—the event is apparently unremarkable at the time. But when Demeter asks her daughter if she ate anything in the underworld, and explains that if she did she will have to return to the underworld part of each year, Persephone replies:

> αὐτὰρ ὁ λάθρῃ
> ἔμβαλέ μοι ῥοιῆς κόκκον, μελιηδέ' ἐδωδήν,
> ἄκουσαν δὲ βίῃ με προσηνάγκασσε πάσασθαι.[128]

> But he in secret
> gave me the seed of a pomegranate, sweet to eat,
> and he forced me, unwilling, with violence to eat it. (411–13)

Where does Hades' supposed violence come from? There are at least two possible answers, and they are not mutually exclusive: first, the difference in the two stories might be the result of the different points of view of the two narrators. That is, Persephone might really have believed that she underwent violence, though it either did not appear so or did not seem worth mentioning to the narrator of the *Hymn*. Second, it may simply be, as Faraone suggests, that Persephone tells the story that she does because she would have been expected by her family and friends to put up some show of resistance.[129] By putting up this front, however, Persephone does not undermine the principle of marriage — rather, she conforms to an absolutely standard expectation of brides in marriage. By portraying herself as resisting the wedding, therefore, she actually supports the institution. And, conveniently, she also masks from all parties the possibility that she is a sexual subject, that in accepting the "seeds" from Hades she has transferred her allegiance to another household, that she is in fact a desiring actor and not just a passive object of violence.[130] We do not actually see Persephone as a subject in this poem; but her "lie" to Demeter suggests that she is covering up precisely such subjectivity.

These artistic depictions are mirrored in Athenian legal structure. The Solonian law on *epikleroi*, as it is quoted in Plutarch, does more than assign the orphaned woman to her nearest male in-law. The law, among other things, contains two interesting provisions:

> εἰς τοῦτο δὲ συντελεῖ καὶ τὸ τὴν νύμφην τῷ νυμφίῳ
> συγκαθείργνυσθαι μήλου κυδωνίου κατατραγοῦσαν, καὶ
> τὸ τρὶς ἑκάστου μηνὸς ἐντυγχάνειν πάντως τῇ ἐπι-
> κλήρῳ τὸν λαβόντα.[131]

> In agreement with this, the bride is to be put in a closed
> room with the bridegroom while eating a Cydonian apple,
> and . . . the one marrying an *epikleros* will go to her[132] three
> times a month in any case. (Solon 20.3)

Faraone suggests that the eating of the apple is a sign of sexual consent, and points out that the law provides for at least a semiregular schedule of intercourse.[133] The purpose of this provision may be no more than to encourage the production of a (preferably male) heir.[134] But the eating of the Cydonian apple at least suggests an awareness of the bride's sexual desires. The law would, in any case, keep men from marrying an *epikleros* for the estate without intending to sleep with her.

Despite these tacit and obscure suggestions of female desire, however, it is clear that the Athenian state viewed it as a threat. A woman's sexual attraction might force a foolish young man into an ill-advised marriage, as the speaker of Isaeus 3 claims:

> ἤδη γάρ τινες νέοι ἄνθρωποι ἐπιθυμήσαντες τοιούτων
> γυναικῶν, καὶ ἀκρατῶς ἔχοντες αὐτῶν, ἐπείσθησαν ὑπ'
> ἀνοίας εἰς αὑτοὺς τοιοῦτόν τι ἐξαμαρτεῖν.[135]

> Indeed, certain young men, being enamored of such
> women, and not having sufficient control over themselves,
> are convinced by lack of thought to make such a mistake
> against themselves. (3.17)

The possibility of such female erotic power leads to the common but tricky question: Is this or that child "from a betrothed wife, or from a hetaira?"[136] *Hetairai* threaten the category of "citizen" precisely because there is not sufficient control of their sexual activity, and hence of their procreative activity. Their adoption of sexual subjectivity (as portrayed in Isaeus 3.17, above) can be parlayed into civic subjectivity—that is, they can slip into the citizenry as producers of legitimate citizens. The result is to threaten society itself—if harlots can be wives, wives will be no better than harlots. The legal texts, however, portray the historical wives as taking on a role rather different from that of women in the tragic texts. Unlike the discontented women of Sophocles' *Tereus*, or Euripides' Phaedra, [Demosthenes] 59.110ff. suggests (hypothetically) that the listeners' wives will protect their position as sequestered within the *oikos*, removed from sexual or civic subjectivity.[137] The two types of text have, therefore, different means of achieving the same social point; but a fear of female erotic subjectivity motivates both.

To see how tragedy contains and neutralizes the possibility of female desire, let us look briefly at Aeschylus's version of the Danaid myth. Detienne's analysis of this story, in particular, finds an element of woman-as-subject in marriage. Although he sees violence as underlying and always potentially present in marriage, Detienne suggests that the acquittal of Hypermestra shows another side of the paradigm: "The pronounced acquitment makes Hypermestra a 'subject under the law'; she is able to ally herself with the man whom she prefers. . . . The marriage of Hypermestra does not have as its purpose the production of children whose legitimacy needs to be confirmed."[138] It is true that this myth emphasizes Hypermestra's right to choose to keep her husband and that the narrative of the marriage focuses on her, not her offspring. But even so, Aeschylus describes this picture of marriage in conventional images that reaffirm Hypermestra's passivity and stability (Aphrodite speaks):

> ἐρᾷ μὲν ἁγνὸς οὐρανὸς τρῶσαι χθόνα,
> ἔρως δὲ γαῖαν λαμβάνει γάμου τυχεῖν·
> ὄμβρος δ' ἀπ' εὐνάεντος οὐρανοῦ πεσὼν
> ἔκυσε γαῖαν· ἡ δὲ τίκτεται βροτοῖς
> μήλων τε βοσκὰς καὶ βίον Δημήτριον
> δένδρων τ' ὀπώραν· ἐκ νοτίζοντος γάμου
> τελεῖθ' ὅσ' ἔστι· τῶν δ' ἐγὼ παραίτιος.[139]

The pure heaven desires to wound the ground,
desire for marriage seizes the earth;
the rains falling from the mating sky
impregnate the earth. The earth gives birth
to flocks of sheep and the livelihood of Demeter [grain]
and the blooming of trees for mortals. From this raining
    wedding
everything that is comes to completion; and of all this I have
    a part. (frag. 44)

Aeschylus allows that Hypermestra desires. Aphrodite justifies that desire, however, with an image of the earth penetrated by rain that renders woman's subjectivity conveniently passive. Even here we see traces of the idea that the woman is wounded, a victim of violence in the erotic union, while she (the earth) desires not so much her mate as the marriage itself. The position of these ideas within the context of the marriage of heaven and earth, as Zeitlin points out, both naturalizes that wounding and compensates the woman for it, by emphasizing her procreative powers.[140] If, as Seaford claims, "the attitude of the Danaids resembles in several respects the attitude associated with the Greek bride or her female companions, but taken to an exotic extreme,"[141] then Hypermestra both overcomes and redeems that attitude. She may not fear marriage, as so many women in tragedy do, but her desire is made so passive that it is no more a threat to male subjectivity (and indeed, in this myth, is less of one) than is the Danaids' fear.[142]

All this suggests that Greek men developed a series of myths emphasizing women's fear of marriage, and normalizing a certain amount of resistance to marriage. And though I do not mean to suggest that this fear and resistance were not present *in fact*, it is important to note that these myths tend to obscure the possibility, also portrayed, of female sexual subjectivity within the legitimate sphere of matrimony. Vase paintings and texts hint at such desire, but similarly bury it under competing images of female decorum and reluctance. In tragedy, when a woman like Hypermestra must justify her desire, the narrative employs images that ensure that the woman will be a stable and pure *object* of desire, which then remains the exclusive province of the male. Once again, I must emphasize that both of these elements are present in masculine texts and are part of masculine culture. Much as we might like to, we cannot extract one side of the picture in order to argue that it (and it alone) represents women's experience.[143] Both sides, rather, represent men's desire. Instead of romantic images being used to help socialize Athenian girls, then, I argue that the vases and texts demonstrate a complex masculine ideology that both posits and contains suggestions of female erotic desire.

In Sophocles' plays, as we shall see, the possibility of female desire is similarly both present and obscure. Sophoclean heroines almost never give voice to desire for a husband or potential husband, and yet they do talk about their desire for marriage, and they do express a wish to be desired. I argue that the inability or unwillingness of Sophocles' dramas to portray female desire — and corresponding subjectivity — at the beginning of marriage parallels the plays' failure to portray the successful transformation from *korē* to *gunē*. At the same time, the moment of desire is, in Sophocles, often a moment of great civic crisis: Deianeira destroying Heracles' household, Antigone undermining Creon, Electra determining to kill Aegisthus herself. In other words, it is the very inexpressibility of female desire — even in a fully legitimate context — that renders it dangerous. Because it is undefined, obscured, it threatens to overturn the stability of masculine transactions and masculine culture.

We end this survey, therefore, with a fundamental paradox. The literary world shows us both more and less of women's transformation in marriage than does the world of legal texts: more, because the literary texts purport to show us the brides' emotional experiences during and after their weddings; less, because these texts, especially tragedy, show the women as having no alternative once they are married. A woman's loyalty to her husband is assured by various textual strategies: she is denied all access to her original family; she either does not have, or seems unaware of, any power of dowry; her *kurieia* is in no sense divided. At the same time, however, we find that the loyalty that this should imply is curiously unexpressed and, when things go wrong, is immediately called into question, both by the male characters in the plays and (as we shall soon see) by the plays' modern critics. Female sexuality lives in a no-man's-land, constantly needed, always suspect, and continuously controlled. We must remember that the "women" we hear speak in Sophocles' plays are not women at all; but to hear Sophocles' version of female discourse and to note where that discourse declares itself unable to speak can be a step toward understanding women's contradictory place in Athenian culture.

Chapter 2 MALE HOMOSOCIAL DESIRE
IN THE *Trachiniae*

> It has been said that he was not in love with Eleanor, and up
> to this period this certainly had been true. But as soon as he
> heard that she loved someone else, he began to be very fond of
> her himself. He did not make up his mind that he wished to
> have her for his wife; he had never thought of her, and did not
> now think of her, in connexion with himself; but he experi-
> enced an inward, indefinable feeling of deep regret, a gnaw-
> ing sorrow, an unconquerable depression of spirits, and also
> a species of self abasement that he — he, Mr. Arabin — had not
> done something to prevent that other he, that vile he whom he
> so thoroughly despised, from carrying off this sweet prize.

ANTHONY TROLLOPE, *Barchester Towers*

Of Sophocles' extant tragedies, the *Trachiniae* focuses
most clearly on the dynamics and implications of marriage. The drama centers on Deianeira and her husband Heracles, and their relationship motivates the principal action. Deianeira, the central character for the first two-
thirds of the play, views every situation that she encounters in the drama in
terms of her marriage, often reminiscing about her wedding day.[1] Her one
decisive act, poisoning the sacrificial robe that will kill Heracles, is a mis-
guided attempt to maintain an exclusive relationship with her husband. In
the midst of all this, as we shall see, there are three other weddings to consider: Heracles' abduction of and implicit marriage to Iole; a parody of wedding rituals in which Heracles is figured as the bride; and Hyllus's promised
wedding to Iole. The text is full of weddings, wedding imagery, and specu-
lation about what it means for men and women to be married.[2]

Not surprisingly, in this play marriage means something different for each
of the characters involved. Tragedies often dramatize the difficulties of mis-
communication between characters, and in this case the drama centers on
the failures of both Heracles and Deianeira to understand how the other
views their mutual relationship. In one sense, Deianeira's marriage constructs her as a subject. That is, she derives an identity, a social position, and
a sense of self from her relationship to Heracles. At the same time, she ex-
emplifies most of the ideas about brides outlined in the previous chapter: she

is fearful of her suitors and reluctant toward marriage, resentful of her position as an alienated wife, and strangely unfulfilled in the course of her married life. I argue that this lack of fulfillment stems precisely from her failure to understand that, from Heracles' point of view, she is not the subject of *his* marriage. Heracles views his wedding to Deianeira as he views virtually every other aspect of his life: as a relationship, whether antagonistic or friendly, with other men. It is an expression of male homosocial desire.

In economies of male homosocial desire, as Sedgwick explains, men establish hierarchical relationships of various types that serve to further the social interests of men.[3] These relationships define the erotic (homo- or hetero-) as springing from a desire for society that is for and between men. So marriage is commonly understood, as Rubin has shown,[4] as two men (the father and the groom) exchanging a woman (the bride).[5] In the most extreme of such cases, the woman involved ceases to be even an object of desire; she is merely an object of exchange. The relationship between men becomes, then, one of the structures by which women are defined as outside of culture. Even a wedding, at the moment of a young woman's personal transformation, may be a transaction in which the woman takes no part as a recognized subject.

I do not mean to suggest that homosocial desire is a transcendental constant of human history. The form that male-male relations takes varies from culture to culture, and from time period to time period. Such relationships are not necessarily homoerotic or homosexual, for example, though they can be.[6] Furthermore, the structure of the desire may be agonistic (as in the case of Heracles and Achelous) or cooperative (as in the case of Heracles and Oineus). In the particularly competitive society of ancient Athens, these relationships are rarely "friendly" — often the participants do their best to harm one another. Although these relationships are characterized by open hostility, it is still useful and accurate to recognize them as a form of the homosocial economy if, in the larger context, this hostility confirms male activity and authority in general. Heracles' relations to other male figures usually take exactly this form.

The presence of homosocial desire also does not preclude the possibility of heterosocial desire — in fact, heterosocial (and particularly heterosexual) desire often becomes a means of enacting the homosocial. I do not mean, therefore, that there is no erotic relationship between Heracles and Deianeira, or between Heracles and Iole. Rather, I suggest that one of the strategies of this play is to privilege the homosocial aspect of those relationships. For Heracles, the defining relation in all of his dealings with women is with another man; for Deianeira, unaware of the importance of these homosocial relations, Heracles' heteroerotic relations with her, Iole, and other women define her social position. The play thus creates a paradigm for marriage of which Deianeira can have only a faulty understanding, because she sees herself as a (passive) center of a heterosocial unit (the *oikos*). From the perspective of the men in the play, however, she is outside of society (defined by and for males) altogether. Heracles lives and breathes male homosocial desire, and for him Deianeira is not so much a person with whom he has a relationship as she is a means of communicating with various male characters. As we shall see, Deianeira's complete failure to understand this form of marginalization constitutes her pathos and her tragedy.[7]

DEIANEIRA'S VIEW OF MARRIAGE

Deianeira's experience of marriage occupies her entire onstage life. When the play opens, she has been married to Heracles for some time; her son, Hyllus, is in the process of becoming an adult. And yet, from her first speech, she talks only of marriage and, much of the time, about the wedding itself. She opens the drama by narrating the story of Heracles and Achelous (9ff.); when she first meets Iole, she wonders if she is unmarried, or has borne children (308); when she learns the truth about Iole, she sets about trying to save her own marriage, and we hear the story of Nessus, who tried to rape her during her journey to her husband's *oikos* (555ff.); and when she learns that her anointed robe has poisoned Heracles, she kills herself by stabbing herself on their marriage bed, an act of penetration that explicitly recalls her intercourse there with Heracles.[8] Clearly, Deianeira understands and expresses herself in terms of her marriage; but as if that transition has never quite been completed, she continually replays it in an endless attempt to gain closure. Her transition to the status of wife, then, is implicitly defined as open, fissured, unstable.

This instability defines the paradoxical nature of marriage for women in tragedy. Deianeira's wedding day, like that of most tragic brides, is far from happy. She does not, however, speak of her marriage as exceptional in kind. Rather, her unhappiness in marriage, from the very beginning, is only exceptional in its particulars. For example, she describes being wooed by the river-god Achelous, and confesses to her fear of marriage: ναίουσ' ἔτ' ἐν Πλευρῶνι νυμφείων ὄκνον[9] / ἄλγιστον ἔσχον, εἴ τις Αἰτωλὶς γυνή ("Living still in Pleuros, I experienced the most painful / fear of marriage, if any Aitolian woman [experienced such]," 7–8). If the *amount* of fear that she feels is unusual, due to the unusual nature of her suitor, the *fact* of it is perfectly regular. Deianeira merely claims to have the worst fear of anyone — not that the fear itself is exceptional.[10]

Moreover, Deianeira laments her marriage in much the same terms most tragic brides use. In a series of images, she and the chorus confirm that, for Deianeira, the wedding has been little more than an alienation from the bride's paternal family. Deianeira tells us that Heracles rescued her from the fate of marrying Achelous, an event that she recalls with some relief. But her description of this pivotal moment is curiously uninformed:

> ὃς εἰς ἀγῶνα τῷδε συμπεσὼν μάχης
> ἐκλύεταί με. καὶ τρόπον μὲν ἂν πόνων
> οὐκ ἂν διείποιμ'· οὐ γὰρ οἶδ'· ἀλλ' ὅστις ἦν
> θακῶν ἀταρβὴς τῆς θέας, ὅδ' ἂν λέγοι.
> ἐγὼ γὰρ ἥμην ἐκπεπληγμένη φόβῳ
> μή μοι τὸ κάλλος ἄλγος ἐξεύροι ποτέ.

> He [Heracles] fell into battle with this one [Achelous]
> and freed me. But I cannot describe the nature of the
>   struggle,
> for I don't know. But whoever was a
> fearless watcher of the sight, perhaps he will say.
> For I sat idle, struck with fear
> lest my beauty discover some grief for me. (20–25)

Here it is, the critical turning point of Deianeira's life; it is not only the moment of her liberation from the horrific river-god, but, in effect, the moment of her wedding. Yet she, fearful, cannot bear to watch, and consequently cannot tell us what it was like. As Deianeira suggested, however, perhaps someone who saw the event can describe it for her; and indeed, the chorus does just that at line 507 and following:

> ὁ μὲν ἦν ποταμοῦ σθένος, ὑψίκερω τετραόρου
> φάσμα ταύρου,
> Ἀχελῷος ἀπ' Οἰνιαδᾶν, ὁ δὲ Βακχίας ἄπο
> ἦλθε παλίντονα Θήβας
> τόξα καὶ λόγχας ῥόπαλόν τε τινάσσων,
> παῖς Διός· οἳ τότ' ἀολλεῖς
> ἴσαν ἐς μέσον ἱέμενοι λεχέων·
> μόνα δ' εὔλεκτρος ἐν μέσῳ Κύπρις
> ῥαβδονόμει ξυνοῦσα.

> τότ' ἦν χερός, ἦν δὲ τό-
> ξων πάταγος,
> ταυρείων τ' ἀνάμιγδα κεράτων·
> ἦν δ' ἀμφίπλεκτοι κλίμακες, ἦν δὲ μετώ-

πων ὀλόεντα
πλήγματα καὶ στόνος ἀμφοῖν.
ἁ δ' εὐῶπις ἁβρὰ
τηλαυγεῖ παρ' ὄχθῳ
ἧστο τὸν ὃν προσμένουσ' ἀκοίταν.
†ἐγὼ δὲ μάτηρ μὲν οἷα φράζω·†
τὸ δ' ἀμφινείκητον ὄμμα νύμφας
ἐλεινὸν ἀμμένει <τέλος>·
κἀπὸ ματρὸς ἄφαρ βέβαχ',
ὥστε πόρτις ἐρήμα.

One had the strength of a river, looking like
a high-horned, four-footed bull,
Achelous of Oiniadae; the other came from Bacchic
Thebes, shaking his bent bow and his spears and club,
the son of Zeus. They met
in the middle, desiring marriage;
Aphrodite alone, well married, was in the middle,
acting as an umpire.

Then there was striking of hands, there was a striking of
    bows,
and a clashing of bull's horns;
there was an intertwining of limbs, there was
a deadly butting of heads and groans from both.
But she, soft and beautiful,
on a shining hillside
sat waiting for her husband.
But I, a mother, say such things [11]
But the fought-over figure (*omma*), a bride,
awaited the *telos* pitiably,
and wandered away from her mother
like a lost calf.[12] (507–30)

Note that the scene as described puts the relationship between Heracles and Achelous squarely in the realm of desire. Aphrodite is in the middle of the two men, who are described as "desiring the bed" (and whose bed, exactly, is not clear). In the antistrophe, the two combatants become confused, their limbs intertwined, so that it is not even clear to whom the clashing "bows" and "horns" belong. These two men are the focus of the scene, the center of the action, and their battle is described in terms that suggest an erotic relationship.

What of Deianeira? As she told us earlier, she is strangely detached from the scene. At the end of the ode, the chorus says that she, a prize, wanders away from her mother like a lost calf. As Seaford points out, the image of a calf separated from its mother is something of a topos in descriptions of weddings.[13] The battle will determine whom Deianeira marries, and so the chorus describes it with imagery that reminds us of weddings. The point of the image, however, is summed up in the description of her as *erēma*, "bereft," a word used of widows and orphans. She is alienated by the battle from both suitors and family members as she waits for her "husband." Deianeira's actual marriage ceremony is not described in the course of the play — the violent contest between two hyper-masculine figures just cited is the only representation of that event. The fight for her hand, then, depicts her wedding as she experiences it: a violent struggle between two men in which she plays no part and that she cannot bear to watch. Little wonder that she suffers a sense of loss.[14]

Moreover, Deianeira's sense of alienation continues as Heracles takes his bride to their new home. The two reach a river, over which Deianeira is carried by the centaur Nessus. This river-crossing is a fateful moment; it marks Deianeira's transference to a new home, her transition to a new state. Not surprisingly, then, as Armstrong has shown, lines 560–63 contain a compact version of the wedding procession. Nessus crosses the river

οὔτε πομπίμοις
κώπαις ἐρέσσων οὔτε λαίφεσιν νεώς.
. . . τὸν πατρῷον ἡνίκα στόλον
ξὺν Ἡρακλεῖ τὸ πρῶτον εὖνις ἑσπόμην.

not rowing with processional
oars, nor with the sails of a ship.
. . . When I first went on the paternal journey
with Heracles, as his bride.

Deianeira speaks of the river-crossing as *patrōion stolon*, a "fatherly procession." Armstrong sees this *patrōion stolon* as a reference to her traditional "'send-off' from her parent's house."[15] What is particularly biting about this description of the procession, however, becomes apparent in 560–61: Deianeira's choice of words, particularly the adjective "processional" (*pompimos*), is significant. She uses the word because she is complaining about the lack of a traditional *pompē* (procession) after her wedding. She has been sent off to her new home without any of the traditional accompaniment, and is instead being carried across the river on the back of a centaur, representative of the very edge of civilization. The point of this complaint becomes even more clear with the end of 563. The sentence admits of two possible translations, depending on the meaning we assign to the word *eunis*: either "When first I went on the paternal journey / with Heracles, as his bride (*eunis*)," or "When first I went on the paternal journey / with Heracles, deprived (*eunis*) [of family]." Given the sarcastic tone of the lines immediately preceding, it is quite probable that this ambiguity of meaning would have been understood by the audience.[16] For Deianeira, to be a bride is to experience separation, and to resent it.

Deianeira's alienation does not end with the wedding: the play presents her transformation from *parthenos* to *gunē* as incomplete, and her integration into her new *oikos* as interrupted. The fears that Deianeira felt before her wedding, for example, and during the battle between Achelous and Heracles (lines 7–8 and 37) have merely been replaced in married life with a new fear: ἐκ φόβου φόβον τρέφω ("I nourish fear from fear," 28).[17] Moreover, when she dies, Deianeira is still trying to establish her place in Heracles' *oikos*. She claims that she will die with Heracles (720), and kills herself on his bed, suggestively stabbing herself in the torso. Even this gesture is a failure, as Loraux argues: "The word 'with' will have meaning only for herself . . . the hero when he is laid low will deny her, condemning her beyond death to the solitude that was her lot in life."[18] In fact, when the nurse describes Deianeira's death, she uses the word *erēmē* ("bereft") at line 905 (cf. 530, cited above).[19] She is literally bereft, since she has apparently killed her husband. As Seaford argues, however, the word is also suitable for Deianeira as a bride who has lost her paternal family and has never been successfully integrated into her husband's.[20] In other words, Deianeira spends the entire play — up to the moment of her death — in a continuous liminal state: "The anxiety of the bride at her ἐρημία, has spilled out over the limits that should have been set to it by the ritual and has engulfed her whole life."[21] Even in death, she is still looking for the completion that her wedding promised but did not deliver.

As we have already seen, our literary texts do not often describe a woman's internal transformation when she undergoes marriage. When women in tragic texts speak of marriage, as in Sophocles' fragment 583, or Euripides' *Medea* 232ff.,[22] they are portrayed as opposed to the marriage in the first place. They would rather have stayed in their fathers' *oikoi*. Deianeira is unique in that she does not speak out against having been the object of a marital transaction. On the contrary, she frequently uses imagery that posits her as an object of desire; what distresses her, it appears, is that she does not occupy the central position that such imagery implies. For example, Deianeira uses a traditional image to describe her marriage, that of the bride as a ploughed field.[23] But here the image is given a twist:

κἀφύσαμεν δὴ παῖδας, οὓς κεῖνός ποτε,
γῄτης ὅπως ἄρουραν ἔκτοπον λαβών,
σπείρων μόνον προσεῖδε κἀξαμῶν ἅπαξ.

And we have borne children, whom he sees then,
like a farmer visiting an outlying field,
only once, during sowing and reaping. (31–33)

The bearing of children, which should integrate Deianeira into her husband's household, and whereby she should, through association with the
goddess Hestia, take on values of "fixity, permanence, and seclusion,"[24] becomes instead another example of Deianeira's isolation and exclusion. She
fairly willingly accepts the passive role of a ploughed field—with its accom-
panying object-status—but not the fact that she is a *marginal* plot of land in
Heracles' eyes.[25]

In Deianeira's second speech (142–50), she uses the other common agricultural metaphor to describe a woman's transformation, characterizing the
unmarried women of the chorus as uncultivated, idyllic flowers.[26]

ὡς δ' ἐγὼ θυμοφθορῶ
μήτ' ἐκμάθοις παθοῦσα, νῦν δ' ἄπειρος εἶ.
τὸ γὰρ νεάζον ἐν τοιοῖσδε βόσκεται
χώροισιν αὑτοῦ, καί νιν οὐ θάλπος θεοῦ,
οὐδ' ὄμβρος, οὐδὲ πνευμάτων οὐδὲν κλονεῖ,
ἀλλ' ἡδοναῖς ἄμοχθον ἐξαίρει βίον
ἐς τοῦθ', ἕως τις ἀντὶ παρθένου γυνὴ
κληθῇ, λάβῃ τ' ἐν νυκτὶ φροντίδων μέρος,
ἤτοι πρὸς ἀνδρὸς ἢ τέκνων φοβουμένη.

. . . thus how my heart is destroyed,
may you never learn, suffering, since now you are
    inexperienced.
For the young [shoot] is nourished in its own
places, and neither the heat of the god,
nor the rain, nor the wind beats down on it,
but it obtains a painless livelihood of pleasure
until that time, when one is called "wife" instead of
    "maiden"
and when one takes her portion of worries in the night,
being frightened either for her husband or for her children.
(142–50)

As Seaford points out, the image of the young girls as plants untouched by
heat and rain evokes a response of pity for the loss of girlhood and privileged

position in her father's home that is implicit in a woman's marriage.[27] That, however, is not the point that Deianeira is making. Deianeira does not directly express regret over her loss of girlhood, though that is implied in her wish that the chorus not experience what she has. Rather, Deianeira is concerned to justify her fear *for* Heracles, despite the recent news that he is on the way home. She assumes that such fear would be incomprehensible to those without experience of marriage. Suggested here is a certain female subjectivity, a notion of Deianeira's personal feelings and desires.[28] But even as she refers to her personal experience, Deianeira suggests that the transformation that the young girls will go through *as she has experienced it* is incommunicable. The chorus will not understand her fears until the chorus members are wives themselves. Deianeira's statement corresponds to this play's reluctance to describe and her own failure to experience the reintegration that marriage is supposed to bring about. Her fear is incommunicable because it is the result of a marriage that has resulted only in apparently endless alienation, in a state of noncommunication.

If Deianeira does not resent her loss of girlhood (as her tragic counterparts, Medea and the women in the *Tereus*, do), we are left with a problem: Why is her marriage one of constant fear and unsatisfied expectations? I suggest that this play presents two mutually exclusive paradigms for marriage, and that Deianeira's model simply has no place in Heracles'. Deianeira sees herself, as lines 31–33 (above) show, as an object of Heracles' desire. She willingly endorses her marriage to Heracles, and even when she questions whether or not that marriage was for the best (27), it is only because she is constantly "worried about him" (29). Although the "(possibly illusory) transition to permanent happiness embodied in marriage"[29] may escape her in the course of this play, she is perfectly willing to embrace the (possible) illusion.[30]

In her view of Heracles, however, there is something that Deianeira does not and cannot see. Earlier I quoted the chorus's description of Deianeira as Heracles and Achelous battle over her: she sits off to one side, "like a calf separated from its mother" (529–30). She is not only bereft of her mother, however; she also sits apart from the battle that is going on. As she herself admits in her version of this scene, καὶ τρόπον μὲν ἂν πόνων / οὐκ ἂν διείποιμ᾽· οὐ γὰρ οἶδ᾽ ("And I could not tell you what the struggle was like; for I do not know," 21–22). Deianeira's blindness here is symptomatic: she cannot look at the aspect of marriage that consists of a fight between two men. What she also does not see, therefore, is that Heracles' relationship with her (and with Iole as well) does not depend on a heterosexual desire for her. Rather, the important relationship in this (and every other) triangle *from*

EXCHANGE AND THE MAIDEN

Heracles' point of view is the homosocial one, in this case between him and Achelous.

Iole will prove a useful point of contact for these two views. For Deianeira sees in Iole a carbon copy of her own relationship to Heracles, and assumes that she is competing with Iole for Heracles' heterosexual desire.[31] From Heracles' perspective, however, his relationship with Iole, like his with Deianeira, is essentially a homosocial one with another man, in this case Iole's father. As we saw in the battle over Deianeira, Aphrodite stands not between Heracles and his future bride, but between the two suitors. In saying this, I do not mean to deny that Heracles has genuine erotic feelings for both women, at some point. I simply mean that, for Heracles, those erotic feelings are not what define the relationship and give it meaning. In Iole, then, Heracles' and Deianeira's perspectives clash head on, and from this clash springs the main action of the tragedy.[32]

HERACLES' CONQUESTS

In Chapter 1 I suggested that for an Athenian, the difference between rape and marriage could be less clear-cut than we might expect. Although rape was publicly denounced (and indeed, was given as a pretext for war in various literary and historical texts), it could at times be privately condoned as a convenient form of marriage for both the groom and the bride's family. Similarly, the wedding ritual seems to have contained vestigial elements of an abduction myth.[33] This play helps confirm that view. To a truly remarkable extent, the experiences of Iole and Deianeira are analogous: Heracles comes and engages in a battle with a man over each of them, and each is then carried over water by a surrogate (though Lichas is more trustworthy than Nessus) to Heracles' home. Both women then experience a similar pain: Deianeira tells us, ἐμοὶ πικρὰς / ὠδῖνας αὐτοῦ προσβαλὼν ἀποίχεται ("Giving me sharp pains for him, he goes away" 41–42). Similarly, Lichas describes Iole's travel:

> ἀλλ' αἰὲν ὠδίνουσα συμφορᾶς βάρος
> δακρυρροεῖ δύστηνος, ἐξ ὅτου πάτραν
> διήνεμον λέλοιπεν.

> But always being pained through the weight of misfortune
> the wretch weeps, from the time when
> she left her windy fatherland. (325–27)

This pain is curiously appropriate to both women since, as Wender points out, *ōdines* are typically labor pangs.[34] Moreover, as several commentators have noticed, Deianeira says of Iole, τὸ κάλλος αὐτῆς τὸν βίον διώλεσεν ("Her own beauty has destroyed her life," 465), recalling her own similar statement about herself (24–25).[35]

Most important, when Deianeira describes Iole, she uses language that posits her as a bride. In fact, much of Deianeira's language is that used *by brides* in other texts to complain about their *own* experience of marriage. In Deianeira's decisive speech, she says:

> κόρην γάρ, οἶμαι δ᾽ οὐκέτ᾽, ἀλλ᾽ ἐζευγμένην
> παρεσδέδεγμαι, φόρτον ὥστε ναυτίλος,
> λωβητὸν ἐμπόλημα τῆς ἐμῆς φρενός.

> For this girl, no, I think no longer, but a yoked woman
> I have received, as a ship captain takes on cargo,
> transacted goods that are abuses of my heart. (536–38)

The image of a bride as an animal who must be yoked is common enough.[36] The word *empolēma* is more pointed. We might compare Sophocles' fragment 583, in which either Procne or Philomela complains of marriage:

> ὅταν δ᾽ ἐς ἥβην ἐξικώμεθ᾽ ἔμφρονες,
> ὠθούμεθ᾽ ἔξω καὶ διεμπολώμεθα[37]

> When we reach puberty, fully thinking,
> we are forced outside and sold into slavery.

Moreover, the reference to a ship captain's cargo recalls the transfer over a body of water that so often marks a literary marriage. Deianeira recognizes, and rightly, that Iole has become what she always expected to be: the traditional bride of Heracles. Segal is correct to point out that Iole's "marriage" violates several civilized norms, since Heracles has not only killed her father but destroyed her entire city.[38] Nonetheless, the language that Deianeira uses to describe this unusually violent transaction can be, and often is, used of brides in "legitimate" marriages.

Deianeira does not recognize the same element in Iole's experience, however, that she fails to see in her own marriage, namely the relation between men that defines the experience. The words that Deianeira uses to describe Iole (above) hold a different meaning for the speaker than they do for Heracles. On the one hand, describing Iole as sold into slavery sets her up as a bride and, therefore, as an object of desire with whom Deianeira must compete. But at the same time, the imagery is all of exchange, especially the reference to Iole as nautical cargo. If we take Deianeira's words more literally than she does, we see that they mark Iole as an object of trade, transacted between men.[39]

Moreover, as smitten as Heracles may be with Iole (and it is well to re-member that we have only Lichas's word for this), he has a longer-standing and, from a masculine standpoint, more important relationship with her father. In Lichas's first explanation for Iole's presence,[40] we are told that Hera-cles sacked Eurytus's city because of a long string of events beginning with a violation of *xenia* ("guest privilege"). Eurytus welcomed Heracles to his "hearth and home" as an old friend. After Heracles got drunk at dinner, Eurytus threw him out, and "from this Heracles' anger began" (262–69). Later, however, the messenger tells a different version, in which Heracles' lust for Iole is the motivating factor in sacking Eurytus's city, and suggests that the reasons that are quoted above are mere trumped-up excuses (359–62, quoted below). Reconciling these two versions has proven difficult. The problem is that the events in Lichas's apparently untrue version are con-firmed elsewhere in the text, while those in the messenger's are confirmed by the very presence of Iole. As Scodel puts it,

> It seems that details of different legends have been mixed
> together so that each part has the ring of familiar, and hence
> true material, but the whole does not cohere. . . . What we
> are told is necessary to the series of events, yet we do not
> know how Heracles fell in love and was refused.[41]

These two versions, however, need not be mutually exclusive, even if the messenger suggests that they are. If we look at these stories in terms of the relations between the men involved, we see that both versions tell of a Hera-cles who is slighted by his homosocial rival, Eurytus. All that has changed is the bone of contention. Seen as expressions of homosocial competition, both are structurally the same story.[42]

Even when the messenger tells of Heracles' passion for Iole (which Lichas is subsequently forced to admit), we should note the element of a dispute between Heracles and Eurytus:

ἀλλ' ἡνίκ' οὐκ ἔπειθε τὸν φυτοσπόρον[43]
τὴν παῖδα δοῦναι, κρύφιον ὡς ἔχοι λέχος,
ἔγκλημα μικρὸν αἰτίαν θ' ἑτοιμάσας,
ἐπιστρατεύει πατρίδα [τὴν ταύτης.

But when he did not persuade her father
to give him his daughter, so that he could have her for his
    secret bed,
he prepared a small complaint as a justification,
and he launched a campaign against her fatherland.
    (359–62)

Heracles' reaction to Eurytus's refusal is clearly excessive. Presumably Heracles need not have destroyed Eurytus's entire city, or earlier killed Iphitus by treachery (270ff.),[44] if his only object were Iole. But that is exactly the point. Heracles' eros for Iole becomes a plausible motivation for the events of the past fifteen months only insofar as it is analogous to Lichas's first version, only insofar as Eurytus's refusal to hand Iole over is a direct insult to Heracles' manhood.[45] The *defining* object of desire for Heracles is not Iole herself (however much he may lust after her), but mastery over his rival, and this element is confirmed by its presence in both versions of the story.

Further, Heracles' devotion to Iole does bear a certain structural similarity to elements in Lichas's first version. In the first story, the point that seems to have really stung is that Heracles was enslaved (*empolētheis*, 250) to Omphale, a woman:

> κεῖνος δὲ πραθεὶς Ὀμφάλῃ τῇ βαρβάρῳ
> ἐνιαυτὸν ἐξέπλησεν, ὡς αὐτὸς λέγει,
> χοὔτως ἐδήχθη τοῦτο τοὔνειδος λαβὼν
> ὥσθ' ὅρκον αὑτῷ προσβαλὼν διώμοσεν.

> He, having been sold to Omphale the foreigner,
> served her for a full year, as he himself says,
> and thus he was stung, taking this reproach,
> so that he swore an oath, attending to himself. (252–55)

Obviously Heracles' slavery to a woman is a reversal of the normal order. But the notion of enslavement also carries connotations of erotic entanglement, in which men are regularly represented as enslaved to their mistresses.[46] When, therefore, the messenger announces that it was not his disgrace before Omphale that spurred Heracles on, but *Erōs* (esp. 354ff.), it sounds not so much like a distinction as a doublet.[47] Heracles attacked Eurytus's city because of his "enslavement" to a woman.[48] The difference between the two enslavements is one that the homosocial economy clearly defines: in the first, Heracles is literally enslaved because of his wrongful actions. In the second, though Heracles may be helpless in the face of *Erōs*, it is Iole who is "sold into slavery" (538; cf. 250 above), and this is clearly Heracles' method of dominating Eurytus. The oath that Heracles swore was ἦ μὴν τὸν ἀγχιστῆρα τοῦδε τοῦ πάθους / ξὺν παιδὶ καὶ γυναικὶ δουλώσειν ἔτι ("to enslave the one responsible for this suffering / together with his child and wife" 256–57). Within the male homosocial economy, Heracles has recovered his mastery.

We can recognize Heracles' abduction of Iole, therefore, as a move of power in the homosocial traffic in women.[49] Nonetheless, the relation between the heterosexual and the homosocial is always characterized by a certain amount of slippage, since the homosocial economy regularly posits a heteroerotic attraction as motivation for what is just as plausibly a power relation between two men. In this instance, the cloaking is doubled. As the messenger tells the story, Heracles made up an excuse to sack the city, his real object being Iole (361). And however appealing this may be as a version of the truth, we must recognize that it does not explain Heracles' quarrel with Iphitus, or his service to Omphale. I suggest, therefore, that this doubling of motivations (eros and anger) mirrors and reverses the double object (mastery over Eurytus, domination of Iole) of Heracles' desire. Both stories about Heracles carry elements of the truth, but neither is singly satisfactory, because Heracles' desire is not single. Heracles' overwhelming lust for Iole is also a justification for, and may be subordinate to, a resentment toward Eurytus. His relationship with Iole is serious; but it is not at the basis of culture as the (assumed) society of this play defines it. Heracles will make his transaction, and, once he does so, Iole becomes mere merchandise to be transported.

Deianeira, therefore, fails to understand the economy at work when she worries about being replaced by Iole as the object of Heracles' desire. Once again using the agricultural metaphor (as well as a specular one) that men usually use to describe marriage, she states:

> ὧν <δ'> ἀφαρπάζειν φιλεῖ
> ὀφθαλμὸς ἄνθος, [50] τῶνδ' ὑπεκτρέπει πόδα.
> ταῦτ' οὖν φοβοῦμαι μὴ πόσις μὲν Ἡρακλῆς
> ἐμὸς καλῆται, τῆς νεωτέρας δ' ἀνήρ.

> Of these [i.e., the young], the eye of man loves to pluck
> the flower, but from these [i.e., the old] he turns away his
>   foot.
> I fear these things, therefore, lest Heracles be called
> my husband, but the *man* of the younger woman. (548–51)

Deianeira sees that Iole has replaced her as an object of erotic desire, but not that, in Heracles' privileged mode of desire, she herself never really has been one.[51] Her marriage has been characterized by nothing so much as Heracles' absence, as he engaged in various agonistic relationships with masculine or hyper-masculine figures. While Deianeira clearly resents these absences, she does not seem to recognize that they are the central aspect of Heracles' life, and not his relationships with her or with other women. This failure to fully understand her marginal status in Heracles' eyes is perhaps the most pathetic aspect of Deianeira.

The subjectivity of women in tragedy is always problematic. Even leaving aside the view from outside the fiction of the play, Deianeira's character within the play is paradoxical. Though she speaks sharply, can act independently, and apparently desires her husband, Deianeira's erotic subjectivity is oddly passive.[52] She almost never directly expresses her desire for Heracles.[53] Instead, she continually posits herself as the object of desire. She desires, in other words, to be desired. This desire for objectivity lies at the heart of Deianeira's decision to use Nessus's potion. Nessus promises her exactly the object status she wants if only she follows his directions:

> ἔσται φρενός σοι τοῦτο κηλητήριον
> τῆς Ἡρακλείας, ὥστε μήτιν' εἰσιδὼν
> στέρξει γυναῖκα κεῖνος ἀντὶ σοῦ πλέον.

> This will be a charm for you over the heart
> of Heracles, so that never looking
> will he love another woman more than he does you.
> (575–77)

Some scholars have missed the extreme conservatism of what Deianeira tries to do here. Segal, for example, very nearly makes her out to be a dangerous radical:

> Deianeira's reliance on a love charm parallels Heracles'
> defeat by bestial lust. She too abandons reason, and surren-
> ders to the dark powers of the beast. Recourse to this magic
> weakens both her logical powers and her moral judgment
> and fuses her with her monstrous double, the husband-
> destroying Clytemnestra or the sorceress, Medea.[54]

But Deianeira is hardly a Clytemnestra or a Medea, stepping into a masculine (monstrous) role. Her desire consistently lacks an active stance. Unlike Clytemnestra, say, she raises no specter of a woman choosing her own man. In fact, when Heracles accuses her, he specifically calls her ἄνανδρος φύσιν ("unmanly in nature," 1062), which I take as a deliberate contrast to Clytemnestra's infamous ἀνδρόβουλον . . . κέαρ ("man-plotting heart," Aeschylus's *Agamemnon* 11).[55] Rather, she wants to fulfill the traditional feminine role, to be desired by her husband, and we must begin here if we are to understand just how her desire disrupts.

DuBois provides a persuasive reading, taking into account the male-male relations that are at stake in this play. Despite the fact that Heracles succeeds in killing his rival, she suggests, "In fact, Nessus' rape of Deianeira is accomplished; through her, he penetrates the circuit of exchange at a crucial moment."[56] Deianeira will later realize that Nessus has "charmed" (*thelgō*, 710) her, which would indicate an insinuation into her relationship with Heracles. But again, the form of this "penetration" is less straightforward than we might assume. Nessus has given her the means, so she thinks, to remain the object of her husband's desire. Nessus charms her toward her husband, not away from him. Precisely because Deianeira trusts in the idea of heterosexual relationships—with Nessus and with Heracles—she kills her husband. She does not realize that the poison Nessus gives her has primarily to do with a homosocial relationship, a relationship in which she has no part except to become a point of attack. As Deianeira realizes too late, it was not *her* relationship with Heracles that the potion was relevant to, but Nessus's:

> πόθεν γὰρ ἄν ποτ', ἀντὶ τοῦ θνήσκων ὁ θὴρ
> ἐμοὶ παρέσχ' εὔνοιαν, ἧς ἔθνῃσχ' ὕπερ;
> οὐκ ἔστιν, ἀλλὰ τὸν βαλόντ' ἀποφθίσαι
> χρῄζων ἔθελγέ μ'.

> For from what, then, in response to what, would the dying
>   beast
> provide me with goodwill, me on whose account he died?
> It is not the case, but desiring to destroy the one who shot
>   him
> he charmed me. (707–10)

Deianeira realizes too late that she played no part in the active desire in this scene; but through deception, she has been made the agent of that desire. As a woman, she is outside of the society in which Heracles and Nessus travel and trade. Ironically, her wish to construct herself as part of it becomes an act of villainy. As this play presents the dangerous moment of Deianeira's wedding procession, she disrupts (homo)society through an entirely passive desire.

This is difficult ground, precisely because when Deianeira thinks that she is most central and stable, she becomes most marginal. She hopes to create an exclusive relationship with Heracles by using the potion, when in fact she is merely the medium of exchange between Heracles and Nessus. This doubling of relations, in which the woman fails to understand her marginal status, is typical of men's homosocial relations and their communications through women.[57] Here it constitutes Deianeira's tragedy. The disparity between her view of herself and Heracles' view of her creates an insoluble conflict, in which Deianeira's (entirely conventional) desires are doomed to failure. She hopes for a central position, and finds instead that she has no position at all.

Exactly how this slippage comes about will be made clear by briefly analyzing the image of the tablets in this play.[58] Twice in the early portion of the play, Deianeira tells us of certain oracles that Heracles left behind before setting off on his most recent journey: at 77ff., she tells us that an oracle said that when Heracles attacked Eurytus's city, he would either die there or live the rest of his life happy. Later, at 155ff., she says that he left a *deltos* with her saying that at the end of fifteen months he would either die or live free from pains (*alupētos*, 168) for the remainder of his life.[59] Already a certain epistemological uncertainty surrounds these oracles; is time the crucial element, or is place? In the end, the real meaning of the oracles defies our expectations. As Heracles recognizes much later, the phrase "to finish his life free from toils" means simply for him to die (1170–72). With this shift of meaning, we see that both options of the predicted future are the same: either Heracles will die, or he will die. The structure of the pronouncements, with an either/or clause, suggests two exclusive possibilities, but as so often with oracles, the "real" meaning turns on the instability of one of these meanings. Nonetheless, each version of the oracles has the typical (for oracles) air of certainty.

It is exactly that air of certainty that Deianeira understands when she uses the word *deltos* in reference to Nessus's instructions to her; she says, παρῆκα θεσμῶν οὐδέν, ἀλλ' ἐσῳζόμην, / χαλκῆς ὅπως δύσνιπτον ἐκ δέλτου γραφήν ("I lost nothing of the oracles, but I saved them / like the indelible writing on a bronze tablet," 682–83).[60] Deianeira's point is that the centaur's instructions are fixed, unchangeable, and stable. In the imagery of her statement, however, Deianeira has become the *deltos*, the tablet on which Nessus wrote. She has become a medium for Nessus's message to Heracles, a symbol communicated between two men, just as she is physically the means of transferring Nessus's poison to Heracles. In trying to create an exclusive relationship with Heracles, she turns herself into the transacted object in an entirely different relationship. Insofar as the other *deltoi* have carried only uncertain meaning, moreover, Deianeira also becomes a signifier of questionable certainty.

In the first place, Deianeira's position as an inscribed tablet carries overtones of a dangerous sexual mobility. The fact that Nessus has "written" on Deianeira like a tablet carries a clear sexual connotation, reinforcing the peril of his attempted rape. This meaning becomes even clearer when we recognize that the word *deltos* can also mean "female genitalia" in Greek. Henderson suggests that the association is primarily because of the triangular shape both of a capital delta and of a woman's pubic area (a sort of three-way pun).[61] All three tragedians apparently made use of this association, and

Euripides provides several interesting parallels to Deianeira. In the *Hippolytus* (see Introduction), Phaedra inscribes a tablet with the (false) story of Hippolytus's rape of her; the tablets here both tell the story and, through their inscription, represent it.[62] In the *Iphigenia at Aulis*, Agamemnon inscribes a tablet with (false) instructions regarding his daughter's marriage. As he wrestles with the responsibility of sending this message, he repeatedly opens and reseals the tablet, which comes to stand for Iphigenia's virginity: "He has sealed up her virginity, breaks it with the promise of marriage, but seals it up again as she is sacrificed as a virgin."[63] Deianeira's reference to herself as a *deltos* (above) implies a similar association.

For Deianeira to say that Nessus has inscribed her, then, is tantamount to admitting that he has sexually penetrated her. And since Nessus tried to do exactly that when he carried Deianeira over the river, such a suggestion carries a certain plausibility. Like the statement that Nessus "charmed" her (710), this image positions Deianeira as sexually suspect. She has been "inscribed" by more than one man. As often in tragedy, this sort of corruption connotes meaning in more than one sphere. Deianeira sends the poisoned robe to Heracles in a sealed package, representing Deianeira's fidelity. But as duBois points out, "Deianeira's seal cannot protect Heracles because she herself has had her seal broken."[64] Just as the robe contains poison rather than a love charm, it is guaranteed by a seal that has already been compromised by another man.

Deianeira's likeness to the tablet, therefore, makes her, like the oracles (and indeed, like all signifiers), unstable.[65] Her fidelity compromised, the robe that she sends carries a message other than what she (or Heracles) thinks. The instability of the woman-as-tablet here, however, is significantly different from that in Euripides. In the *Iphigenia at Aulis* as well as in the *Hippolytus*, the tablets themselves are a lie: Agamemnon is going to sacrifice Iphigenia, not marry her to Achilles, and Hippolytus has not raped Phaedra. Deianeira, however, practices no deception. She simply does not understand what Nessus means when he says that if she follows his instruction, Heracles will never look at another woman again (575–78, above). The medium of writing itself is at fault.[66] Deianeira's attempt to solidify Nessus's instructions by "inscribing" them, then, has the opposite effect. It renders her, as an inscribed tablet, unwittingly deceptive, a signifier of unsure meaning.

The image of Deianeira-as-*deltos*, therefore, has several mutually supporting effects. Deianeira values her relation to the centaur. She trusts that she is the recipient of a true and valid gift from him. She does so, moreover, in order to recapture an exclusive relation with her husband. Instead, she defines herself as marginal to the relations that she is valuing: Sexually, she becomes a shared rather than an exclusive object. Socially, she becomes a pure signifier, the tablet on which meaning is inscribed, in a play where interpretation of such tablets is notoriously tricky. And in terms of the plot, she becomes the *deltos*, whose shifting meaning (like the oracle) she brings to pass, and hence elucidates, by becoming the medium for Nessus's poison. On all three levels she is excluded from the *loci* of meaning and power of masculine society. Deianeira is absolutely correct when she suggests that it was Nessus's relation to Heracles that mattered all along (707–10, above). She may have been the object of some desire, but far more importantly, she was the unstable, destructive mode of communication between two men.

Heracles' reaction to the news that Nessus and not Deianeira has killed him further confirms her marginal position in his formulation of the world. At first Heracles is unable to accept the fact of his dying, expressing disbelief that he could be killed by a woman (see below). Once Hyllus mentions Nessus, however, Heracles immediately relates a third (and final) oracle (1157ff.), that he was to be killed by someone no longer living (1160). Heracles' oracle could as easily refer to Deianeira at this point, since she, too, is no longer living.[67] But Heracles' interpretation — that the oracle refers to Nessus — affirms itself because it makes sense to him in homosocial terms. In fact, from this point forward Heracles ceases to mention Deianeira.[68] What appeared to be a conflict between a man and a woman is resolved in this play into a relationship (admittedly antagonistic) between two men.[69] Nessus has had to cross a fairly significant boundary — death — in order to kill Heracles, but that is less of a cognitive problem than the idea that "a woman, being a female, and not manly in nature" (1062), did the killing. Deianeira's apparent deed has proven to be merely a communication from another male figure, and as a pure medium (of meaning, and of poison) she can now be ignored in favor of the homosocial relationships from which she is excluded throughout. All of her apparent heterosexual contacts melt away in the face of (male) culture.

That is not, of course, Deianeira's experience. She only recognizes the homosocial economy after she has unwittingly killed her husband. The difference between Deianeira's subjective experience and the one that this play forces upon her, then, constitutes her tragedy. We see her pathos particularly in a line that has puzzled commentators for some time. The nurse tells us that just before killing herself, Deianeira cries out, complaining of τὰς ἄπαιδας ἐς τὸ λοιπὸν οὐσίας ("the childless future," 911).[70] The line does not make sense: Deianeira's children are grown, and surely she was not planning on having more. Kamerbeek suggests that "ἄπαις οὐσία is for her the negation of existence itself," so that this becomes an announcement of her death. This is surely unnecessarily obscure for a woman who, to her knowledge, has no audience. Easterling suggests (but does not put in her text) two "bold" emendations that make *Heracles'* death the point of the line. I suggest, rather, that this is simply Deianeira trying again, as she has all her life, to put herself in a traditional but central role within the *oikos*. She laments the lack of future children because future children would make her a "mother" again, would supposedly make her marriage something other than the alienation it has been. Her line does not seem logical; but the language of masculine society gives her no vocabulary with which to express her desire outside of this traditional role.[71] She has no place in which to make sense.

Wohl has analyzed the effect of Deianeira's experience in theoretical terms that I find particularly apt:

> Her attempt to enter into the arenas of male subject-
> formation — gift exchange, competition, even a heroic
> death — valorizes the same structures that reproduce her
> subjection. If, in the process, the inevitability of these struc-
> tures and categories of self is challenged and alternatives are
> imagined, this critique is ultimately foreclosed and, along
> with it, the female subject that might have been built upon
> such a critique.[72]

Deianeira's lack of coherence in her death scene might be seen as a moment of resistance, however buried, to the homosocial economy of the play. By lamenting a house that will be childless in the future, she suggests a perspective at which the rest of the play has only hinted. The failure of her dying words to make sense, however, reinforces the incomprehensibility, instability, and incommunicability of this "woman's" perspective. Ultimately, any resistance to the masculine point of view is circumscribed by the inexpressibility of female subjectivity. Deianeira, wife and mother, laments from the only emotional position that she has been able to occupy in this play — that of a new bride whose transition is necessarily incomplete.

HERACLES' EXPERIENCE OF MARRIAGE

With Deianeira off the stage, the actor who played her probably reappears as Heracles. He is raving, sick, and near death. He will never meet his wife onstage. His presentation, too, reinforces the idea of homosocial desire. The one time that Heracles mentions his marriage to Deianeira, here, he refers to it as τὸν Οἰνέως γάμον ("the marriage of Oineus," 792).[73] It is not that he has no relationship with Deianeira — we are also told that he cursed τὸ δυσπάρευνον λέκτρον ("the ill-mated bed," 791) — but he views the social institution of marriage, as he does all other relationships, as a relation between men.

As a result, Heracles finds it inconceivable that he has been killed by a woman (cf. 1058ff.)—this is not the sort of relation that he can comprehend.[74] In trying to understand it, therefore, Heracles takes two directions. First, he tries to deal with Deianeira as if she were Nessus or Achelous—to make her the object of a homosocial competition. Second, he suggests that he has undergone a gender change: in line 1071 he declares that he cries out "like a maiden" (*parthenos*), and at 1075 he calls himself "female" (*thēlus*). He takes this idea so far that he experiences his pain as a sort of mock wedding, with himself in the role of the bride. In the first strategy, then, he makes Deianeira his equal; in the second, he makes himself hers, and in so doing suggests a male view of her pain and isolation.[75]

In his first attempt to make sense of his current predicament, Heracles makes several lists of the traditional enemies who did *not* kill him—all male, except for Hera.[76] In 1048–49 he lists Hera and Eurystheus; then, in a frustrated expression of incomprehension,

κοὐ ταῦτα λόγχη πεδιάς, οὔθ' ὁ γηγενὴς
στρατὸς Γιγάντων, οὔτε θήρειος βία,
οὔθ' Ἑλλάς, οὔτ' ἄγλωσσος, οὔθ' ὅσην ἐγὼ
γαῖαν καθαίρων ἱκόμην ἔδρασέ πω·
γυνὴ δέ, θῆλυς οὖσα κἄνανδρος φύσιν,
μόνη με δὴ καθεῖλε, φασγάνου δίχα.

And not the spear on the battlefield, nor the earth-born
army of Giants, nor the beast's violence,
nor Greece, nor any foreign-tongued land, nor any
of the lands I came to as a purifier could do this at all,
but a woman, being female, and unmanly in nature,
alone she killed me, without a sword. (1058–63)

As the repetitions of the idea "woman" in 1062 mount up, followed by the details that she was alone, and swordless, we sense Heracles' growing confusion. To be killed by such an enemy is utterly beyond his ken. Finally, after another list of the external enemies (1092–1100), he decides how to deal with this one: just like all the rest. Heracles announces to Hyllus,

προσμόλοι μόνον,
ἵν' ἐκδιδαχθῇ πᾶσιν ἀγγέλλειν ὅτι
καὶ ζῶν κακούς γε καὶ θανὼν ἐτεισάμην.

Only let her come,
so that she may learn to announce to everyone that
I exact punishment from those who are evil, whether I am
    alive or dead.[77] (1109–11)

EXCHANGE AND THE MAIDEN

As Reinhardt comments on the scene, "He wishes to meet and conquer the poor woman just as if she were his last enemy and the worst monster in his fabulous world (1107ff.)."[78] Heracles can only understand her by making her a part of the homosocial context that her passive desire has disrupted.

While this is going on, Heracles also redefines his relation to Hyllus, in an attempt to exclude Deianeira's mediation between them.[79] Just before asking Hyllus to bring Deianeira to him so that he can kill her, Heracles says, ὦ παῖ, γενοῦ μοι παῖς ἐτήτυμος γεγώς, / καὶ μὴ τὸ μητρὸς ὄνομα πρε-σβεύσῃς πλέον ("Boy, become my truly-born son, / and do not honor the name of your mother more [than mine]," 1064–65). As I discussed earlier, one of the most common fears of female subjectivity in ancient Greece seems to have been a fear of the wife's ability to falsify a child's paternity. It is typical of patriarchal societies to try to control female reproduction, and that is exactly what has happened here.[80] Deianeira has, for Heracles, taken on an untrustworthy aspect; he conceives of her as an enemy, and is baffled by her apparent destruction of (homo)society. He responds, therefore, by reasserting his paternal bond with Hyllus, trying to create thereby a purely male bond with his son that excludes Deianeira's part in Hyllus's birth.[81]

That bond, moreover, continues to be important to Heracles even after he has forgotten about Deianeira. As soon as Hyllus mentions Nessus (1141), Heracles accepts the centaur as his killer. Once he does so, Heracles worries about only two things: the funeral pyre, and Hyllus's marriage to Iole.[82] Heracles is still in great pain, but the world is now comprehensible to him. Deianeira participated in his death, but so long as she does not claim the subjectivity implicit in originating the poison, she does not threaten his world order. She does still possess a disturbing power, however, implicit in her control of paternity. When Hyllus shows himself reluctant to follow Heracles' instructions concerning the funeral pyre, Heracles responds harshly: εἰ δὲ μή, πατρὸς / ἄλλου γενοῦ του μηδ᾽ ἐμὸς κληθῇς ἔτι ("If not, then be the son / of another man, and do not call yourself mine," 1204–5). Again, the question of Hyllus's behavior—as defined by unquestioned deference to Heracles' wishes—determines the validity of his birth. Deianeira may not have turned Heracles world upside-down. She is no longer named. She does, however, still silently threaten Heracles' position as a husband, and specifically his male-male bond with his son: if Hyllus does not prove himself to be Heracles' offspring, then Heracles cannot know who the boy's real father is.

As the example of Deianeira has shown, then, women as go-betweens are a threat to the men within homosocial culture. The desire to be desired, however conventional and acceptable, can have disastrous consequences. As a result, Heracles institutes a new *oikos*, but with an important difference. As duBois points out, the marriage of Hyllus and Iole that Heracles sets up is endogamous: "The second part of the narrative stresses the continuity of the hearth . . . Iole is passed vertically, from father to son, rather than horizontally, as is Deianeira."[83] There will be no need for Iole to be transported over a liminal body of water by a second party. Her moment of transition to a new *oikos* will be internal, controlled, and without any of the implied sexual dangers that Deianeira's contained.

Segal, Sorum, and others at least cautiously approve of Heracles' emphasis on the family here: "He affirms . . . the importance of the family unit."[84] We should note, however, that this marriage is strictly a masculine affair; it will take place in accordance with "the finest of all laws, to obey the rule of the father" (1177–78). Another homosocial bond is thus created between two men who exchange a woman, but this one without any threat from outside elements.[85] And Iole, whose silence is perhaps her outstanding feature, is the perfect emblem for the male homosociality that this new form of marriage creates. All of the uncertainties of communication that marked Deianeira, all of the dangers of exchange that she posed by wanting to fulfill a highly traditional role, have been resolved into a father-son relationship in which marriage is the exchange of a silent woman who lives within the house. Insofar as this wedding resolves the anxieties about marriage expressed in this play, it is a resolution that reinstates culture as masculine with all the subtlety of a poke in the eye with a sharp stick.[86]

Is it, however, a resolution? Segal suggests in nonspecific terms that there is a certain lack of closure "on the human level" at the end of the play; Foley is more specific, noting, "We are left with the feeling that cultural order has been recreated at too high a price."[87] The play clearly indicates that not all is well with Heracles' new all-male *oikos*. Hyllus reacts with a horror that we can safely assume the audience shares to Heracles' insistence that he marry Iole: οἴμοι. τὸ μὲν νοσοῦντι θυμοῦσθαι κακόν, / τὸ δ᾽ ὧδ᾽ ὁρᾶν φρονοῦντα τίς ποτ᾽ ἂν φέροι; ("Alas! To be angry with a sick man is base, / but who could bear to see him thinking such things?" 1230–31). Hyllus's reason for disgust is not fear of quasi-incest; rather, he is appalled at the suggestion that he marry the woman whom he holds responsible for both his mother's death and Heracles' condition (lines 1233–37). But Heracles simply does not see things that way; he responds in terms that invoke male-male bonds with Hyllus again: ἀνὴρ ὅδ᾽ ὡς ἔοικεν οὐ νεμεῖν ἐμοὶ / φθίνοντι μοῖραν ("It seems that this man will not give me / my portion, though I am dying," 1238–39). In short, Heracles may "reinstate the *oikos*," but he does so in an act that simply disregards the woman, and that demonstrates the *oikos* to be a violent and divisive space. We can celebrate Hyllus's marriage to Iole only by disregarding his (and our own) aversion to such a household.[88]

Finally, when Heracles arrives onstage, howling mad, he also provides a comment on marriage. Not only does he suggest that he is a woman (as noted above, lines 1071 and 1075), his entrance is a parody of a wedding. When he says that he "cries out like a *parthenos*," the word carries more than a change of gender; a *parthenos* is a young girl of marriageable age. At 148, we should remember, Deianeira describes the transformation of marriage as the change from *parthenos* to *gunē*. Moreover, when Heracles announces that he will reveal his tortured body, he says, δείξω γὰρ τάδ᾽ ἐκ καλυμμάτων ("I will show you these things from under my veil," 1078). Seaford has seen in this a grim parody of the *anakaluptēria*.[89] Heracles is experiencing marriage as a bride.

I have argued that throughout this play, Heracles represses the "other" sex, defining women as outside of subjectivity. At the end of the play, however, this repressed difference returns to the surface, and Heracles is forced to experience himself as feminine.[90] What does it mean, then, that his experience is one of unspeakable pain, in which everything that he values most is cut away to the extent that he is unsure even of where he is (984)? Has this been Deianeira's experience? When we recall the sense of alienation that has characterized Deianeira's marriage, and the incommunicability of her experience, the two portrayals are not irrevocably distant. If this play has not shown Deianeira's life of alienation to be a pleasant one, however, in Heracles' experience as a bride, at least, the drama seems aware of that unpleasantness. The idea of Heracles as a weak and crying bride is a paradox; so, the play seems to suggest, is the idea of a bride as an object of desire *and* an object of exchange. Even a bride who accepts her passive, fertile role in the *oikos*, the *Trachiniae* warns, may find herself so painfully marginal in a society that defines itself by homosociality and endogamy that she loses all sense of herself.

Still, this mock wedding points as well to its own failure as a critique: women's suffering, it seems, is most meaningful when it is experienced by a man. Deianeira's long years of waiting evoke sympathy, her death may evoke pity. Heracles reduced to a wailing woman, however, is tragic. His "wedding," then, echoes the movement of both tragedy and marriage as ideologies: it calls attention to the woman's experience, grants her a momentary voice, only to translate that experience into an expression of subjectivity that is by and for men. Rather than cultural order being restored at "too high a price," we are forced to recognize that, for the woman, cultural order as defined by marriage *is* the price for social identity. The marriage may bring order, but at the exclusion of woman-as-subject. Should she try to interject herself into her husband's society, should she assume the minimal subjectivity of desiring to be desired, she runs the risk of destroying the *oikos*, herself, or both.[91]

Chapter 3

E L E C T R A ,   N E V E R   A   B R I D E

> *The little sacrifices of society are all made by women as are*
> *also the great sacrifices of life. A man who is good for anything*
> *is always ready for his duty, and so is a good woman always*
> *ready for a sacrifice.*

ANTHONY TROLLOPE, *The Small House at Allington*

Electra presents the critic with a unique difficulty. Hers is one of the longest, most continuous stage presences in all of Athenian drama; yet it is curiously difficult to discover exactly what she does. Though she maintains a powerful hatred against her father's killers, Electra's is not an active role. Before Orestes' arrival, she appears to do little other than wait for him. Though Clytemnestra complains that she is always running wild, she does not seem to take any actions, other than mourning, on her own. After Orestes arrives, she runs the risk of giving the game away several times with her emotional outbursts, and Orestes repeatedly silences her. As far as stage action goes, the plot of the play is almost entirely ruled by Orestes' "plot" to kill his father's murderers, and Electra's function in this central deed is both unspecified and contradictory.[1] As a result, the large majority of readings of the play focus not on Electra, but on her brother Orestes, and on the moral issues that surround his homecoming.

A few analyses have focused on Electra and her role.[2] As these readings demonstrate, however, it is difficult not to slip into vague statements about Electra's femininity and thus naturalize her lack of an *active* role in the plot. Segal, for example, notes Electra's lack of involvement in the public world of the play only to conclude, "In her commitment to emotion more than to principle, to the intensely personal bond to *her father* as much as to 'justice' in the abstract, Electra shows herself deeply feminine."[3] Leaving aside the implicit understanding of femininity here, such statements tend to neutralize whatever it is that Electra does. Her purpose in this play, it seems, is simply to reveal herself *as herself*. It turns out that she is—reassuringly—a woman, and at that point both her meaning and her ability to do anything other than emote come to an end. It benefits us little to conclude that Electra is "deeply feminine." So, it might be argued, is Chrysothemis, or even Clytemnestra (in this drama). *If* Electra is feminine, we must seek out the distinguishing marks of that femininity.

A more promising approach has been to argue that in some way Electra's speech is a form of action. Woodard, for example, assigns the part of male rationality to Orestes, and of female emotion to Electra. He then valorizes the emotive content of her laments, commenting, "She commands a language moving beyond logic."[4] But what does this mean, this language that goes beyond logic? In part, as Seaford and Kitzinger have shown, Electra's lament—which exists entirely in words—functions as a critique of Aegisthus's rule.[5] And while it may not have the direct appeal of Orestes' plot of revenge, it, too, is a form of resistance, particularly suited to a woman, and one that the male characters (including Orestes) continually undercut.

Surprisingly, however, when Electra speaks, she envisions an active role for herself in this drama, and in some ways she fulfills that vision. Significantly, the actions that Electra takes as well as those she contemplates are continually expressed in terms of her marital status. Though she is unmarried, then, the ideology of marriage is still active in constructing her as a subject. This aspect comes particularly to the fore because Sophocles emphasizes Electra's relationship with Clytemnestra, giving the two women a face-to-face *agōn* in which they argue, among other things, about the proper role of married women. Through their attacks on one another, Electra and Clytemnestra dramatize contradictory roles for women in the *oikos*. Insofar as this play is about Electra, it turns on her understanding of those roles, and on the way that those roles are defined by the male characters in the play.[6]

In order to understand Electra, therefore, we must look at her role in the *oikos*: we must consider what she thinks of marriage, and how she views her own unmarried state. When we look at what she says in the play, we find a pattern of three complaints. First, she complains about the killing of her father (cf. 86ff., 201ff., 558ff., etc.). Second, she resents the fact that Clytemnestra and Aegisthus are lovers (cf. esp. 271ff., 561–62). Third, she complains that she is herself still unmarried, and thus is forced to live with Clytemnestra and Aegisthus (cf. 164, 187, 961ff., etc.). The first two complaints clearly go hand in hand. The third, though less obviously so, also depends on the other two: Electra's unmarried state is a result both of her devotion to her dead father and of Clytemnestra's affair with Aegisthus (though the latter reason is not mentioned until quite late in the play). At the same time, Electra sees

Clytemnestra's affair as a continuing affront to the king's household, and ultimately to marriage itself. Electra's failure — or perhaps refusal — to marry is, in part, an answer to this affront. In short, by remaining unmarried, Electra positions herself in a state of social limbo. Betwixt and between states, she proves difficult to control, and maintains for herself a certain potential for disruption. If marriage is a moment of high subjectivity for a woman, Electra seems determined to hold that moment in perpetuity, and thus create room for herself to act.

Here again, I see Sophocles' play exploring particular legal and social forms of Athenian marriage. As we shall see, Electra's complaints about marriage represent her according to a certain model — the ideal daughter, dedicated, even after death, to her father and his bloodline. Indeed, I argue that Electra understands her position in terms closely analogous to that of the *epikleros* in fifth-century Athens. At the same time, her position is in various ways extreme; she is not a paradigm to be imitated by young Athenian women. She does, however, provide a stark contrast to Clytemnestra, the paradigmatic "bad wife" whose allegiances stray outside her husband's *oikos*. The play as a whole functions as ideology, then, in that Electra and Clytemnestra define a range of possibilities covered by the idea of being "unmarried," and by implication map out the proprieties of marriage and its function within the *oikos*.[7] Between their extremes lies the position of normalcy defined, implicitly, as marriage.

ELECTRA THE UNMARRIED

Sophocles' emphasis on Electra's unmarried state is not an innovation in the myth (though it may be for tragedy). As Kamerbeek points out, the ancients saw Electra's name as a pun on ἄλεκτρος:

> According to Aelianus *v.h.* IV 26, II 71 the lyric poet Xanthus . . . λέγει τὴν Ἠλέκτραν τοῦ Ἀγαμέμνονος οὐ τοῦτο ἔχειν τοὔνομα πρῶτον ἀλλὰ Λαοδίκην. ἐπεὶ δὲ Ἀγαμέμνων ἀνῃρέθη, τὴν δὲ Κλυταιμνήστραν ὁ Αἴγισθος ἔγημε καὶ ἐβασίλευσεν, ἄλεκτρον οὖσαν καὶ καταγηρῶσαν παρθένον Ἀργεῖοι Ἠλέκτραν ἐκάλεσαν διὰ τὸ ἀμοιρεῖν ἀνδρὸς καὶ μὴ πεπειρᾶσθαι λέκτρου (cf. P.M.G. 700P.).[8]

> According to Aelianus *v.h.* IV 26, II 71 the lyric poet Xanthus ". . . says that Electra the daughter of Agamemnon did not hold that name [i.e., Electra] at first, but rather Laodike. When Agamemnon was killed, and Aegisthus married Cly-

temnestra and became king, the Argives called the *parthenos* 'Electra,' as she was unbedded (*alektros*) and growing old, because of her having no share of men, and not being experienced in the wedding bed (*lektron*).

In this play, however, Electra complains about her unmarried state far more than she does in other versions, and notably more than in Aeschylus's play. Only once in the *Choephoroi* does Electra mention her hypothetical wedding (486–87). In Sophocles' play, her lack of marriage is Electra's constant refrain. Early in the drama, she regards it simply as an unrealized potential, one that is in danger of slipping away. At her first mention of marriage, she criticizes Orestes for never coming to avenge Agamemnon:

> ὅν γ᾽ ἐγὼ ἀκάματα προσμένουσ᾽ ἄτεκνος,
> τάλαιν᾽ ἀνύμφευτος αἰὲν οἰχνῶ,
> δάκρυσι μυδαλέα.

> Untiring, childless, waiting for him,
> I live continually unmarried, a wretch
> dripping with tears. (164–66)

Her potential ability to bear children is exactly parallel to Orestes' potential return—and both opportunities seem in danger of being extinguished with the passing of time.[9]

At the next mention of Electra's perpetual eligibility, however, she also points out her mistreatment at the hands of Aegisthus:

> ἅτις ἄνευ τεκέων[10] κατατάκομαι
> ἇς φίλος οὔτις ἀνὴρ ὑπερίσταται,
> ἀλλ᾽ ἀπερεί τις ἔποικος ἀναξία
> οἰκονομῶ θαλάμους πατρός, ὧδε μὲν
> ἀεικεῖ σὺν στολᾷ,
> κεναῖς δ᾽ἀμφίσταμαι τραπέζαις.

> I who, without children, am wasting away,
> over whom no loving husband stands guard,
> rather like some unworthy foreigner
> I take care of the tomb/bedchamber of my father, and thus,
> in a shameful cloak
> I stand by empty tables. (187–92)

Electra is without proper male guardians, she has no decent clothes or food, and, as part of this same pattern of treatment, she has not married and has not borne children. She has been prohibited, in effect, from making the transition to married, adult life. The reference to Electra standing by the empty tables is a clear indication of her perpetual minority. Typically, a recently married bride laments the loss of her former place at her father's tables. So Iphigenia, whose sacrifice in Aeschylus's *Agamemnon* has been shown to be described in terms of a marriage,[11] is described in part: . . . ἐπεὶ πολλάκις / πατρὸς κατ᾽ ἀνδρῶνας εὐτραπέζους / ἔμελψεν . . . ("When many times / she sang in the well-tabled men's banquet hall / of her father," *Agamemnon* 243–45). Similarly, shortly before Oedipus laments that his daughters will be unable to marry, he describes their life as *parthenoi* in his house. He points out that they were never far from his table, and always shared in whatever food he had. All the more tragic, then, that they will never be able to marry (*Oedipus tyrannus* 1462–65).[12] For Electra to stand perpetually at her father's table, then, represents a perversion of norms, a denial of her still valid potential as a bride. This perversion is emphasized all the more by the fact that her father is dead, the table empty. Her lack of marriage creates a pattern of her mistreatment. Her parents (or, in this case, her stepparent) are responsible for seeing that she has an opportunity for marriage, and Electra's statement amounts to a critique of Aegisthus as an evil stepfather. Orestes sums it up rather nicely, when he finally recognizes Electra: φεῦ τῆς ἀνύμφου δυσμόρου τε σῆς τροφῆς ("Alas for your unmarried, ill-fated nurturance," 1183).

Later in the play, Electra will blame her childless state on Aegisthus's fear of her offspring, though at this point Electra's nonmarriage is simply a symptom of general ill-treatment. It is far from clear that Electra wants to marry, however. From Electra's perspective, Aegisthus's abuse stems specifically from her own dedication to her dead father, which she is hesitant to give up. In line 190 (above), Electra says, οἰκονομῶ θαλάμους πατρός ("I take care of the *thalamos* of my father"), and she offers this as a cause of her degraded condition. She implies that Aegisthus treats her badly — as well he might — because she will not let the memory of Agamemnon die. Electra's continual state of mourning, through which she recalls her father, is also a continuous indictment of Aegisthus as his killer.

Electra's dedication to Agamemnon is not merely that of a daughter, however. This passage places particular emphasis on Electra's potential as a bride. Although the word *katatakomai* ("I am wasting away") refers explicitly to the fact that she has borne no children and is running out of time to do so, it can have erotic connotations,[13] so that her very word for wasting away almost suggests its opposite, an erotic union. *Thalamos* can mean bedchamber as well as tomb, and when unmarried young women talk of tending to *thalamoi*, bridal connotations cannot be far off.[14] In addition, when Electra interrupts Chrysothemis's dedication from Clytemnestra, she offers her *zōma*

(452), "the symbolical offering of her virginity" to Agamemnon.[15] In a sense, Electra is married to her dead father. This "marriage," however, renders Electra liminal sexually as well as socially. She continuously and deliberately walks the line between *parthenos* and *gunē*. Her "marriage" to her father (as she cares for his *thalamos*) is precisely that which prevents her from normal familial connections, from successfully marrying into another household.[16] Now we can see the full implications of her bridal stance before the empty tables of her father. Her status as a *korē* is a state of permanent transition, dedicated to her father in an unmarried marriage.[17] Like Antigone's, Electra's connections are with the dead, whom she cannot reach, while maintaining those connections necessarily precludes any chance of normal relations with her living family, now ruled by Aegisthus.

Well into the play, Electra and Clytemnestra have a formal argument about their respective behaviors. Clytemnestra is concerned to justify her relationship with Aegisthus, while Electra argues for her own dedication to Agamemnon. In making her argument, Clytemnestra champions, somewhat surprisingly, the cultural bonds of marriage. Clytemnestra particularly resents her husband's killing of Iphigenia, and significantly interprets this event not only as a failure to recognize her maternity, but as evidence of Agamemnon's overstrong ties to *his* brother. In lines 536–47 she complains bitterly about Agamemnon's actions, asking if he had killed *her* daughter for *his* brother's sake, and wondering if Menelaos had no children to sacrifice himself. In the eleven lines, she mentions Menelaos by name no less than three times. She finishes by accusing Agamemnon of valuing his own *oikos* (i.e., the one he had formed with Clytemnestra) less than his bonds with Menelaos: ἢ τῷ πανώλει πατρὶ τῶν μὲν ἐξ ἐμοῦ / παίδων πόθος παρεῖτο, Μενέλεω δ' ἐνῆν; ("Or was desire for children from me disregarded by your all-destroying father, / while desire for such from Menelaos was present?" 544–45).

In Electra's version of the story, however, Agamemnon sacrifices Iphigenia because of an offense against Artemis (576). We should note, moreover, that before making this argument, Electra allies herself with Artemis: [18]

> ἐροῦ δὲ τὴν κυναγὸν Ἄρτεμιν τίνος
> ποινὰς τὰ πολλὰ πνεύματ' ἔσχ' ἐν Αὐλίδι·
> ἢ 'γὼ φράσω· κείνης γὰρ οὐ θέμις μαθεῖν.

> Ask the huntress Artemis why
> she held back the many winds at Aulis,
> or rather, I'll tell you. For it is not right [for you] to learn of
>   her. (563–65)

Electra claims a special connection with the goddess, a connection in which Clytemnestra apparently cannot partake. Artemis, it seems, encapsulates the paradox that Electra is living: she is the virgin goddess, but as Burkert notes, "The virginity of Artemis is not asexuality as is Athena's practical and organizational intelligence, but a peculiarly erotic and challenging ideal." [19] Her virginity always rests on the verge of marriage or rape, and she assists in marriage and childbirth. Moreover, in a common version of the myth, she owes her virginity to her father.[20] Electra, similarly, is a virgin who tends to her father's *thalamos*. She also takes on Artemis's maternal aspect, as she seems to have nursed her brother, Orestes, as a youth:[21] when she thinks he is dead, she laments,

> οἴμοι τάλαινα τῆς ἐμῆς πάλαι τροφῆς
> ἀνωφελήτου, τὴν ἐγὼ θάμ' ἀμφὶ σοὶ
> πόνῳ γλυκεῖ παρέσχον.

> Alas for my long-ago nurturing,
> useless, which I provided to you often
> with sweet difficulty. (1143–45)

Like Artemis, Electra is a virgin bride and a virgin mother, indelibly linked with the father.[22]

Though this identification with Artemis and the concern for her sanctity does not exactly justify Agamemnon's action, Artemis's sexual purity (which, we might remember, comes from her alliance with *her* father) does allow Electra to call into question Clytemnestra's fidelity:

> λέξω δέ σοι,
> ὡς οὐ δίκῃ γ' ἔκτεινας, ἀλλά σ' ἔσπασεν
> πειθὼ κακοῦ πρὸς ἀνδρός, ᾧ τανῦν ξύνει.

> I will tell you
> how you did not kill with justice, but the persuasion
> from an evil man drew you, with whom even now you are
>   living. (560–62)

Clytemnestra's promiscuity is presumably the reason that she cannot ask anything of Artemis (565), and at 593–94 Electra portrays this promiscuity as a violation of Clytemnestra's *oikos*-bonds with Agamemnon: οὐ γὰρ καλὸν / ἐχθροῖς γαμεῖσθαι τῆς θυγατρὸς οὕνεκα ("For it is not good / to have sex with [be married to] enemies for the sake of a daughter"). Electra, then, takes Agamemnon's fidelity to his own *oikos* more or less for granted, and perhaps suggests that his sacrifice to Artemis demonstrates this fidelity. In her account, Clytemnestra is the one who has violated *oikos*-bonds, marrying Agamemnon's enemy. At the same time, of course, Electra sets herself up as an Artemis figure, devoted to her father and (by implication) sexually pure.

Electra, therefore, represents and champions a certain model of the *oikos*, and it is one we have seen before. With her virginal marriage, virginal motherhood, and absolute devotion to the *oikos* as embodied in her father (all supported by her alliance with Artemis), Electra creates a vision of the *oikos* parallel to the myth of Hestia: "Through the goddess of the hearth, the function of fertility . . . can appear as the indefinite prolongation of the paternal line through the daughter, without a 'foreign' woman being necessary for procreation."[23] Electra's *anumpheia*, then, is multiply motivated. It is both a part of Aegisthus's mistreatment of her and a part of her revenge on Clytemnestra and Aegisthus. Through it, she creates an endogamous household, in which she defends Agamemnon's bloodline by tending to his *thalamos*.[24]

In this reading, Electra's "perpetual liminality" does not just create pain for her. It also provides her with a source of power. We have already seen that by her allegiance to her father, she attacks Clytemnestra's treachery toward him (593–94). Winnington-Ingram further suggests that by constantly mourning Agamemnon, Electra has psychologically persecuted Clytemnestra for years.[25] More specifically, however, Electra claims that by living as she does, she harms Clytemnestra and Aegisthus:

> ἐπεὶ δίδαξον, ἢ μάθ' ἐξ ἐμοῦ, τί μοι
> κέρδος γένοιτ' ἂν τῶνδε ληξάσῃ γόων.
> οὐ ζῶ; κακῶς μέν, οἶδ', ἐπαρκούντως δ' ἐμοί.
> λυπῶ δὲ τούτους, ὥστε τῷ τεθνηκότι
> τιμὰς προσάπτειν.

> Then tell me, or learn from me, what gain
> I would obtain from leaving off of these mournings?
> Do I not live? Badly, I know, but sufficiently for me.
> And I hurt them, so as to attach some honor
> to the dead man. (352–56)

And in fact, her stance on the threshold seems to pain them most of all: Clytemnestra's first words to her are,

> ἀνειμένη μέν, ὡς ἔοικας, αὖ στρέφῃ.
> οὐ γὰρ πάρεστ' Αἴγισθος, ὅς σ' ἐπεῖχ' ἀεὶ
> μή τοι θυραίαν γ' οὖσαν αἰσχύνειν φίλους.

> Let loose again, as it seems, you wander around,
> for Aegisthus is not present, who holds you in check always
> lest, being out of doors, you shame family and friends.[26]
> (516–18)

It is by now a commonplace that young Athenian women were not supposed to be out in public without a guardian, and this sort of concern seems to inform Clytemnestra's reaction to Electra. But it is important to remember why, exactly, women were ideally to be kept indoors. When young women in myth are outside unattended, they tend to be abducted (and possibly raped).[27] Such a position emphasizes the latent sexual potentialities of the young unmarried woman. Electra capitalizes on this understanding: she constantly tries to be outdoors, and thereby points out her status as a *korē* (as the chorus calls her, 464). By doing so she brings shame to Clytemnestra and Aegisthus, who cannot keep her in check, and actively maintains her potential to produce offspring. She is not just *alektros*, she aggressively positions herself as *alektros*, so that the potential for her becoming married always remains close to the surface.[28]

CLYTEMNESTRA THE (UN)MARRIED

Electra is not the only person in the play described by the adjective *alektros*. The word applies to Clytemnestra as well—though in such a way that we cannot help but think of Electra. In lines 472 and following, the chorus predicts that a Fury will soon avenge Agamemnon's death:

ἥξει καὶ πολύπους καὶ πολύχειρ ἁ
δεινοῖς κρυπτομένα λόχοις
χαλκόπους Ἐρινύς.
ἄλεκτρ' ἄνυμφα γὰρ ἐπέβα μιαιφόνων
γάμων ἀμιλλήμαθ' οἷσιν οὐ θέμις.

It will come, many-footed, many-handed
hidden in terrible ambushes,
a bronze-footed Fury.
For she came upon an unmarried, unbedded striving
for blood-stained marriage by those for whom it was not
right. (489–94)

The idea of a Fury is not new to the play; at 275ff., Electra wondered why Clytemnestra did not fear an avenging Fury for her sexual promiscuity: ἡ δ' ὧδε τλήμων ὥστε τῷ μιάστορι / ξύνεστ', Ἐρινὺν οὔτιν' ἐκφοβουμένη ("She is so bold as to sleep with this pollution, / fearing no Fury," 275–76). When, therefore, the chorus announces that a Fury is on the way, we expect to hear some reference to that suggested revenge—and for the space of two words, the chorus fulfills our expectation: ἄλεκτρ' ἄνυμφα (492). We hear those words *as* "Electra unmarried," who is coming as a Fury to avenge her mother's infidelity.[29] She, after all, has done little but speak ill of her mother and Aegisthus since the play began.

When the lines continue, however, it turns out that the adjective does not refer to Electra at all; it modifies *hamillēmata*, "striving" [for marriage]. Clytemnestra's new marriage, then, is both *alektros* and *anumphos*, just as Electra described herself earlier.[30] Clearly the two words have a different sense here, and the chorus describes Clytemnestra's union as "unmarried" not because of a lack of experience on her part, but because her new "marriage" defies the patrilineal nature of marriage. Clytemnestra and Electra, then, define opposite poles on the axis of being unmarried.[31] Electra's lack of marriage, as we have seen, represents Hestia's model of the household, the endogamous marriage to the father. Clytemnestra's marriage to Aegisthus suggests the opposite.

While Electra remains devoted absolutely to her father, Clytemnestra devalued her husband so much that he became replaceable, and his bloodline powerless, as Segal has pointed out: "Usurping the masculine authority of the house, Clytemnestra transmits that authority not to the son of her womb but to her lover, an older male who prevents the legitimate heir from acceding to his father's property."[32] Electra specifically complains about Aegisthus's usurpation of her father's throne, clothes, libations, and bed (266ff.). In addition, in this play Electra makes the unlikely suggestion that Clytemnestra and Aegisthus might have children of their own:[33]

> ἥτις ξυνεύδεις τῷ παλαμναίῳ, μεθ' οὗ
> πατέρα τὸν ἀμὸν πρόσθεν ἐξαπώλεσας,
> καὶ παιδοποιεῖς, τοὺς δὲ πρόσθεν εὐσεβεῖς
> κἀξ εὐσεβῶν βλαστόντας ἐκβαλοῦσ' ἔχεις.

> You who sleep with this murderer, with whom
> earlier you killed *my* father,
> and with whom you produce children, and those
>   [children] who were honored
> previously, and who were born honorably, you throw out.
>   (587–90)

Clytemnestra's marriage, then, is deliberately figured as absolute exogamy. She has annihilated her husband and transferred his property and political power to an external male with whom she *may* even produce new heirs. Electra, by privileging her father for so long, hopes to see this same property and power transferred to an internal male, Orestes. These two possibilities, then, define the range of meaning for the adjective *alektros*. Electra's lack of marriage stems from an absolute devotion to Agamemnon, while Clytemnestra's "nonmarriage" defies his bloodline outright.

Sophocles' unusual treatment of the Furies further clarifies this polarity. As Winnington-Ingram points out, the idea of Furies avenging sex crimes seems to be unique to this play.[34] Also remarkable is the idea that the Furies would avenge Clytemnestra's killing of Agamemnon, though the drama makes no mention of them in reference to the matricide. Aeschylus's *Eumenides* 605 makes it explicit, after all, that the Furies did not avenge Agamemnon's death because there was no blood tie between Agamemnon and Clytemnestra. We must understand that, in Electra's eyes, Clytemnestra's crime *is* a crime against blood ties — Electra sees the *oikos* as Agamemnon's, and considers that Clytemnestra has violated this *oikos* as defined by the paternal line through the daughter and son. She continues to violate it by sleeping with Aegisthus — hence the suggestion (275, above) that the Furies avenge adultery.

One of the more puzzling passages in this play, that describing Clytemnestra's dream, illustrates precisely why Clytemnestra fears Electra's continued ties to Agamemnon.[35] Chrysothemis relates the dream:

λόγος τις αὐτήν ἐστιν εἰσιδεῖν πατρὸς
τοῦ σοῦ τε κἀμοῦ δευτέραν ὁμιλίαν
ἐλθόντος ἐς φῶς· εἶτα τόνδ' ἐφέστιον
πῆξαι λαβόντα σκῆπτρον οὑφόρει ποτὲ
αὐτός, τανῦν δ' Αἴγισθος· ἔκ τε τοῦδ' ἄνω
βλαστεῖν βρύοντα θαλλόν, ᾧ κατάσκιον
πᾶσαν γενέσθαι τὴν Μυκηναίων χθόνα.

The story is that she saw a second coitus
with your — and my — father,
as he came to her in the light. Then, seizing the scepter that
he carried then, he struck the hearth [with it],
the scepter which Aegisthus now holds. And up out of this
a teeming shoot grew up, with which all
the Mycenaean earth was overshadowed. (417–23)

The dream is puzzling because, unlike its counterpart in Aeschylus's *Choephoroi*, it serves no immediate purpose.[36] That is, it does not set up the recognition scene between Orestes and Electra, and it does not explicitly suggest the matricide, as does the dream in the *Choephoroi*. Even more important, however, the dream is not immediately terrifying. In this regard, Sophocles' drama sharply contrasts with Aeschylus's version. Clytemnestra's dream in the *Choephoroi* (527–33), with its image of a snake sucking blood mixed with mother's milk, inevitably evokes a visceral response. But as Devereux notes about Sophocles' treatment, "This dream's capacity to frighten the one who dreamed it is *not* due to its *manifest* content. . . . Its truly frightening content becomes evident only *after* it is *interpreted*." [37]

Once one has interpreted the dream, of course, one can see in it a threat to Clytemnestra. The scepter represents Agamemnon's procreative power; its flowering suggests that Orestes is coming into manhood. If Orestes overshadows all Mycenae, then Aegisthus's rule (and Clytemnestra's) is doomed to a short life. There is more to this dream, however; and a close reading of its structure, as well as consideration of its sources, help to see why it posits such a palpable and material threat to Clytemnestra.

In his analysis of the dream, Devereux compares it to a list of Greek and Near Eastern dreams in which a king's wife or daughter produces vines or trees of uncontrolled growth from her genitalia. A parallel set of dreams involves women urinating such a quantity of water that it floods the land. [38] Among the narratives of such dreams are the two of Astyages in Herodotus (1.107–8), and Devereux suggests that Clytemnestra's dream has the same meaning as Astyages'. [39] He is mistaken. The point of King Astyages' dream (as well as his second dream, of the urination variety) is that his daughter's offspring threatens Astyages himself. [40] Clytemnestra's dream foretells the opposite, structurally speaking: it is not her genitalia that flower, but rather her husband's scepter, with her genitalia functioning only as a locus for its fertility. Moreover, the flowering scepter threatens not the king (Agamemnon), but Clytemnestra, as Electra makes immediately clear: οἶμαι μὲν οὖν, οἶμαί τι κἀκείνῳ μέλειν / πέμψαι τάδ' αὐτῇ δυσπρόσοπτ' ὀνείρατα ("I think, indeed I think it was a concern to *him* [Agamemnon] / to send this ill-omened dream to her," 459–60).

Sophocles has taken a common type of dream, then, and changed its usual function. Rather than demonstrating anxiety over female powers of reproduction, the dream becomes one that champions paternity. To see exactly how and why the dream threatens Clytemnestra, moreover, we must consider its *syntagmatic* as well as its *paradigmatic* order. [41] Structurally speaking, the dream narrates the same event twice: first, Clytemnestra dreams that Agamemnon comes to her and has intercourse with her. [42] Then she dreams about Agamemnon driving his scepter into the hearth, and its consequent flowering. Both sequences represent the king having intercourse. When we look at the two versions in sequence, however, it becomes clear that the second version is more abstract. As such, it replaces Clytemnestra with a hearth, and thus replaces the private act of copulation with a public, political (and perhaps violent?) fertilization of the *oikos*. [43] As Devereux puts it, "On the basis of Vernant's analysis of the function of the hearth, it could reasonably be argued that the hearth represents the *Queen's* feminine parts *better* than do the actual organs of the *woman* Klytaemnestra." [44] I believe that the dream suggests exactly that, so that as the dream represents the *oikos*, it writes Clytemnestra the person out of the picture, and subsumes her in the fertility function of the hearth.

In brief, what Sophocles does to the typical form of this dream is parallel to what happens to Clytemnestra within the dream. Normally, dreams of this type symbolize a powerful female fertility. Here, by contrast, the narrative sequence of the dream changes the female part of that fertility into the hearth, allowing an endogamous *oikos* in which the father directly generates the son. And Clytemnestra, who has (in this play as elsewhere) held and transferred political power to the man of her choice through her sexuality, is eliminated from the procreative powers of the *oikos*. It is no wonder that she is terrified. The dream foretells the success of the sort of *oikos* that Electra has championed. Just a few lines earlier, in fact, Electra chided Chrysothemis: νῦν δ᾽ ἐξὸν πατρὸς / πάντων ἀρίστου παῖδα κεκλῆσθαι, καλοῦ / τῆς μητρός ("But now when it is possible to be called / the child of the best of all fathers / you are called [the child] of your mother," 365–67). For Electra, the dream foretells elimination of the mother from the *oikos*, an act to which all her energies are devoted. She does not realize that *her* model of the *oikos*, with its "indefinite prolongation of the paternal line through the daughter," [45] will ultimately result in her own alienation as well—when she becomes a wife rather than a daughter. Electra's normalizing version of marriage, inevitably, is one that denies female erotic subjectivity.

ELECTRA THE *epiklēros*

I have so far presented a static Electra, a cerebral representative of a certain paradoxical model of marriage. But of course Electra the character—her mode of action, her plans, her vision of herself—changes in the course of the drama. Her most noticeable change occurs when she believes that Orestes is dead. Now, for the first time in the play, when she complains of being childless, she does not merely reproach Aegisthus for general mistreatment. At this point she also tells Chrysothemis that they both are childless and will remain so because Aegisthus fears their offspring:

> ἦ πάρεστι μὲν στένειν
> πλούτου πατρῴου κτῆσιν ἐστερημένη,
> πάρεστι δ᾽ ἀλγεῖν ἐς τοσόνδε τοῦ χρόνου
> ἄλεκτρα γηράσκουσαν ἀνυμέναιά τε.

καὶ τῶνδε μέντοι μηκέτ' ἐλπίσῃς ὅπως
τεύξῃ ποτ'· οὐ γὰρ ὧδ' ἄβουλός ἐστ' ἀνὴρ
Αἴγισθος ὥστε σόν ποτ' ἢ κἀμὸν γένος
βλαστεῖν ἐᾶσαι, πημονὴν αὑτῷ σαφῆ.

For you it is possible to groan,
having been deprived of the property of your paternal
    wealth,
and it is possible to grieve that you are growing old
for so many unbedded, unmarried years.
And you should not have hope of these things, that
you will achieve them sometime. For that man is not so
    clueless,
Aegisthus, as to allow your or my offspring ever
to bloom, a clear calamity for him. (959–66)

Note, too, that, for the first time, Electra speaks of being deprived of their father's wealth (960, above). As Juffras points out, "Electra links their inability to wed with the loss of their inheritance."[46] And here, for the first time, she unveils a plot to kill Aegisthus herself (with Chrysothemis's help, if she can get it), with no mention made of killing Clytemnestra.

There are, of course, perfectly good reasons for Electra's change of heart. With Orestes dead (as she thinks), only she and her sister remain to avenge Agamemnon. And, as several scholars have pointed out, if she were to kill Clytemnestra first, the (presumably) stronger Aegisthus would find out and kill her, leaving the revenge only half-completed.[47] These reasons, however plausible, are never voiced by Electra. On the contrary, Electra's talk of producing heirs to Agamemnon's throne, her complaint at being deprived of her inheritance, and her sudden resolve toward active rather than passive resistance all point to one thing: with Orestes dead, she has become an *epiklēros*.

Earlier, as I have argued, Electra's power depended on her sexuality remaining latent and metaphorical. Only by maintaining a liminal stance as the virgin bride/virgin mother could she champion the paternal model of the *oikos*. With Orestes dead, however, her inherited bloodline (like that of an *epiklēros*) changes from latent to active. In fact, the chorus uses strangely legal language to describe Electra when Orestes arrives and asks to be announced: ἥδ', εἰ τὸν ἀγχιστόν γε κηρύσσειν χρεών ("Here she is, if you need to announce it to the closest one," 1105). The line is rather banal (though not impossible) if we take *anchistos* as simply meaning "near at hand." But it makes perfect sense if taken as a legal statement: with Agamemnon and Orestes dead, Electra's *anchisteia* is now in force — she is the "nearest" heir of Agamemnon's *oikos*.[48] She and Chrysothemis are now active representatives of Agamemnon's public power — provided, as the law on *epiklēroi* specifies, that they get married. And it is in exactly these terms that Electra proposes the bold act of killing Aegisthus: ἔπειτα δ᾽, ὥσπερ ἐξέφυς, ἐλευθέρα / καλῇ τὸ λοιπὸν καὶ γάμων ἐπαξίων / τεύξῃ ("Then as you were born, you will be called / free for the rest of your life, and you will achieve / a worthy marriage," 970–72). Aegisthus has become the primary target, then, not only for the reasons listed above, but because he stands in the way of Electra regenerating Agamemnon's bloodline. As her latent ability to continue the *oikos* has become active, so has she, abandoning her stance of passive liminality for one of action and (literal) marriage.

Obviously, this contains a certain contradiction for Electra. She has spent the play arguing that the bloodline is paternal, and passes through the male alone (cf. esp. lines 394–96). Now she is caught in the recognition that it can pass through the female. Sophocles did not invent this paradox. It is exactly the paradox of the Athenian citizen woman: In the official language of Athenian law, a woman's bloodline belongs both to her father and to her husband.[49] Unfortunately for Electra, once she finds her political fertility to be active, she begins to resemble Clytemnestra, and her "unmarried" state becomes a threat of dangerous sexual mobility.[50]

Clytemnestra killed her husband and transferred his public power to another man; Electra intends to kill Aegisthus and then retransfer Agamemnon's power to someone else (ultimately to her offspring). The patrilineal image of Clytemnestra's dream, in which the woman is subsumed into the hearth, does not sit well with the role Electra envisions for herself:

τίς γάρ ποτ᾽ ἀστῶν ἢ ξένων ἡμᾶς ἰδὼν
τοιοῖσδ᾽ ἐπαίνοις οὐχὶ δεξιώσεται,
"ἴδεσθε τώδε τὼ κασιγνήτω, φίλοι,
ὣ τὸν πατρῷον οἶκον ἐξεσωσάτην . . .
τώδ᾽ ἔν θ᾽ ἑορταῖς ἔν τε πανδήμῳ πόλει
τιμᾶν ἅπαντας οὕνεκ᾽ ἀνδρείας χρεών."

For what citizen or stranger, then, seeing us,
would not receive us with such praises as these:
"Look, friends, the two sisters
who saved their paternal household . . .
we must all honor them in the festivals
and throughout the city, on account of their bravery
    [manliness]."
(975–983)

Significantly, Electra identifies her allegiance: she is saving her *paternal* household, as is appropriate for an *epiklēros*. Nonetheless, Electra imagines herself and her sister as heroes in a public spotlight, a role not generally thought acceptable for Athenian women.[51] Juffras suggests that the image Electra envisions is of a public statue of the two girls, "On a parallel with the paired statues of Harmodius and Aristogeiton that stood in the Agora from the fifth century on."[52] Whether or not we accept this interpretation, Electra clearly believes that she will be praised for her *andreia*, her "manliness" (983). We can hardly help thinking of Clytemnestra's "man-counseling heart" (Aeschylus's *Agamemnon* 11). In short, we might well apply Segal's critique of lines 1415ff. to this passage: "Electra moves from the perpetually lamenting *mater dolorosa*, Procne or Niobe, to a different mythic paradigm: the destructive, vengeful female, the Clytemnestra of the *Agamemnon*, whose act she here symbolically repeats."[53]

The remarkable thing about Electra's experience, however, is that she gets to act both ends of the paradigm: early on she is the faithful daughter who ensures endogamy; later she becomes the active, vengeful woman whose potential marriage carries with it the father's political clout. Electra dramatizes the ideological paradox of citizenship for the Athenian woman. As a wife, she is called on to continue her husband's *oikos* selflessly, but her sexuality is always suspect; and as a daughter in her father's *oikos*, she carries a latent bloodline that can become active at any time. She is figured simultaneously as the ensurer of culture (through reproduction) and, as Gould puts it, "as [a point] of weakness in the solidarity of the community, and as forming strong and fast-wrought ties with incomers who are also subverters of order."[54]

THE RETURN OF ORESTES

Paradoxically, Electra's role in Orestes' return (which is also the return of the patrilineal *oikos*) is figured as exactly the sort of dangerous autonomy that Gould describes (above). Orestes does not return to his *oikos* as Orestes, but disguised as a stranger.[55] At the same time that Electra is championing her father's bloodline, then, she is also forming a "fast-wrought tie" with a stranger who will subvert the *oikos*, at least as Aegisthus and Clytemnestra define it. Her position is a structural paradox, to the extent that she occupies both poles of the axis of being "unmarried" at precisely the same moment. She is both pure virgin and an autonomous possessor of her father's *oikos*, one who will transfer that *oikos* to an outsider.

Electra has not yet fully experienced, however, the horror that Clytemnestra feels when her procreative powers are coopted and restructured as endogamy within the masculine rule of the household. When Orestes returns, Electra is finally and decisively separated from Agamemnon's *oikos*, as fully as if Aegisthus continued to rule. We have already seen that the play figures Orestes' return metaphorically as rebirth, with Electra in the role of mother (cf. especially lines 1133ff.). Ironically, however, this rebirth results in Orestes stepping in and denying, on various levels, Electra's ties of *philia*. Though the confusion here is typical for recognition scenes, lines 1209ff. do not bode well for our heroine:

Ηλ.	ὦ τάλαιν' ἐγὼ σέθεν,
	Ὀρέστα, τῆς σῆς εἰ στερήσομαι ταφῆς.
Ορ.	εὔφημα φώνει· πρὸς δίκης γὰρ οὐ στένεις.

El.:	I am wretched over you,
	Orestes, if I am to be bereft of your burial.
Or.:	Be quiet. For you do not mourn justly. (1209–11)

Mourning for her dead father has been Electra's most significant role up to this point, the one way that she has been able to harm Clytemnestra and Aegisthus. Now Orestes, however momentarily, denies this role. In the following scene, moreover, Orestes will repeatedly squelch his sister's emotional outbursts (cf. especially 1238, 1288ff.).[56] Electra is keen to celebrate the return of her "dear brother" (just as she was keen to lament his "death"), but Orestes sees such celebration only as endangering *his* chances for regaining his inheritance.

At the same time, Electra ceases to take an active role in the plot, as Woodard cogently notes.[57] Electra will be outside when Orestes kills Clytemnestra, as lines 1402–3 make clear. And when Aegisthus enters, she asserts perhaps too strongly her knowledge of Orestes' actions, and her connection to him: ἔξοιδα· πῶς γὰρ οὐχί; συμφορᾶς γὰρ ἂν / ἔξωθεν εἴην τῶν ἐμῶν γε φιλτάτων. ("I know. For how would I not? For I would have to be / outside of the fortunes of my closest friends/relatives," 1448–49).[58] In a very real sense, she *is* "outside of the fortunes of her closest friends/relatives." Orestes is a practical avenger.[59] He has little time for laments, and his matricide barely seems a moral problem for him in this play. Orestes will kill Aegisthus simply because Aegisthus has taken control of his rightful inheritance.[60] As Sorum puts it, "Orestes perceives a different family than that seen by Electra, who is concerned with kinship and its obligations."[61] Orestes sees the house, and the family, in public, political terms; and (now that her role as *epiklēros* is over) Electra has no part to play within those terms.

Indeed, in a basic way, Orestes' return makes it impossible for Electra to succeed using her former methods.[62] She is shown onstage lamenting the death of Orestes in what should be a poignant and moving scene, a scene that helps cement her identification with Agamemnon and his household. But as Kitzinger has pointed out, the entire scene is written so that Electra's words do not ring true. We know, as does Orestes, that Orestes is not dead, and this creates an odd disjunction. The very emotive power of Electra's lament, the thing that should guarantee the authenticity of her strength of character, instead makes her into a liar, and the lament plays like a grisly joke. Orestes' return makes her a fool, at the same time that Orestes wrests political and familial power away from her.

It is curious how many critics assume that once Orestes is on the throne, all will be well for Electra. Linforth, for example, suggests, "Electra, relieved of all her cares, can look forward to the gentle life of a princess of the house."[63] It is worth noting with Segal that Electra's position in Agamemnon's *oikos* is structurally unchanged at the end of the play: "She is left once more confronting the House, alone, standing 'before the doors of her father' exactly as she was at the beginning."[64] She has, like a remarried *epiklēros*, successfully transferred her father's political power to her (metaphorical) offspring. As a result, she stands once more at the threshold, excluded from the culture that the *oikos* represents, just as she has been excluded from the active plot of the play.

The final words of the chorus, if we accept them to be genuine, serve only to emphasize Electra's isolated state as the play closes:

> ὦ σπέρμ' Ἀτρέως, ὡς πολλὰ παθὸν
> δι' ἐλευθερίας μόλις ἐξῆλθες
> τῇ νῦν ὁρμῇ τελεωθέν.

> Seed of Atreus, what great suffering you have come through
> with difficulty, to freedom,
> having been perfected by this effort. (1508–10)

I agree with Calder that the lines are addressed to Electra, and that she specifically is meant by "seed of Atreus."[65] Though now free, however, Electra has in no way been "perfected."[66] She remains unmarried, childless, and excluded from the *oikos* of Agamemnon.[67] The chorus's words must ring ironic. They assert a closure at the end of the play, but that sense of closure directly contradicts the visual impact of the scene before us. The doors of the house are closed, indeed, but Electra is not within them. She remains outside, in the open space of the theater, possibly unsure of where to turn next. We have not even heard Orestes kill Aegisthus, so that Electra's continued presence onstage (as she stood onstage for the killing of Clytemnestra) sug-

gests that the principal action of the play is not yet complete. Her potential —
for marriage, for childbirth, for action — remains unresolved, and furthermore, Orestes has taken no clear charge of her as her new guardian. In short,
everything about the last scene stands in the way of the closure that the chorus pronounces, at least so far as Electra is concerned.

Electra, therefore, remains in limbo just as her position in society embodies a paradox. In this drama she has had two choices: a dangerous move
toward the autonomy of Clytemnestra, or the self-annihilation implicit in her
faithful devotion to her father. By championing the endogamous view of the
oikos represented by the Hestia myth and legislated in the epiklerate, she has
enabled Orestes' return and, on some level, the return of order to the house.
She fails to realize (within the bounds of the play) that once so enabled,
Orestes will coopt both house and drama from her.[68] The *oikos* may well be
restored for Orestes; but the play gives no indication that Electra will par-
ticipate in Orestes' restored position. The paradox of the woman's role in
the (re)generation of that *oikos* becomes Electra's tragedy, just as it was her
mother's nightmare.

Chapter 4

FAMILY MATTERS
IN THE *Antigone*

*The chief impression produced upon Isabel's mind by this criti-
cism was that the passion of love separated its victim terribly
from every one but the loved object. She felt herself disjoined
from every one she had ever known before.*

HENRY JAMES, *The Portrait of a Lady*

Although the *Antigone*[1] contains one of the most famous
marriage-to-death scenes in Greek literature, previous scholarship has not
usually seen issues of marriage as central to the play.[2] Rather, interpreters
have focused on the question of justice, taking Creon and Antigone as representing opposing and separable aspects of the law (usually defined as civic
and divine, respectively).[3] Creon, it is usually argued, oversteps the bounds
of proper kingship when he forbids Antigone to bury her brother. Antigone
upholds this right on grounds of religious authority, and thus becomes a
martyr in her death. Creon, meanwhile, pays the price for his foolishness
through the loss of his family, the very thing that he denied Antigone. The
interpretations that take such a focus, however, do not explain why the marriage theme comes into the play in the first place. The relationship that
causes all the difficulty is that of Antigone and her dead brother; why, then,
does Sophocles raise the question of Antigone's marriage to Haemon, and
why does her death take on the imagery of matrimony and erotic union?[4]

One point is clear: the theme of marriage is not incidental to the central conflict of the play.[5] By the middle of the drama, the moral and legal
problem of what to do with Antigone is being posed explicitly in terms of
her marriage. Ismene asks Creon the question quite baldly: ἀλλὰ κτενεῖς
νυμφεῖα τοῦ σαυτοῦ τέκνου; ("But would you kill the bride of your own
child?" 568). In Creon's divisive scene with Haemon, similarly, both speakers
address the issue of whether Haemon's loyalties lie with his father or his be-

trothed (e.g., 637–38, 648–51). Most importantly, Antigone's death scene has little to say about the justification or condemnation of the heroine's actions, but a good deal to say about her experience of marriage and perceived place in her family. We know from a scholiast that Sophocles was not unique in portraying an engagement between Haemon and Antigone.[6] But this makes the late introduction of the theme (not to mention Antigone's complete disregard for Haemon in the play) and its apparent irrelevance to the question at hand all the more puzzling.

In this play, then, we are not dealing with a marriage that is essential to the plot. Ideologies, however, function on the margins as well as in the centers of social structures. In the course of this drama, marriage becomes a node of conflicting power relations: it is the site of conflict between father and son, niece and uncle, and, through their alliances, citizen and enemy. By looking closely, then, at the characters' assumptions about marriage in general, and at Haemon's proposed marriage to Antigone in particular, we are provided with a lens through which to view the other conflicts of the play. Regardless of which characters we sympathize with, this play makes a series of shifting and contradictory definitions of the family a nexus around which other questions — of duty, of pollution, of justice — take shape.

At the same time, we should recognize that marriage provides Antigone with a way of thinking. In her decision to bury her brother against the order of Creon, both she and Creon use language that remind us of marital union. When caught in her crime and facing a punishment of death, Antigone again calls to mind the marriage that she will never have. For Antigone, as for the other heroines we have seen so far, moments of strong personal voice, moments when she can be seen as the subject of her own actions, are likened to and linked to her (real or potential) marriage. And like the tragedy itself, Antigone's "marriage" to death will eventually close down on her character, silencing the voice that it appears to create.

CREON THE FAMILY MAN

Many critics have argued that Creon represents the interests of the state, as opposed to those of the family.[7] It is not always easy, however, to determine exactly where the family leaves off and the city begins in fifth-century Athens.[8] More importantly, as we shall see, Creon clearly does have an interest in the family — it is merely a question of how he defines that family. A key scene is the argument between Creon and his son Haemon. Once Antigone has been captured, Haemon approaches his father to plead for her release. Creon sees this exchange in explicitly familial terms. He begins his conversation with Haemon with a question:

ὦ παῖ, τελείαν ψῆφον ἆρα μὴ κλυὼν
τῆς μελλονύμφου πατρὶ λυσσαίνων πάρει;
ἢ σοὶ μὲν ἡμεῖς πανταχῇ δρῶντες φίλοι;

Child, I hope you have not come raving mad at your father,
having heard the final vote concerning your soon-to-be
    bride?
Or am I your *philos* no matter what I do? (632–34)

Creon is, for whatever reason, seriously concerned about his relations with
his son. Moreover, he describes those relations as a form of *philia*.[9] As standard readings of this play would have it, Creon defines *philoi* in terms of
service to the state, Antigone in terms of family ties.[10] This is not strictly true.
As Haemon approaches, Creon worries about Haemon's treatment of him as
a father. Admittedly, he will use his model of the family shortly to describe
successful civic government (659–60), but that does not erase the familial
concern present here.

Haemon seems to recognize Creon's concern, and answers his questions
with a little speech that should please his father:

πάτερ, σός εἰμι· καὶ σύ με γνώμας ἔχων
χρηστὰς ἀπορθοῖς, αἷς ἔγωγ' ἐφέψομαι.
ἐμοὶ γὰρ οὐδεὶς ἀξιώσεται γάμος
μείζων φέρεσθαι σοῦ καλῶς ἡγουμένου.

Father, I am yours. And you give me straight advice,
which I, for my part, will follow.
For no marriage will be worth more to me
than to be guided by your sound leadership. (635–38)

He explicitly states his dedication, not to Creon as ruler of Thebes, but to
his father as an advisor in the matter of marriage. And this is a role that Creon
takes seriously.[11] In a generalizing statement a few lines later, he gives Haemon advice on choosing a bride:

μή νύν ποτ', ὦ παῖ, τὰς φρένας γ' ὑφ' ἡδονῆς
γυναικὸς οὕνεκ' ἐκβάλῃς, εἰδὼς ὅτι
ψυχρὸν παραγκάλισμα τοῦτο γίγνεται,
γυνὴ κακὴ ξύνευνος ἐν δόμοις.

Do not ever, child, throw away your mind for pleasure
on account of a woman, knowing that
this becomes a cold embrace,
an evil wife sleeping with you in the house. (648–51)

Obviously Creon has Antigone in mind. He may be misjudging her, but it seems foolish to doubt that he genuinely thinks she would make a bad wife. We see the same motivation in his response to Ismene's question (above): κακὰς ἐγὼ γυναῖκας υἱέσι στυγῶ ("I hate evil wives for sons," 571). The drift of Creon's words, moreover, implies that Antigone's danger lies in a sexual desirability. As a *parankalisma* ("embrace") in line 650, she is clearly figured as a bedmate, a notion further implied by *suneunos* ("bedmate") in the next line. Creon wants particularly to warn Haemon against her false physical charms (false, since she will be a "cold" embrace). What is especially bad about such a wife, as the language in 650–51 shows, is that she is *in the house*, in a privileged and intimate position. Above all else, then, Creon fears that the desirability of Antigone will create discord in his relations with Haemon. It is crucial, therefore, that he set the father-son bond as prior in importance to that of (potential) husband and wife.[12]

We know that Demosthenes found Creon's opening speech to be a model for a good ruler.[13] Creon's advice on marriage, too, probably struck a responsive chord. Athenian men were evidently concerned with the possibility that sexually desirable women could sway a young man's senses and cloud his judgment. Isaeus warns, for example, that young men who lack self-control might be led astray by the wrong sort of woman.[14] The mistake that such men may make is in agreeing to marry sexually desirable women even though their citizenship is questionable, and their class is not suitable for the men marrying them. Ultimately, then, a woman's sexual attractions are a threat to the state, whether the danger is in falsifying citizenship (as is the case in Isaeus 3) or merely in undermining masculine authority (as is the case in the *Antigone*). Creon is not anti-family, any more than is Isaeus. Rather, Creon sees the family as necessary for the city, but also as potentially destructive of order within the city. If the husband chooses a woman for a wife because of her sexual desirability, rather than in accord with his father's wishes, then the formation of a new family becomes a threat to the masculine hierarchy. In other words, Antigone presents a double threat here. As the person who buried Polyneices, she undermines Creon's political authority, but as an unmarried, potentially seductive woman, she has access to a momentary subjectivity and could subvert Creon's family.

The question, then, is what sort of family Creon envisions. At his most extreme, Creon resembles Heracles in the *Trachiniae*. He sees his family as a succession of men, for whom women present a perhaps necessary but dangerous and suspect mediation.[15] At times (as above) he merely tries to control that mediation. In other places, he tells a story of civilization that excludes women altogether. In fact, in his next speech Creon will borrow from Hesiod to draw his ideal image of society:

τούτου γὰρ οὕνεκ' ἄνδρες εὔχονται γονὰς
κατηκόους φύσαντες ἐν δόμοις ἔχειν,
ὡς καὶ τὸν ἐχθρὸν ἀνταμύνωνται κακοῖς
καὶ τὸν φίλον τιμῶσιν ἐξ ἴσου πατρί.
ὅστις δ' ἀνωφέλητα φιτύει τέκνα,
τί τόνδ' ἂν εἴποις ἄλλο πλὴν αὑτῷ πόνους
φῦσαι, πολὺν δὲ τοῖσιν ἐχθροῖσιν γέλων;

For this reason men pray to sow
obedient offspring to have in the house
so that they will ward off enemies by doing them harm,
and will honor friends [16] equally with their father.
And whoever begets unhelpful children,
what would you say, except that he has sown
troubles for himself and much laughter for his enemies?
      (641–47)

We find several interesting features here: men, explicitly, pray for obedient offspring, but implicit in Creon's formulation is the idea that children will obey their fathers. The only real question is whether these children will honor the father's *philoi* as much as they do the father (643–44). Even more interesting, however, are the last two lines quoted above, because they remind us of Hesiod's *Works and Days*:

παρθενικὴν δὲ γαμεῖν, ὥς κ' ἤθεα κεδνὰ διδάξῃς,
[τὴν δὲ μάλιστα γαμεῖν, ἥτις σέθεν ἐγγύθι ναίει]
πάντα μάλ' ἀμφὶς ἰδών, μὴ γείτοσι χάρματα γήμῃς.
οὐ μὲν γάρ τι γυναικὸς ἀνὴρ ληίζετ' ἄμεινον
τῆς ἀγαθῆς, τῆς δ' αὖτε κακῆς οὐ ῥίγιον ἄλλο.[17]

Marry a young woman, so that you can teach her good
      manners,
[and especially marry one who lives near to you,]
looking at everything, all around, lest you marry a source of
      joy for the neighbors.
for a man carries off nothing better than a good wife,
nor anything more painful than an evil one. (699–703)

Sophocles has taken the potential instability of a wife who, if bad, will amuse the neighbors, and has transferred it to the offspring. The move is not unlikely, since indeed a bad wife might be expected to produce bad, or even illegitimate, children. Creon's speech, however, rewrites the danger of marriage as a danger to the relationship of father and son. Unlike Hesiod, who advises merely to choose a "maiden" and try to control her, Creon bypasses the woman altogether, focusing his attention on controlling his (male) children.

Similarly, when it comes to the issue of whom Haemon will marry, Creon makes it clear that, in his eyes, the woman is the replaceable party in a marriage; for when Ismene asks him point blank, "But will you kill the bride of your own child?" he responds, ἀρώσιμοι γὰρ χἀτέρων εἰσὶν γύαι ("[Yes], for the lands of others are plowable," 569). Creon's line would call to mind the Athenian wedding formula (above, Chapter 1).[18] But it also makes clear the construct that the formula implies: the woman in marriage is an object of exchange for the purpose of bearing children, and as such, she can be painlessly traded in without damage to the identity of the *oikos*.[19] Creon's views of Antigone may be in part politically motivated. But they also fit the stock views of women held by men in patrilineal, homosocial society.

Toward the end of Haemon's scene with his father, Creon emphasizes the importance of his direct bond with Haemon, and again tries to deny Antigone's sexual dominion over his son:

| **Αἰ.** | εἰ μὴ πατὴρ ἦσθ᾽, εἶπον ἄν σ᾽ οὐκ εὖ φρονεῖν. |
| **Κρ.** | γυναικὸς ὢν δούλευμα, μὴ κώτιλλέ με. |

| Hae.: | If you were not my father, I would have said you aren't thinking well. |
| Cr.: | Since you are a woman's slave, don't fawn on me. (755–56) |

The idea that Haemon is "enslaved" by his eros is again a stock characterization, but one that emphasizes through exaggeration the dangers of female sexuality.[20] If Haemon is going to let that woman mediate between them, Creon seems to suggest, then their father-son relationship is in peril. Desperately, at the end of the exchange, Creon suggests that he will have Antigone killed in front of Haemon, the clearest possible attempt to create a bond with his son that excludes his son's fiancee. When we consider the tendency for women to be portrayed as sacrificial victims at the moment of their marriage (e.g., Iphigenia), we might even see this as an attempted sacrifice, one that will restore Creon's optimum order.[21] It will remove Antigone, and in forcing Haemon to watch her death, it will implicate his approval—or at least his acceptance—of that death, in obedience to his father.

This view of the family contrasts sharply with the view put forth by Antigone, a view that she hints at from the first line of the play. Antigone begins, Ὦ κοινὸν αὐτάδελφον Ἰσμήνης κάρα ("Dear Ismene, my sister of the same parents"). This might emphasize no more than her closeness to her sister. Segal, however, has noticed a pattern of kinship words especially prevalent in Antigone's speech.[22] At 466–67, she refers to Polyneices as "from my mother," and at 511 she argues, οὐδὲν γὰρ αἰσχρὸν τοὺς ὁμοσπλάγχνους σέβειν ("For it is not at all shameful to honor those from the same *splanchna*"). *Splanchna* means, literally, "womb." In short, Antigone "makes kinship a function of the female procreative power,"[23] and the first line of the play also fits into this category. Segal points out that *adelphos* comes from *a*- ("same") and *delphys* ("womb"). At this point Antigone still seeks the help of her sister, and so includes her in the *maternal* line by which she defines the family. Later, when she has dismissed her sister as weak-hearted, she still sees the king's bloodline as going through herself (though only through herself). About to go to her death, Antigone invokes the chorus: λεύσσετε . . . / τὴν βασιλειδῶν μούνην λοιπήν ("Look at the only remainder of the king's line," 940–41). Her definition of the family, both hers and her parents', grants specific powers of kinship to the female. Creon's idealized father-son lineage, then, directly opposes Antigone's implicit recognition of female mediation and participation.

Creon, therefore, defines the family differently than does Antigone. In his talk with Haemon, he tries to create a male homosocial line similar to that established by Heracles at the end of the *Trachiniae*. As several commentators have pointed out, however, Creon's political power is all too dependent on the maternal lineage that Antigone implies.[24] He states, in his first speech, ἐγὼ κράτη δὴ πάντα καὶ θρόνους ἔχω / γένους κατ᾽ ἀγχιστεῖα τῶν ὀλωλότων ("I hold all the power and the throne / through my close relationship to the dead," 173–74). *Anchisteia* is, of course, a specific legal term defining the order of inheritance within a family. Though we cannot assume that Creon is bound by fifth-century Athenian law, he bases his power on a familial relationship and uses terminology that would certainly recall inheritance disputes for the audience.[25] What that terminology does not state, but must be understood to mean, is that Creon's right to the throne comes to him through his sister, Jocasta. He has no patrilineal relation to the two dead brothers.

The importance of Creon's *anchisteia* becomes even more clear when we hit a wickedly funny pun about twenty lines later. Creon here makes the public proclamation to which Antigone had referred at the beginning of the play: καὶ νῦν ἀδελφὰ τῶνδε κηρύξας ἔχω / ἀστοῖσι παίδων τῶν ἀπ᾽ Οἰδίπου πέρι ("And now, having announced these things I hold their brother-announcements, / for the citizens concerning the children of Oedipus," 192–93). Notice that for Creon, the two dead warriors are sons of Oedipus, not of Jocasta. His decree, however, is "from the same womb" (*a-delphos*) as the things he has just been saying. Many will not agree that the word *adelphos* calls to mind the idea of a womb; Kamerbeek (ad loc.) translates the phrase in this context as "in full accord with these principles." In the light of the familial definitions that appear in this passage, and in the light of Antigone's appeal in the first line to her *autadelphos* sister, however, I take *adelphos* as meaning (at least) "brother to" these principles. To understand the word as such is to recall the relationship that Creon specifically refuses to acknowledge in his decree: the relationship of Polyneices and Eteocles as brothers, whom Antigone will address as "from the same womb." Creon's proclamation, like his power, is matrilineal, however much he might like to overlook that fact. He cannot exclude female mediation.

THE ODE ON MAN [*sic*]

Recently Sourvinou-Inwood has argued that, by and large, the chorus of the *Antigone* agrees with Creon.[26] Certainly the first choral ode (100–61) shows the proper pro-Theban spirit. The chorus's second song, which comes immediately after it has heard about the mysterious burial of Polyneices, supports the picture of Creon that I have been presenting. It does so, moreover, on a level beyond the chorus's recognition. Let us take the ode in context: Creon made his commandment, as the last lines of his first speech make clear, in an attempt to maintain order within the city: ἀλλ' ὅστις εὔνους τῇδε τῇ πόλει, θανὼν / καὶ ζῶν ὁμοίως ἔκ γ᾽ ἐμοῦ τιμήσεται ("But whoever is well-minded toward this city, dying / or living he will be honored similarly by me," 209–10). Now someone has overturned that commandment. The chorus responds to this first challenge to order with an ode celebrating the foundation of civilization. Humankind, we learn in successive stanzas, has crossed the seas, domesticated animals, created shelter, learned language, and created laws. Two aspects of this story are unusual: first, the ode presents the transition from a state of nature to a state of culture as largely positive; and second, this transition takes place entirely without reference to gender. The first strophe and antistrophe are particularly interesting in this regard:

> πολλὰ τὰ δεινὰ κοὐδὲν ἀν-
> θρώπου δεινότερον πέλει·
> τοῦτο καὶ πολιοῦ πέραν
> πόντου χειμερίῳ νότῳ
> χωρεῖ, περιβρυχίοισιν
> περῶν ὑπ᾽ οἴδμασιν, θεῶν
> τε τὰν ὑπερτάταν, Γᾶν
> ἄφθιτον, ἀκαμάταν ἀποτρύεται
> ἰλλομένων ἀρότρων ἔτος εἰς ἔτος,
> ἱππείῳ γένει πολεύων.

κουφονόων τε φῦλον ὀρ-
νίθων ἀμφιβαλὼν ἄγει
καὶ θηρῶν ἀγρίων ἔθνη
πόντου τ' εἰναλίαν φύσιν
σπείραισι δικτυοκλώστοις,
περιφραδὴς ἀνήρ· κρατεῖ
δὲ μηχαναῖς ἀγραύλου
θηρὸς ὀρεσσιβάτα, λασιαύχενά θ'
ἵππον ὀχμάζεται ἀμφὶ λόφον ζυγῷ
οὔρειόν τ' ἀκμῆτα ταῦρον.

There are many amazing things, but none
more amazing than humankind.
This is the thing that crosses the grey sea
with the storming south wind,
crossing beneath the swells that crash all around;
and it wears away the oldest of gods,
the imperishable never-tiring Earth,
when the plows go back and forth year after year,
as it [humankind] turns the soil with the race of horses.

And snaring the tribe of
thoughtless birds man leads them,
and also the races of wild animals,
and the breeds of the salt sea,
with his close-coiled nets,
man [does this], very thoughtful.
By contrivances he controls
the mountain-goings of
field-dwelling animals,
and he binds the mane of
the shaggy-necked horse to the yoke,
and the tireless mountain bull. (332–52)

The ode is curious. It makes no reference to heroes or ancestors, does not
call up familiar narratives from Greek prehistory. It seems firmly rooted in
the present. Segal sees the ode, therefore, as a celebration of rationalism:
"The Ode on Man . . . is the only ode in the play without mythical allusions.
It is as if the spirit of reason, extolling itself, displaces myth as the principal
mode of understanding and structuring reality." [27] Segal overlooks, however,
the fact that for the Greeks (and no less for us), the progress of civilization is
a myth. By this I do not mean to suggest that in some vague, unspecified way

progress has not been all to the good. I mean, quite specifically, that the Greeks had constructed a mythological narrative of the progress of civilization. The ode is simply another retelling of this common story: it is a restatement of the end of the Golden Age, as told by Hesiod. At lines 42ff. of the *Works and Days*, Hesiod lists the toils that would not be necessary had not Prometheus stolen fire from Zeus and given it to mortals:

> Κρύψαντες γὰρ ἔχουσι θεοὶ βίον ἀνθρώποισιν.
> ῥηιδίως γάρ κεν καὶ ἐπ' ἤματι ἐργάσσαιο,
> ὥστε σε κεῖς ἐνιαυτὸν ἔχειν καὶ ἀεργὸν ἐόντα·
> αἶψά κε πηδάλιον μὲν ὑπὲρ καπνοῦ καταθεῖο,
> ἔργα βοῶν δ' ἀπόλοιτο καὶ ἡμιόνων ταλαεργῶν.

> For the gods hold back livelihood from humans, hiding it.
> For easily would you produce in a single day
> enough to satisfy yourself for a year, without working,
> and immediately you would put your rudder away over the
>   smoke,
> and the work of cows and long-toiling mules would
>   disappear.[28] (42–46)

These are, of course, the two common signs of the end of the Golden Age: men must plough the earth and sail the seas to make their living — exactly the two achievements that Sophocles' ode praises. Simply put, Sophocles has taken the typically pessimistic story of humanity's fall and presented it as an optimistic foundation of civilization.[29]

The last antistrophe of the ode continues in this vein, celebrating man as σοφόν τι τὸ μηχανόεν τέχνας ὑπὲρ ἐλπίδ' ἔχων ("being wise at devising skills beyond expectation," 365). And here we become particularly aware of what Sophocles has left out of his rewriting of the myth. In Hesiod's version, Prometheus's theft of fire is a theft of *technē*, skill that (since Zeus hides it as punishment for humans, 49–50) makes life easier. In return for this theft, Zeus gives the human race a gift: Pandora (57–58). Pandora will be the first wife, and as Pucci says, "The creation of Pandora occurs as the last act of a series of incidents that lead mankind from its 'natural' godlike life to 'culture' and the mortal life of toil."[30] With Pandora comes, in broad terms, *difference*: from now on, sexual reproduction replaces spontaneous autochthony, agriculture replaces the self-producing bounty of the earth, and physical space is divided into inside and outside.[31] Insofar as Greek myth sees culture as a step down, it associates culture with the female.[32]

The chorus of the *Antigone*, however, tells a curiously genderless history of the development of culture. The achievements of humankind (however ambiguous) do not depend on the difference introduced, in Hesiod's version, by women and marriage. They simply happen, to our benefit. This gender-less history, nonetheless, has a gendered subtext, one that becomes all the more clear when we look at specifics. The images that the chorus uses to describe the rise of civilization are also images often used to describe marriage, or at least erotic domination by men. Two passages in particular fall into this category. First, we are told that humans plough the earth, turning up the soil (338–41). Greek myth often uses the image of the earth ploughed to describe the civic and familial fertility desired in marriage; in fact, it is echoed in Creon's line 569 (discussed above).[33] A similarly agrarian metaphor surfaces a few lines later in the chorus's ode when we hear about successfully yoking both horses and mountain bulls (350–52). Again, brides (as well as grooms) are often said to be "yoked" when they are married, and brides in particular are often associated with horses.[34] The fact, therefore, that women do not appear in this myth of civilization is all the more remarkable. This ode does essentially what Creon does: it creates a vision of the city in which women do not figure, and in which the theme of marriage is suppressed. The ode, like Creon, champions the masculine role (in yoking, taming, etc.) while eliding the gendered context of that which must be yoked or tamed.

The play itself makes a similar move. Whether or not the idea of an erotic relationship between Haemon and Antigone was part of the tradition, the *Antigone* has been keeping a secret from us. Until we reach line 568, we have no clue that Antigone is betrothed to anyone. The silence is so remarkable that Goheen speaks of the "suppression" of "a developed erotic sub-plot."[35] This is not to say that Sophocles was trying to suppress the role of erotics in his own play, in which case he might have done a more thorough job of it. Rather, the play suppresses Antigone's betrothal because suppression of the female role in civilization (as in the case of the first stasimon) is one of the key themes of this play.

This reading of the first stasimon helps explain its connection to the action surrounding it, a task that scholars have not always found easy. Shortly before the choral ode, Creon asks the hapless guard, τί φής; τίς ἀνδρῶν ἦν ὁ τολμήσας τάδε; ("What are you saying? What man was it who dared to do this?" 248). Creon (like Heracles in the *Trachiniae*) is thinking of possible dissenters as men.[36] No women, he implies, act in his city. But, just as Antigone disrupts his view of his family later, and just as Pandora is a disruption of the Golden Age in Hesiod, Antigone enters at the end of the first stasimon as the woman who is disrupting Creon's rule. The chorus can barely comprehend the spectacle:

εἰ δαιμόνιον τέρας ἀμφινοῶ
τόδε· πῶς <δ'> εἰδὼς ἀντιλογήσω
τήνδ' οὐκ εἶναι παῖδ' Ἀντιγόνην;

My mind is split at this awful sight;[37]
and how, knowing her, can I argue the opposite,
that this is not the child Antigone? (376–78)

The chorus's two-mindedness is the emotional correlative of the ode it has just sung. Unknowingly, the chorus suppressed woman in its myth of civilization, and unknowingly, Creon suppressed her as a possible source of chaos in the city. Now that suppression has exploded; Antigone, betrothed of Haemon and sister of Polyneices, has entered the civic realm.

ANTIGONE'S WEDDINGS

Antigone plainly represents a threat to civic order at this entrance. Significantly, her disruption is figured from the first in terms that position her as a potential bride. After Antigone has been captured, Creon says of her: σμικρῷ χαλινῷ δ' οἶδα τοὺς θυμουμένους / ἵππους καταρτυθέντας ("I know that high-spirited horses / are tamed with a small bit," 477–78). As well as carrying connotations of dangerous wildness, the horse image also implies that Antigone is an object (at least potentially) of erotic desire. *Parthenoi* are regularly described as wild horses that must be broken, particularly in lyric poetry.[38] Compare, for example, Anacreon frag. 417:

πῶλε Θρηκίη, τί δή με λοξὸν ὄμμασι βλέπουσα
νηλέως φεύγεις, δοκεῖς δέ μ' οὐδὲν εἰδέναι σοφόν;
ἴσθι τοι, καλῶς μὲν ἄν τοι τὸν χαλινὸν ἐμβάλοιμι.[39]

Thracian filly, why, looking at me crosswise,
do you flee from me pitilessly, and seem to think that I have
   no skill?
Know this, I would put the bit on you beautifully. (1–3)

Creon's desire to break Antigone, therefore, is not as simple as it seems. On one level, his image posits her as an animal, an object to be tamed. At the same time, however, it points to her potential as an erotic object, the very thing that Creon most fears will corrupt his son (see especially lines 648–51 above).

Moreover, the guard hints at Antigone's potential role as a wife and mother when he tells of her capture. He describes her as a bird who cries over the loss of her young:

ἡ παῖς ὁρᾶται κἀνακωκύει πικρῶς
ὄρνιθος ὀξὺν φθόγγον, ὡς ὅταν κενῆς
εὐνῆς νεοσσῶν ὀρφανὸν βλέψῃ λέχος.

The child was spotted, and she cried out sharply
with the shrill voice of a bird, as when, the bedding empty,
the bird looks at the nest/bed bereft of hatchlings. (423–25)

Again, the play shows Antigone valuing her brother according to a specifically maternal relationship, the very relationship that Creon so carefully avoids. The bird image does more, however, than momentarily construct Antigone as a mother. The words *lechos* and *eunēs*, which here seem to refer to the nest in the bird metaphor, are more commonly used of a marriage bed. A few lines later, the guard will use a word from the realm of hunting (*thērometha*, 433) as he describes capturing this "bird." Once again, the image is one that carries specific erotic connotations: so many vases portray young men pursuing *parthenoi*, spears in hand, that Sourvinou-Inwood states, "Indeed, in Athenian mentality the capture of wild animals was generally associated with the erotic sphere."[40] In one compact image, then, Antigone is figured both as a wild *parthenos* who needs to be captured and tamed, and as a mother who grieves the loss of her young.

The chorus amplifies and underlines Creon's fear of Antigone a second time, in the ode immediately following the scene between Creon and his son. They sing an ode to Eros that ushers in the idea of Antigone's marriage to Hades.[41] In the course of the ode, they blame the strife that we have just witnessed between father and son on the god:

σὺ καὶ τόδε νεῖκος ἀνδρῶν
ξύναιμον ἔχεις ταράξας·
νικᾷ δ' ἐναργὴς βλεφάρων
ἵμερος εὐλέκτρου
νύμφας.

And you hold this quarrel
between blood-kin, shaking it up.
Manifest desire from the eyes
of a well-bedded bride
is victorious. (793–97)

Whether or not the chorus is correct in its analysis is of little concern.[42] What matters is that it sees Antigone as a potential source of strife between father and son. Perhaps even more important (and unusual), the chorus sees eros as operating *within* the institution of marriage: desire sits specifically on the eyebrows of "a well-bedded bride" (796–97). Antigone is a threat to male society even within marriage because Haemon's physical attraction to her interferes with his relation with his father (cf. the discussion of Isaeus 3, Chapter 1 above). As often, moreover, the chorus does more than reflect Creon's fears; it predicts his downfall. The ode begins, "Eros unconquerable in battle" (781). Creon will indeed find this disruptive force beyond his ability to control.

As a potential bride, however, Antigone presents a certain paradox. A central part of getting married, for the woman, is her rupture from her original *oikos* and integration into a new one. In refusing to leave Polyneices unburied, Antigone expresses a solidarity with her birth family that denies this very experience:

> φίλη μετ' αὐτοῦ κείσομαι, φίλου μέτα,
> ὅσια πανουργήσασ'· ἐπεὶ πλείων χρόνος
> ὂν δεῖ μ' ἀρέσκειν τοῖς κάτω τῶν ἐνθάδε.

> *Philē* I will lie with him, with my *philos*[43]
> having done everything that is holy. For it is necessary for me
> to please those below for a longer time than those here.
> (73–75)

This paradox is consistent, however, with a certain set of expectations for *parthenoi* in fifth-century Athens; it makes sense insofar as Antigone, like Electra, is in the position of an *epiklēros*. This structure is never made explicit in the play (though the mention of *anchisteia* in 173 hints at it), but it goes far toward explaining Antigone's actions.[44] The *epiklēros*, as we have seen, passes her father's inheritance on to her husband (who, like Haemon, should be a near relative). Her potential "divided *kurieia*" is made actual. She stands at a paradoxical moment, when the paternal line is passed matrilineally, when the woman is a subject in legal as well as personal terms. No wonder, then, that Antigone tends to define the family with matrilineal terms, actively champions the part of her birth family, and is simultaneously figured as a potential bride. Antigone is living the paradox of the *epiklēros*, and this ambivalent structure constitutes her position in her moment of subjectivity.[45] Her potential as a carrier of her family's bloodline, made most evident when the guard casts her in the role of Polyneices' mother, is therefore congruent with, even dependent on, a dedication to her paternal family.[46]

Unlike Electra's marriage, however, Antigone's does not remain indefinitely *in potentia*. In some way, in fact, Antigone gets married twice — once to Hades and once to Haemon. It is well known that Antigone is portrayed as a "bride of death." Most commentators on Antigone's death scene have done little, however, beyond pointing out that her position has a real correlative in Greek culture: *parthenoi* who died were often portrayed as "married to death," as if the one transition could stand in adequately for the other.[47] The apparent equation of these two *telē*, however, is not so straightforward. As we have seen, an element of death is often present in real marriages. The metaphor emphasizes the woman's change of state: the girl who existed before dies, and is replaced by the woman that she has become.[48] Suggesting that an unmarried woman has married death, however, also indicates that the *parthenos* has left life in some way incomplete, and her marriage to death is an attempt, doomed to failure, to achieve that closure. Thus we find that a number of tombstones lament that a woman has died *instead of* getting married, and the inscriptions regret this waste of potential.[49] This common construction does not substitute one *telos* (death) for another (marriage), but aligns these two possibilities as polar opposites. These women will never be brides, will never be "perfected" into the state of being a wife and mother. In the *Antigone*, Sophocles creates an Antigone who fits both sides of this complex relation with uncanny closeness: she marries death, as does Persephone, while still alive, and yet she insists on her lack of marriage, on her unfulfillment.[50] She both marries and does not marry death, and the result is an isolation more extreme even than that of those other women in Greek literature whose marriages are in some way incomplete.

Let's consider the complex structure of Antigone's nonmarriage. First we should note the many lines that suggest that Antigone's death is a marriage (to Hades).[51] Both Antigone and the chorus refer to the cave as a bridal chamber: at 804, the chorus calls it a *thalamos*,[52] and at 891 Antigone begins her penultimate speech, ὦ τύμβος, ὦ νυμφεῖον ("Oh tomb, oh marriage chamber"). Antigone's central declaration, moreover, runs as follows:

> ἀλλά μ᾽ ὁ παγ-
> κοίτας Ἅιδας ζῶσαν ἄγει
> τὰν Ἀχέροντος
> ἀκτάν, οὔθ᾽ ὑμεναίων
> ἔγκληρον, οὔτ᾽ ἐπὶ νυμ-
> φείοις πώ μέ τις ὕμνος ὕ-
> μνησεν, ἀλλ᾽ Ἀχέροντι νυμφεύσω.

> But Hades where all must lie
> leads me, still living, to the edge
> of Acheron.
> I have no share in bridal songs,
> nor does anyone sing the bride hymn

outside my bridal chamber,
but I will marry Acheron. (810–16)

In addition to the statement that she will marry Acheron, the passage makes Antigone, as Segal points out, into a Persephone figure.[53] She is distinct from the *parthenoi* who are said to be married to death in that she will go to Hades while still alive (811, 836). She becomes more than a representative for the maiden who dies young, then. She also represents, through her association with Kore, the women who get married and so "die" a symbolic death.[54] Antigone's entrance into her *thalamos* is a tragic correlative to the "normal" bride's entrance into her new home.

Insofar as Antigone is going to meet death, however, she bitterly resents the fact that she is *not* going to be married and is not undergoing marriage rites. In addition to her complaint in lines 813–16 (above), she states toward the end of the first kommos:

> ἄκλαυτος, ἄφιλος, ἀνυμέναι-
> ος <ἁ> ταλαίφρων ἄγομαι
> τὰν ἑτοίμαν ὁδόν.

> Unwept, without friends, without marriage,
> I who am wretched am led
> down the road that is prepared for me. (876–78)

It is not just that her death is represented as a marriage. The death that she predicts for herself calls to mind the laments that we find on the gravestones of unmarried young women. It removes the possibility of marriage for Antigone, and denies her any successful transition to adult life. It seems that Sophocles has juxtaposed the two representations of death-as-marriage to create a paradox: death is both the cruel force that prevents fulfillment in marriage, and the sign that a transformation has been made, a marker of the new bride's successful integration in the new household.

Ultimately this paradox remains unresolved. If anything, Antigone's place, in the family and in the world, becomes only more and more problematic. She describes her placement in the cave as a lack of integration on the most basic level:

> ἰὼ δύστανος, βροτοῖς
> οὔτε <νεκρὸς> νεκροῖσιν
> μέτοικος, οὐ ζῶσιν, οὐ θανοῦσιν

> Look, the wretch, not a corpse
> among mortal corpses
> sharing house with neither living nor dead. (850–53)

The rock chamber, as Reinhardt points out, "becomes an image of her half-way position, her rootless hovering."[55] Moreover, the word *metoikos* is particularly interesting in this context. Though it looks as if it should mean "sharing a house with," and indeed, LSJ gives it this meaning for this passage, every other citation of the word in LSJ has the sense of someone who has settled somewhere from abroad. Athenians in the fifth century commonly used the word in a specific legal sense, to refer to the class of resident aliens. It is not enough, then, to realize that Antigone "shares a house" with neither living nor dead; the diction of the passage suggests that even if she did, she would be an outsider.[56]

Moreover, because Antigone's death/marriage stems in part from a dedication to her paternal family, her entrance into the underworld comes to represent a failure to marry as much as it does a marriage. Like Electra, she refuses to abandon her ties with her blood family, even though her family is dead. In structural terms, this dedication directly opposes the experience of Persephone, who is forced to abandon her (living) family for a marriage in the underworld. Unlike Kore's journey, Antigone's trip to the underworld represents a union of sorts with her blood family rather than a severance from them via marriage.[57] Here again, however, Antigone realizes late in the game what her alliance with her dead parents signifies. She uses the word *metoikos* a second time: πρὸς οὓς ἀραῖος ἄγαμος ἅδ' / ἐγὼ μέτοικος ἔρχομαι ("I go to them an alien / cursed, unmarried," 867–68). She will be with her father and mother, but again the implicit idea of a metic suggests alienation, lack of full integration. In the same breath, she laments the fact that she will be *agamos* (867). Remaining with her parents, then, is a restatement of her marginal position as a *parthenos* who will not wed.[58] Neuberg suggests, "She is forced to choose the blood family at the expense of the marriage-family, ending up in a void between them, which for a woman is also death."[59] I see it the other way around. Antigone's death signifies a void, a lack of resolution or integration of any kind.

It may seem odd that Antigone's lament, one of the most famous and arguably among the most powerful speeches by a female character in Greek tragedy, should be characterized by such instability, such lack of integration. I would argue, however, that this portrayal is exactly consistent with the view of female subjectivity that I have found throughout this study. Both this tragedy and Antigone's "marriage" give her a voice. At the same time, however, Antigone's speech renders her a "stranger" who finds no completion in her marriage. As was the case with Deianeira in the *Trachiniae*, Antigone's experience of marriage is both final and endlessly alienating; ultimately, her experience can only be rendered as incommunicable, foreign.

At the end of Antigone's lament over her death come some of the most controversial lines in the play. In lines 904–20, Antigone states that she would not have done for a husband or a child what she did for her brother, because with her parents dead Polyneices could not be replaced. A long line of scholars have found these lines so disruptive to their readings of the play that they have argued for excision.[60] The lines are consistent, however, with the values that Antigone expresses throughout the drama. As Murnaghan says, "The speech marks the moment when Antigone first confronts the loss of marriage and motherhood that her willingness to sacrifice her life for the sake of burying her brother entails."[61] Antigone exhibits here that dedication to her birth family that the endogamous model of marriage requires of an *epiklēros*. In so doing, however, she also reveals the inherent paradox of that model — that because of her unfailing devotion to her (dead) family, she cannot cross over to another *oikos* and transmit that line. Whereas the *epiklēros* possesses the bloodline only in order to pass it on, Antigone's possession of the bloodline is self-annihilating.[62]

The hypothetical situation of Antigone's speech, too, reverses the normal perception of gender roles in marriage. Murnaghan points out that "the aspect of marriage that she especially emphasizes — the possibility of replacing one participant in it with someone else — is central to its character as an institution."[63] Marriage is, essentially, a rite of successive substitutions: the woman's *kurieia* is transferred from her father to her husband; the woman symbolically replaces the *korē* who existed before; and the woman becomes a substitute for the goddess Hestia within her new house. In all of these substitutions, typically, the woman is the mobile, unstable, changing element. Antigone's speech, however, emphatically figures the husband as replaceable:

> πόσις μὲν ἄν μοι κατθανόντος ἄλλος ἦν,
> καὶ παῖς ἀπ' ἄλλου φωτός, εἰ τοῦδ' ἤμπλακον,
> μητρὸς δ' ἐν Ἅιδου καὶ πατρὸς κεκευθότοιν
> οὐκ ἔστ' ἀδελφὸς ὅστις ἂν βλάστοι ποτέ.

> There would be another husband for me, should the first die
> and a child from another man, if I should be bereft of this
>   one,
> but since both my mother and father lie in Hades,
> there is no other brother who would sprout up ever. (909–12)

Not only can she get a new husband if the first dies, but she suggests that, if a child dies, she can get more *from another husband*. The logic is strained here; we expect her to say that, if a child dies, she can have more, presumably with the same husband. But instead she formulates the passage so that the husband is replaced in both cases. Just as earlier, when Antigone defined her family in specifically female terms, the woman becomes the stable center of marriage via her ability to produce children.

The real problem, then, is that Antigone threatens to usurp male subjectivity. Like the earlier paradoxes surrounding Antigone's "marriage," however, the gynocentric model that Antigone proposes also calls attention to its own inevitable failure as cultural critique. The passage, as has long been realized, is probably based on the story of Intaphernes' wife in Herodotus (3.188ff). But the borrowing seems clumsy.[64] Whereas Intaphernes' wife could actually choose one relative whose life would be spared, Antigone takes the issue of replaceability to new heights. If we work out the logic of her speech, she is saying, "I would not break the law to bury a husband, because I could always get another husband, and bury him." The thought is so disjunctive that Fowler, who accepts the lines, calls them "just another of Sophocles' lapses."[65] But Murnaghan suggests rather that the failure of the two texts to mesh *should* disturb us. The sterility of Antigone's logic, she argues, matches the sterility of the situation in which she finds herself.[66] I suggest we take Murnaghan's argument a step farther: the disruption that comes about because these two texts are clumsily related actually deconstructs the notion of replaceability for which Antigone argues. Just as the story from Herodotus does not make sense when transplanted, husbands (or, for that matter, wives) are not replaceable, at least not without creating serious and complex emotional rifts.[67] The passage problematizes, therefore, Antigone's separation of blood ties from marriage ties. At the same time, it shows the difficulty inherent in marriage itself, since the mobile party (typically the bride) already experiences marriage as a type of substitution, which carries with it a lack of integration: the bride in ancient Greece fails to substitute completely for the goddess Hestia. The woman is figured as a replacement, a mimesis, and so is doomed to the role of imperfect substitute.[68]

As Neuberg points out, Creon first raises the issue of replaceability in marriage at line 569, so that Antigone is here "using his own concept against him."[69] She does pose a threat to Creon specifically in that she makes Haemon the mobile element in marriage. Creon fears that Haemon might side with her against his own father, and this does eventually happen. When Creon goes to the *thalamos* to release Antigone, he finds that Haemon is already there, and Antigone already dead. Haemon rushes at his father, misses, and then kills himself in yet another scene that recalls marriage: κεῖται δὲ νεκρὸς περὶ νεκρῷ, τὰ νυμφικὰ / τέλη λαχὼν δείλαιος ἔν γ' Ἅιδου δόμοις ("Corpse lay upon corpse, and the wretch achieved / his[70] marriage rites in the house of Hades," 1240–41). The tableau is certainly erotic.[71] Some commentators have even seen in the scene a certain redemption of marriage in the play: Seaford states, "But here inasmuch as Haemon and Antigone are bought together in death . . . the τόπος [of marriage-as-death] is in part reversed."[72] I take a rather bleaker view.

Haemon's "marriage," like Antigone's marriage to death, is a perversion of the normal structure of the wedding, in which the bride leaves her house and processes to the groom's. Instead, this marriage makes Haemon the mobile element. Such a notion fits nicely, of course, with Antigone's status as an *epiklēros*, her insistence on matrilineage, and her formulation in lines 904–20. Haemon's marriage, therefore, represents exactly the disruption of ties that Creon feared earlier. His dedication to Antigone demonstrates "the failure of the political tie of the male band to pull the youth away from the mother to the city and a return to the womb as the underground cavern."[73] This marriage, then, is as much a disrupter of civic, social bonds as a creator of them.

Moreover, we must ask ourselves what the marriage to Haemon represents for Antigone. It can hardly be accidental that Antigone never once betrays an awareness of Haemon's existence in the course of the play.[74] She meets him only after she is already dead and has forcefully dedicated herself to her paternal family. This marriage, then, duplicates her earlier marriage to Hades, which was marked by a lack of marriage rites and a failure of fulfillment.[75] Haemon kills himself in his father's presence because of his bride, furthermore, and thus the scene posits Antigone as a danger to society because of her marginal position vis-à-vis the living and vis-à-vis the family. The marriage is both one of extreme endogamy, in that the *epiklēros* dies in dedication to her birth family, and one of extreme exogamy, in that it draws the groom away from his birth family.[76] Haemon's "marriage" to her in death, then, only increases our sense of Antigone's isolation, and our awareness that we do not know her experience.

CONCLUSION, BY WAY OF THE FOURTH STASIMON

In my reading, this play illustrates the dangers implicit in marital connections, and the failure of various models of marriage to contain those dangers.[77] I have treated two odes in the course of my argument, and, by way of concluding, I shall treat one more. The fourth stasimon has long presented a problem for readers.[78] It tells the stories of Danae, Lycurgus, and Cleopatra (not named in the ode); the relation of these three stories to one another, and to the play as a whole, is far from clear.[79] I suggest that all three of these stories explore the difficulties of containing female sexuality, and two of them specifically within the context of marriage. Previous scholars have not seen this as a connection, however, because the perspective shifts from episode to episode. In the first stanza we see a woman who is unsuccessfully contained; in the second, we see a man who fails to contain female passion and is punished in like kind for the attempt; in the third, we see the disruption that a replaced and marginalized woman effects on the stability of the *oikos*.

Danae's story is that of a *parthenos* whose father tries to enclose her so as to prevent marriage:

> κρυπτομένα δ᾽ ἐν τυμβή-
> ρει θαλάμῳ κατεζεύχθη·
> καίτοι <καὶ> γενεᾷ τίμιος, ὦ παῖ παῖ,
> καὶ Ζηνὸς ταμιεύεσκε γονὰς χρυσορύτους.

> Hidden away in a tomblike
> *thalamos* she was yoked
> although she also was of honorable family, child, child,
> and she received deposits of Zeus's golden-raining seed.
> (946–50)

Obviously, the enclosure fails; Zeus's golden-raining seed impregnates her even within her tower. But at the same time, the ode suggests that Danae was already married, as soon as she was placed in this interior space: her enclosure, like Antigone's, is a *thalamos*. Moreover, the verb that describes her enclosure, *katazeugnumi*, suggests the common "yoking" image of marriage.[80] She becomes vulnerable, it seems, through the attempt to make her impregnable. This is one of the paradoxes of historical marriage, as witnessed by various legal battles: it tries to insure a lack of access to the wife, but in so doing charges her with erotic potential. In Danae's case, that potential turns toward a paradigm of the good wife. Locked in her tower, she guards and nourishes Zeus's "golden seed," just as Athenian wives were to guard and nourish both children and household properties. Antigone, on the other hand, emphasizes the dangerous side of the contained woman: her containment is deadly, for herself and for Haemon, over whom she exercises erotic power.[81]

The next episode shifts the focus to a *male* figure who attempts to control female sexuality. Lycurgus is also "yoked," as a punishment for trying to stop a group of Maenads from worshiping Dionysus (955). Dionysus is always associated with *mania*, and specifically with uncontrolled female passion.[82] Various commentators have, therefore, seen a connection between

Lycurgus's attempts to curb the maenads and Creon's attempts to control Antigone.[83] Lycurgus, not unlike Danae's father, is trying to contain a threat of female sexuality. His action, however, results only in his being restrained himself. As such, he is a model not only for Creon but for the doctrine of exclusion that he represents.

Finally, we come to the episode of Cleopatra (who is never named), the most complex of the three vignettes. Cleopatra suffers through her children, who are probably blinded by their stepmother:[84]

Ἄρης δισσοῖσι Φινείδαις
εἶδεν ἀρατὸν ἕλκος
τυφλωθὲν ἐξ ἀγρίας δάμαρτος
ἀλαὸν ἀλαστόροισιν ὀμμάτων κύκλοις
ἀραχθέντων ὑφ᾽ αἱματηραῖς
χείρεσσι καὶ κερκίδων ἀκμαῖσιν

κατὰ δὲ τακόμενοι μέλεοι μελέαν πάθαν
κλαῖον, ματρὸς ἔχοντες ἀνυμφεύτου γονάν.

Ares
saw the accursed, blinding wound
struck against Phineidos's two sons
by the wild wife,
the vengeful orbs of their eyes,
having been pierced by the bloody
hands and with the points of loom-pins

and wasting away, miserable, they mourn their miserable
    sufferings,
having [their] birth from an unmarried mother. (970–80)

Diodorus (4.44.3) tells a version of this myth that includes Cleopatra's imprisonment, and many commentators have focused on this as the theme that links the story to the other two.[85] But the ode itself does not mention this, and it is fair to doubt that the chorus has it in mind. The familial relations in this episode are clear, however, and worth considering. First, the stepmother has apparently replaced Cleopatra in such a way that the children resent the replacement—hence the "vengeful eyes" of 974. We are reminded of Creon's doctrine of the replaceability of the female (569), and here see the complications of such a model. The woman who is a wife is also a mother, and that relation, unlike that of husband and wife, is not one of cultural contract and cannot be replaced by one of cultural contract. Second, the stepmother in the story is figured as the opposite of female virtue in that the shuttle, the instrument of weaving, becomes a weapon against children.[86] The model that presents a woman as a replacement in the home, it seems, also allows the woman a certain dangerous power. Her very lack of connection to the children makes her wifely virtues suspect.

Finally, the children's fate is sealed by their birth to an *anumpheutos* woman. Kamerbeek translates this word "ill-wedded," but the one other time Sophocles uses it (*Electra* 165) it means "unwedded."[87] I suggest that it has that meaning here, in the sense that Cleopatra is no longer married. Her marriage was apparently not fully successful as a *telos*. In addition, Cleopatra grew up on the wild side of culture: τηλεπόροις δ' ἐν ἄντροις / τράφη θυέλλησιν ἐν πατρῴαις ("In far-distant caves / she was nurtured, in her father's winds," 983–84). Through her association with the cave, and her status as *anumpheutos*, Cleopatra reminds us directly of Antigone.[88] Marriage has made both women marginal rather than central; each has been displaced rather than integrated into culture.

Most important, the ode does not tell us what Cleopatra undergoes once that displacement has occurred—we are not even sure, in fact, if she is alive or dead while her children are blinded.[89] Instead, we are abruptly invited to reflect on her birth and upbringing: ἁ δὲ σπέρμα μὲν ἀρχαιογόνων / <ἦν> ἄνασσ' Ἐρεχθεϊδᾶν ("But she was offspring of the ancient race / of Erechtheids, ruling over them," 981–82). Her position as ruling over her city, and especially as a descendent of Erechtheus, reminds us of another *epikleros* in tragedy, Creusa in Euripides' *Ion*.[90] Yet with Cleopatra, unlike with Creusa, we have no notion of what she experienced, how she felt, or what she did on finding herself outside of culture just when she seemed most secure within it. The chorus can only attempt to describe her position through a return to her origins. In a similar way, Antigone's marriage ceases to be a marriage, and becomes only a return to her origins:

> οἵων ἐγώ ποθ' ἁ ταλαίφρων ἔφυν·
> πρὸς οὓς ἀραῖος ἄγαμος ἅδ'
> ἐγὼ μέτοικος ἔρχομαι.

> To those from whom once I, suffering, was born
> unmarried, accursed,
> I go, a metic. (866–68)

This move, for Antigone as for Cleopatra, signifies a failure of the institution of marriage; more important, it ultimately fails to describe that failure. Once Antigone is dead, and once Cleopatra is replaced, we see them only as vague and indistinct, things that once were but are not now within our experience. We do see the material effect that such failure has: Haemon dies over Antigone, and Cleopatra's children look accusingly at her replacement and are blinded. The processes of regeneration have been disrupted.[91] Ultimately, then, this episode demonstrates the inability of marriage to contain woman's mobility; as (necessarily) marginal to culture, a woman always has the potential to be "outside" even when she has been locked "inside," to remain at the margins and, from there, to pull the center off-balance.

The *Antigone*, then, represents the dangers and paradoxes of female mediation. For Creon, the woman's place in reproducing culture is at best suspect, at worst to be suppressed altogether. He tries desperately and unsuccessfully to create a bond with his son that will be stronger than Haemon's bond with his betrothed, Antigone. For Antigone, the woman at the center of this cultural mediation, marriage is no less problematic. Her attempt to define her own family in matrilineal terms, giving herself a central position in relation to both her brother and her potential husband, involves her in inevitable paradox. She cannot remain dedicated to her birth family (as she must, in order to carry Oedipus's line as an *epiklēros*), since this, for her, means that she cannot marry. Her death becomes a marriage — to a point — but Antigone also experiences it as a failure of marriage. Her integration is nowhere complete. Even among her birth family, for whom she has sacrificed everything, she describes herself as a metic. Her death resolves nothing, her marriage fails as a *telos*, and finally the play makes her own attempt to position herself in the center of culture into a statement of absolute marginality. Moreover, though we witness her apprehension about her coming death/marriage, we still know nothing of her experience after she enters the *thalamos*. It may be argued that this is simply a by-product of Antigone's death; but this play, by making Antigone's marriage into a death, places that experience beyond our ken. No wonder Creon fears the female as mediator. The woman-as-subject in that role remains for us, as for him, outside of the realm of knowledge.

The *Antigone* is one of the few plays of Sophocles for which we have a relatively firm date. Though the evidence is anecdotal, most scholars place it at about 442. Seen in the light of the developments of the mid-fifth century, the ideological representations I have just described take on an aspect of social critique. Pericles had, just ten years earlier, seen legislation through the Athenian assembly that dramatically redefined citizenship, and ultimately limited access to citizen women. Women who were not citizens, who were legally "outsiders," became, as the speeches of the fourth century show, a potential threat to both family and state through their erotic wiles (which were all the more erotic because foreign). Here in Sophocles' play, we are invited to see that any woman — even the king's daughter, loyal to her natal family — could be defined as suspect, foreign, an intruder. At the same time, we are invited to see that once women were defined as such, any and all attempts to control that "foreign" influence must have been marked by the very instability and uncertainty that marked the women themselves.

Chapter 5   T H E *Ajax,* O R M A R R I A G E
BY DEFAULT

> *There is no binary division to be made between what one says
> and what one does not say; we must try to determine the differ-
> ent ways of not saying such things, how those who can and
> those who cannot speak of them are distributed, which type of
> discourse is authorized, or which form of discretion is required
> in either case. There is not one but many silences, and they are
> an integral part of the strategies that underlie and permeate
> discourses.*
>
> M I C H E L F O U C A U L T , *The History of Sexuality,* vol. 1
> (trans. R. Hurley)

QUESTIONS OF BIRTH

The Athenian state in the fifth century was obviously concerned with questions of birth.[1] In a basic legal sense, parentage defined
what it meant to be a citizen: a citizen was the child of two *astoi,* and hence
a descendent of the original autochthonous Athenians. Such children, and
only such children, were entitled to full inheritance rights and full participation in civic institutions. Of course, Greek tragedies are rarely set in Athens and do not often deal directly with questions of citizenship. On a con-
ceptual level, however, questions about citizenship could be played out in
dramas by raising questions of birthright, familial membership, and membership in the state (whether an oligarchy, quasi-democracy, or military
camp) represented in the play. Such plays not only represent the Athenian
ideology of citizenship (ensured by political endogamy), they also provide
justification for it, in that inclusion in the state was clearly modeled on the
definition of the family.[2] Sophocles' *Ajax* serves exactly this function. More
than any other Greek tragedy, the *Ajax* raises questions about birth, legitimacy, and the relation between parentage and social status. In the end,
however, the play confirms the existence of an aristocratic ideal maintained
(however democratically) by members of a noble bloodline.[3]

It may seem odd to suggest that Ajax (and his family), who comes from
Salamis, should be chosen to explore questions of Athenian citizenship. We
should remember, however, that Ajax was one of the eponymous heroes of
the ten tribes in post-Kleisthenic Athens.[4] Sophocles has gone to some length

to associate Ajax with Athens in this play, and what is more, he does so in terms that call to mind ideas about birth. When Ajax is about to die, he calls upon (among other things) κλειναί τ' Ἀθῆναι, καὶ τὸ σύντροφον γένος ("Famous Athens, and the race raised with me," 861). Perhaps even more striking, at Tecmessa's first entrance she addresses Ajax's sailors thus: ναὸς ἀρωγοὶ τῆς Αἴαντος, / γενεᾶς χθονίων ἀπ' Ἐρεχθειδᾶν ("Sailors of Ajax's ship, / from the race of Erechtheus-born-of-earth," 201–2). Not only are the sailors thus allied with the Athenians; the naming of Athens as the "race of Erechtheus" belongs to a specific conception of citizenship.[5] As Loraux has shown, the naming of Athenians "Erectheids" calls to mind their supposed autochthonous birth (explicitly referred to here), which serves to deny the interference of women in the production of Athenian citizens.[6] Here, the fact that Salamis only became part of Athens in the sixth century is apparently of little import. Having become Athenians, the Salaminians now partake fully in the tradition of Athens's beginnings.[7] The fact that Ajax's sailors are "Erectheids," therefore, provides a specifically Athenian context for questions concerning Ajax's marriage and offspring.

The exact status of Ajax's marriage will occupy the bulk of this chapter. It is important to note, however, that the play is shot through with questions of legitimacy. The scenes with Ajax's half-brother Teucer provide several key examples: After Ajax has killed himself, the Atreidae, put out by his ungentlemanly conduct, deny his right to burial. Teucer arrives on the scene and argues for that right, but finds Agamemnon and Menelaos unwilling to enter into a discussion. Most critics have found the petty bickering in this second half of the play problematic at best, and a variety of explanations have been forwarded to explain the tone.[8] Rather than discussing the situation of Ajax, and how his past behavior affects his current status, Agamemnon in particular resorts to an ad hominem attack, belittling Teucer because of his birth. It may well seem that Sophocles has introduced this debate for no other purpose than to show the Greek leader's base character.[9] But Agamemnon's low character and the terms in which he chooses to make his argument mark a central theme in the play. The attack on Teucer, like many other scenes in the drama, makes the supposedly fixed category of noble birth unstable, a site of struggle that various characters manipulate for their own ends.

In the first place, we should note that every major hero in the drama (except Ajax) has his birth called into question at some point. Early in the action, for example, the chorus (made up of Ajax's quasi-autochthonous sailors) call Odysseus the son of Sisyphos, a suggestion that his mother was not faithful to Laertes.[10] That this suggestion is at least in part politically motivated is confirmed at the end of the play. Once Odysseus has spoken in Ajax's defense, and assured his right to a burial, Teucer calls him ὦ γεραιοῦ σπέρμα Λαέρτου πατρός ("O seed of respected father Laertes," 1393). Odysseus's birth seems, paradoxically, to depend on his behavior rather than the other way around. Similarly, in response to the insults that Agamemnon hurls at him, Teucer attacks the Atreid family history, ending with a suggestion that Agamemnon's mother was an adulteress:

αὐτὸς δὲ μητρὸς ἐξέφυς Κρήσσης, ἐφ' ᾗ
λαβὼν ἐπακτὸν ἄνδρ' ὁ φιτύσας πατὴρ
ἐφῆκεν ἐλλοῖς ἰχθύσιν διαφθοράν.

You yourself were born from a Cretan mother;
your father, finding a foreign man with her,
sent her out as prey for the mute fishes. (1295–97)

Again at 1311, Teucer will suggest that both Menelaos and Agamemnon have slept with Helen. From the perspective of the heroes who side with Ajax, then, the heroes who side with the Atreids are marked by unsure birth and questionable sexual mores. In these insults, the category of birth itself is not brought into question; rather, the ill manners of the heroes result in the conclusion that they must not be wellborn.

Another set of insults, however, has a more radical function. In the debate over Ajax's body, when Menelaos is abusing Teucer, Teucer answers with a different rhetorical tack:

οὐκ ἄν ποτ', ἄνδρες, ἄνδρα θαυμάσαιμ' ἔτι,
ὃς μηδὲν ὢν γοναῖσιν εἶθ' ἁμαρτάνει,
ὅθ' οἱ δοκοῦντες εὐγενεῖς πεφυκέναι
τοιαῦθ' ἁμαρτάνουσιν ἐν λόγοις ἔπη.

No longer, men, would I wonder at a man
who, being of no importance with respect to birth, errs,
when those seeming to be wellborn
make such erroneous speeches. (1093–96)

He does not question the nobility of Menelaos's birth (except perhaps in the word *dokountes*, "seeming"), but rather questions the efficacy of birth as a guarantee of noble character, a theme that the play echoes repeatedly. Indeed, if we agree with most commentators, Teucer is absolutely correct: Sophocles presents the supposedly noble Atreidae as petty, abusive tyrants.[11] In the new democratic Athens, it seems, the role of birth in determining status must still be worked through.

Teucer is at the center of many of the play's controversies about birth and character. Teucer's birth, however, is not suspect. Nobody ever suggests that his mother was unfaithful, or even of low birth. Why, then, is he treated as an inferior throughout the play? The abuse that he receives on account of his birth stems from the peculiar marginal social position that Teucer occupies, a position, moreover, that Athens gave new legal definition in the fifth century. Teucer's problem is that he is a *nothos* (as he calls himself at 1013).[12] In archaic times, *nothoi* are simply the product of a man and a woman who is not his recognized wife. Often the woman occupied a lower social position, having been captured or won in battle, for example. The woman passed on her lower social standing to her son, so that *nothoi* occupied a marginal position; they were recognized in the paternal household, but in contrast to fully legitimate children (or *gnēsioi*) did not hold full familial rights. Solon is credited with legislation that formally restricted the right of *nothoi* to inherit, although some texts suggest that *nothoi* could do so if there were no *gnēsioi* offspring.[13]

Teucer's position as a *nothos* would have been particularly resonant, moreover, in the middle of fifth-century Athens, where such social categories had recently been redefined.[14] I refer, of course, to the change in marriage laws introduced by Pericles in 451/50.[15] Under these laws, a citizen of Athens could only be produced by two citizens. As Patterson has argued, children of a citizen man and noncitizen woman, regardless of social standing, would be classified as *nothoi* under this new legislation:

> What had been a purely social definition now took on legal form: Thus, using the language of family and inheritance, any union between an Athenian and non-Athenian could be at best *pallakia* and its offspring *nothoi*. . . . Pericles' law established a legitimacy requirement for the polis itself.[16]

Under this law, such *nothoi* could neither inherit their fathers' property nor claim citizenship. The production of *gnēsioi*, therefore, had become democratized, and the parents' citizen status became more important in determining a child's position than their wealth. This requirement marks a sharp break from archaic times, in which marriages seem to have taken place between upper-class members of different cities with some regularity, as represented in the genealogies of nearly all the Greek heroes, and of such notables as Pericles himself.[17] Whereas Teucer's mother, under different conditions, might have produced *gnēsioi* sons in archaic times, under the new Athenian law she could not.[18]

So, in this play, Ajax is Telamon's son by his legitimate wife; Teucer is his son by Hesione, given to Telamon as a spoil of war. Teucer clearly still maintains some status in Telamon's household: Ajax's dependence on him to take care of Tecmessa and Eurysakes makes that clear (688–89). But it is equally clear that Teucer's birth marks him as socially inferior, and that his character is suspect as a result. Teucer imagines his father, on seeing him return from Troy without Ajax, reviling him specifically in terms of his mother's status:

ποῖον οὐκ ἐρεῖ κακὸν
τὸν ἐκ δορός γεγῶτα πολεμίου νόθον,
τὸν δειλίᾳ προδόντα καὶ κακανδρίᾳ
σέ, φίλτατ' Αἴας, ἢ δόλοισιν, ὡς τὰ σὰ
κράτη θανόντος καὶ δόμους νέμοιμι σούς.

What nasty thing will he not say?
[Will he not call me] a *nothos*, begotten from a spear of war,
[saying] that I betrayed you, most beloved Ajax, by
    wretchedness or cowardice,
or by treachery, so that I could rule over your kingship
and your household once you died. (1012–16)

In this imagined and unjust scenario, Teucer's alleged poor character is perceived as a natural product of his mother's social circumstances. What is more, he is assumed to have murdered Ajax in order to better his own position, a position that was fixed as long as Telamon's *gnēsios* son, Ajax, remained alive.[19]

Similarly, Agamemnon makes a great deal of the social circumstances of Teucer's parentage. At no point does he question Teucer's noble blood as such; he merely attacks him because his mother was a spear-captive (τὸν ἐκ τῆς αἰχμαλωτίδος, 1228). He ends by suggesting that, far from being able to demand burial for Ajax, Teucer is not even fit to speak:

οὐ σωφρονήσεις; οὐ μαθὼν ὃς εἶ φύσιν
ἄλλον τιν' ἄξεις ἄνδρα δεῦρ' ἐλεύθερον,
ὅστις πρὸς ἡμᾶς ἀντὶ σοῦ λέξει τὰ σά;
σοῦ γὰρ λέγοντος οὐκέτ' ἂν μάθοιμ' ἐγώ·
τὴν βάρβαρον γὰρ γλῶσσαν οὐκ ἐπαΐω.

Will you not be moderate? Learning who you are by birth,
will you not bring another man here, a free man,
who will speak on your behalf to us in place of you?
I would not like to learn anything more from you,
since I do not understand your barbarian speech. (1259–63)

Agamemnon exaggerates, of course. Nothing about Teucer's speech has marked him as a barbarian, nor is there any suggestion elsewhere that he is not free.[20] Agamemnon is suggesting, however, that he has received these characteristics from his mother, just as he receives his status as *nothos* from her. In effect, Agamemnon is employing the fifth-century definition of *no-thos* in his insult: the suggestion that Teucer is foreign (βάρβαρον γλῶσσαν, 1263) would have had little bearing on his freedom under the archaic definition of *nothoi*. It is rather a product of Athens's new policy of citizens marrying citizens. Teucer is admirably suited, therefore, to bring up questions of birth and character. He occupies a position that is neither fully legitimate nor illegitimate; and he comes from noble stock, yet is abused as ill-born. Like so many Sophoclean characters, he stands in an ambiguous position, and his character serves to question the categories that define that position.

Sophocles, I argue, is playing on this new legal construction, by making Teucer a central character and forcing a *nothos* to enter into competitions with the wellborn heroes (who largely act less nobly). Sophocles emphasizes, moreover, that the category of *nothos* itself is a challenge to the notion of noble blood, as each *nothos* in the play occupies that position *despite* the noble birth of his mother. Teucer's mother's nobility (as defined by birth) is not under attack. On the contrary, we learn that she was a queen, and Teucer describes himself as ἄριστος ἐξ ἀριστέοιν δυοῖν ("born from two noble lines," 1304). Rather, her circumstances alone have placed her in a diminished social status. Patterson goes so far as to suggest that line 1304 plays on words to emphasize this new, purely legal definition of *nothos*:

> It seems to me just possible that when Teucer insists . . . that although *nothos* he is *aristos* born from two *aristoi* . . . the Athenian audience would have remembered Pericles' law: "no one shall have a share in the city who is not born from two *astoi*" (*Ath. Pol.* 26.4).[21]

Teucer insists on a nobility for himself that stems from an out-of-date system: he has noble blood. In the new climate of the mid-fifth century, such considerations give way to the purely economic and political standing of the parents in question. Hesione's position as a spear-captive — and hence as foreign — creates a diminished social standing for her son, so much so that Agamemnon does not even consider him fit to speak. As for Hesione herself, she is a type we have seen before in Sophocles, a woman with power but no authority. Her position determines her son's, but she is passive in this process, a spear-captive who has no control over her status. In this regard she will prove an analogue to Tecmessa.

In this play, then, Sophocles is concerned not just with marriage, but with specific forms of marriage, and the particular effect of new legal definitions of marriage and citizenship. We have seen in previous chapters that Sophocles tends to fix on a particular aspect of subjectivity (usually female) and to bring out its internal contradictions. As we shall see, he does the same with the notion of the *nothos* here. The *Ajax* demonstrates not only the complex and contradictory nature of that identity, but also its implications for women. For if women (as I have argued) are largely defined according to their relationships to men, this new category of semi-citizens must affect the women who give birth to them. Such is the case with Tecmessa: by giving birth to Eurysakes, she finds herself interpellated into a specific subject and citizen status.

TECMESSA'S POSITION, TECMESSA'S STATUS

Tecmessa is a woman in an unpleasant spot. Captured and enslaved by Ajax, her position in the Greek camp is entirely dependent on her relationship with him, and throughout the first half of the play, she does everything she can to present that relationship as both legitimate and important to Ajax. Most critics have implicitly accepted Tecmessa's self-presentation, and see her purely as a loving wife without ulterior motive. Many also believe her unquestioningly when she states that, in the past, she had Ajax's favor (808).[22] Very little in the play suggests that Ajax shares this picture of their relationship, however; if he loved her in the past (which I do not consider certain), he has few words for her now, and they are usually demanding and surly.[23] In fact, he specifically denies her the intimacy that she claims, privileging instead his relations with other men.

One of the most remarkable scenes in all of Greek tragedy, for example, occurs when Tecmessa tells the story of Ajax's madness to the chorus. The depiction of an interior scene at night, and conversation between a hero and his bedmate, is extremely rare. Tecmessa describes it thus:

> κεῖνος γὰρ ἄκρας νυκτός, ἡνίχ' ἕσπεροι
> λαμπτῆρες οὐκέτ' ᾖθον, ἄμφηκες λαβὼν
> ἐμαίετ' ἔγχος ἐξόδους ἕρπειν κενάς.
> κἀγὼ 'πιπλήσσω καὶ λέγω, "τί χρῆμα δρᾷς,
> Αἴας;"

> For he, in the depth of night, when the evening-time
> torches no longer burned, taking his two-edged spear
> he planned to make a pointless excursion.
> But I rebuked him and said, "What are you doing, Ajax?"
> (285–89)

Though we must bear in mind that this is Tecmessa's account, we can infer that Tecmessa was sleeping with or near Ajax (not necessarily to be assumed), and moreover that their relationship is of such closeness that she is unafraid to question his comings and goings. This is an intimacy indeed. Ajax's response, however, is both impersonal and harsh:

> ὁ δ' εἶπε πρός με βαί', ἀεὶ δ' ὑμνούμενα·
> "γύναι, γυναιξὶ κόσμον ἡ σιγὴ φέρει."
> κἀγὼ μαθοῦσ' ἔληξ', ὁ δ' ἐσσύθη μόνος.

> But he said to me that oft-spoken little saying,
> "Woman, silence brings decoration to a woman." [24]
> And I, having learned, left off while he went out alone.
>   (292–94)

Not only does Ajax refuse to answer Tecmessa's question, he does so by quoting what seems to be an aphorism (293).[25] He does not speak to her tenderly, or even personally.

Ajax, it seems, is not interested in what Tecmessa has to say, even in her version of events. This holds true in the scene that follows: once Ajax is on the stage, he repeatedly ignores Tecmessa, though he asks for his son (339), and then for Teucer (342). When Tecmessa asks him to hear her (368), he tells her to leave (369). Finally, Tecmessa insists on the closeness of their relationship: ὅταν κατεύχῃ ταῦθ', ὁμοῦ κἀμοὶ θανεῖν / εὔχου· τί γὰρ δεῖ ζῆν με σοῦ τεθνηκότος; ("When you pray for these things, pray for me to die as well; / for why should I live once you have died?" 392–93). Once again, however, Ajax ignores this suggestion, and in fact offers an alternative: ἔρεβος ὦ φαεννότατον, ὡς ἐμοί, / ἕλεσθ' ἕλεσθέ μ' οἰκήτορα, / ἕλεσθέ μ' ("Dark underworld, most light to me, / take, take me as a house-dweller, / take me," 395–97). Where Tecmessa sees herself bound to Ajax in death, Ajax sees himself sharing a house only with death itself. He takes no notice of Tecmessa's appeal in the lines that follow. When he does finally agree to speak with her (527–28), he first demands her obedience, and then uses the opportunity to ask for his son again. For Ajax, Tecmessa is a link to his son, a troublesome mediator in masculine relations; he does not see himself as bound to her.

This is a harsh picture, and critics have again been quick to blame Ajax for such treatment of his "wife." So, for example, Poe: "The pity that we feel still is very intense; but it is shifted in large part to Tecmessa. And toward Ajax we feel, besides pity, a certain anger which is aroused by his callousness toward her."[26] But such critics have missed a crucial point, a point that

Tecmessa is desperate to alter, namely that she is not his wife, and that the closeness of her bond to the hero is of her own manufacture.[27] Before Ajax's pivotal speech at 646ff., no one speaks of Tecmessa in terms that suggest legitimate, recognized marriage to Ajax. The one exception is (perhaps) line 292, when Ajax addresses her as *gunē*. But given the pejorative tone of the line, the word might just mean "woman" there; and in any case, we must remember that it is Tecmessa who relates that story. Instead, the chorus refers to her, on her first entrance, as a λέχος δουριάλωτον (211). Granted, the term *lechos* can be used to refer to a married wife, but more generally it simply means "bedmate," and here, combined with the epithet "spear-won," it implies less than full status in Ajax's household. We have already seen that such terminology implies low social status in the case of Teucer ("this *nothos* born from a spear of war," 1013; cf. Agamemnon's insult at 1228, τὸν ἐκ τῆς αἰχμαλωτίδος, "the son of a spear-prize"). We might even compare the δορίληπτος ("spear-snatched") cattle of lines 145–46. Though the chorus says that Ajax esteems Tecmessa (212) (and this may or may not be true), she is a spear-captive, not unlike Briseis in the *Iliad*.[28] She is the (perhaps very valuable) property of Ajax—little more. Most important of all, she speaks of herself as a *doulē* (489), a female slave, which means that her son will have the same status as Teucer. He will be a *nothos*.[29]

This is the social context, then, in which we must read Tecmessa's great speech (485–524). She tries to convince Ajax not to kill himself, arguing that if he does so he will destroy her and their son. The speech is charged with high feelings, and most modern interpreters have taken it as an emblem of Tecmessa's female character: emotional, lacking in reason, and bordering on incomprehensible.[30] Such readings, while often sympathetic to Tecmessa, do her a disservice. Tecmessa's entire speech is a practical, rhetorical attempt to change her status in Ajax's eyes. She declares her loyalty to Ajax, despite the fact that she is his slave (489–91), and supplicates him in terms suitable for a wife: καί σ᾽ ἀντιάζω πρός τ᾽ ἐφεστίου Διός / εὐνῆς τε τῆς σῆς, ᾗ συνηλλάχθης ἐμοί ("And I supplicate you by Zeus of the domestic hearth, / and by your (marriage) bed, in which you have had intercourse with me," 492–93). At the end of her speech, moreover, she tries to redefine the category of noble birth in order to secure her own position:

> ἀλλ᾽ ἴσχε κἀμοῦ μνῆστιν· . . .
> ὅτου δ᾽ ἀπορρεῖ μνῆστις εὖ πεπονθότος,
> οὐκ ἂν γένοιτ᾽ ἔθ᾽ οὗτος εὐγενὴς ἀνήρ.

> But remember me . . .
> whoever, being well treated, does not remember it,
> no longer would he be wellborn. (520–24)

She literally tries to make her relationship with Ajax the basis for his lineage, a "persuasive redefinition" of nobility.[31] Like Teucer, Tecmessa makes class into a potentially unstable category, one that she can use to create a valid social position for herself.

If Tecmessa is a figure like Briseis or Hesione, however, that is not the model that Sophocles has her choose for herself. An interesting poetic sleight-of-hand takes place in Tecmessa's speech to Ajax at 485–524. In addition to the surface arguments that Tecmessa makes, her speech is parallel in several places to *Iliad* 6.390–502, in which Andromache pleads with Hector not to abandon her, his wife, as he goes off to war.[32] Obviously, Tecmessa cannot be said to be aware of this. The audience certainly would be, however, and the extended allusion begins to take on a life of its own. The arguments that both Tecmessa and Ajax make are subtly supported by the positions that they unwittingly take through analogy to the epic, and we must consider the effect of this meta-argument as well as the one that each character consciously makes.

The three points in Tecmessa's speech that echo the *Iliad* (501–3, 510–13, 515–18) strengthen Tecmessa's social standing, implicitly casting Tecmessa and Ajax in the roles of Andromache and Hector, respectively. This becomes a powerful suggestion that Tecmessa's legitimate place is by Ajax's side. We must notice, however, that the allusions to the *Iliad* are a rhetorical device, and involve a bit of careful deception. While readers have often noted that Ajax does not act like Hector here, few have pointed out that Tecmessa is not, properly speaking, socially parallel to Andromache. In fact, in one of the key parallel passages, Tecmessa lets this difference slip. Tecmessa imagines the insults that she will receive from one of her future masters: "ἴδετε τὴν ὁμευνέτιν / Αἴαντος, ὃς μέγιστον ἴσχυσε στρατοῦ" ("'Look at the bedmate / of Ajax, he who had the greatest strength of the army,'" 501–2). When Hector predicts similar abuse of Andromache (6.460–65), he calls her his *gunē*, a proper word for wife; Tecmessa realizes that she is only the *homeunetis* ("bedmate") of Ajax, at least to outside observers.[33] Sophocles makes the comparison to Andromache, but also deftly undercuts it, hinting that Tecmessa's status is not so exalted as that of her epic predecessor.

Perhaps the most astounding of Tecmessa's argumentative flourishes comes in her final comparison to the *Iliad*. At *Iliad* 6.428, Andromache makes her famous appeal: Ἕκτορ, ἀτὰρ σύ μοί ἐσσι πατὴρ καὶ πότνια μήτηρ / ἠδὲ κασίγνητος, σὺ δέ μοι θαλερὸς παρακοίτης ("Hector, you are therefore father and honored mother to me, / and brother, you who are my young (blooming) bedmate," 6.428–29). She says this because, as she has just explained, Achilles killed her father, and Artemis her mother (after Achilles had captured and released her). Tecmessa is in a rather different position, since Ajax is her capturer, rather than her rescuer; and so when she echoes Andromache, the comparison is strained:

σὺ γάρ μοι πατρίδ᾽ ᾔστωσας δορί,
καὶ μητέρ᾽ ἄλλη μοῖρα τὸν φύσαντά τε
καθεῖλεν Ἅιδου θανασίμους οἰκήτορας.
τίς δῆτ᾽ ἐμοὶ γένοιτ᾽ ἂν ἀντὶ σοῦ πατρίς;

For you destroyed my fatherland with your spear,
and another fate snatched my mother and father
down to the deadly house of Hades.
What fatherland, then, could there be for me other than
    you? (515–18)

In this deft verbal transformation, Tecmessa has rendered her enemy and captor (Ajax) into her Hector-like protector from such enemies. In so doing, of course, she redefines her own relation to him. We have seen that brides often lament the loss of their fatherland, or contact with their parents, on marriage (see Chapter 1). In the Homeric model, that loss is turned to emphasize the closeness of the couple. The husband has fully replaced those things which the bride lost and acts as substitute for them. Here, Tecmessa similarly implies that she is fully integrated into Ajax's household, even though it was Ajax's destruction of her natal family that has made that integration necessary.

The difficulty of the transformation, however, leaves some seams showing: as has been noted, Tecmessa cannot quite bring herself to call Ajax father, mother, and brother—she stops short at "fatherland."[34] Perhaps more importantly, the syntax of 516–17 is odd.[35] What does it mean that Ajax destroyed Troy, but "another fate" killed her mother and father? Jebb suggests that the ambiguity allows Tecmessa to avoid reproaching Ajax for the death of her parents, and he has been tentatively followed by Stanford. In any case, I believe that the strained logic of the passage arises from the difficulty implicit in Tecmessa's redefinition of her relationship to Ajax. He has not wooed her from her parents, after all, but has taken her as a spoil of war. Tecmessa wishes to establish intimacy, but cannot call him "father and mother," or even "fatherland," in the same breath that she names him a murderer. So she glosses over that aspect of their relationship, twisting and turning her model to make Ajax into her "fatherland." Once again, Sophocles sets up the comparison, but simultaneously shows us how unlike Hector and Andromache these two are. Tecmessa is not just a wife begging for the life of her husband, but also a character in desperate straits, maneuvering— however justifiably—for status.

As has also been amply noted, Ajax does not play his part in the Homeric drama that his companion's speech sets up. Tecmessa, for example, rather than Ajax, worries about her being captured and enslaved.[36] Nor does Ajax express any pity for her at the end of her speech.[37] It has generally been taken that this scene, for these reasons, stands to the detriment of Ajax. He is revealed as a brutish lout, without proper care for his delicate and respectable wife. I do not mean to suggest that Tecmessa deserves what she gets, because she is only a spear-prize anyway. But I do wish to point out that this passage is a formal debate, in which she is far from a passive victim. In fact, the assumption that she *is* Ajax's full-fledged wife has allowed critics to overlook the strength of her character. She shows considerable political savvy in trying to make herself into Ajax's legally recognized companion, and Sophocles bolsters that attempt by having her unknowingly compare herself to the most famous and faithful of Trojan wives. That Ajax refuses to acknowledge her may be cruel, and certainly the Homeric allusion backs him into an uncomfortable comparison. But he is not a failed Hector, except through an analogy that does not quite fit. He is abandoning a spear-prize, not a wife, Tecmessa's forceful allusions notwithstanding.

In one respect, however, Ajax does conform to the Homeric model that Tecmessa evokes, namely in his relationship to his son. Although Ajax may have little respect for Tecmessa herself, he does clearly care for young Eurysakes. On one of the rare occasions when he speaks to Tecmessa, he orders that she bring him *his* boy: κόμιζέ νύν μοι παῖδα τὸν ἐμόν, ὡς ἴδω ("Bring me now my boy, so I can see him," 530.) When the boy arrives, Ajax echoes the same scene from the *Iliad* that Tecmessa had, praying for his son's future:

> ὦ παῖ, γένοιο πατρὸς εὐτυχέστερος,
> τὰ δ' ἄλλ' ὁμοῖος· καὶ γένοι' ἂν οὐ κακός. . . .
> ὅταν δ' ἴκῃ πρὸς τοῦτο, δεῖ σ' ὅπως πατρὸς
> δείξεις ἐν ἐχθροῖς οἷος ἐξ οἵου 'τράφης.
> τέως δὲ κούφοις πνεύμασιν βόσκου, νέαν
> ψυχὴν ἀτάλλων, μητρὶ τῇδε χαρμονήν.

> Son, may you be luckier than your father,
> but in all other things similar. And you will not be base. . . .
> But when you reach this [i.e. adulthood], it will be necessary
> to show your enemies what sort of a man you are, and from
>   what sort of father.
> Until then, feed on the light breezes,
> nourishing your young spirit and charming your mother
>   here. (550–59)

The prayer, especially lines 550–51, recalls Hector's for Astyanax at *Iliad* 6.476–81.[38] While some scholars have seen in line 559 evidence for Ajax's genuine concern for Tecmessa, I see little to suggest that he thinks of her, except in that she has produced Eurysakes.[39] It is Ajax's only mention of Tecmessa in the entire scene, and the emphasis throughout the speech is on the growth of his son into a man like his father. In short, Sophocles' echo of Homer here suggests that Ajax, like Hector, recognizes his *son* as part of a family; but in Ajax's version of the *Iliad*, the wife is all but elided from the model.

This elision of Tecmessa's position becomes even more clear as the scene progresses. Ajax entrusts his son to Teucer, and the language he uses is significant: τοῖον πυλωρὸν φύλακα Τεῦκρον ἀμφί σοι / λείψω τροφῆς ἄοκνον ("I leave a strong gate-guard for you, Teucer, / unstinting in nurturance," 562–63). *Trophē*, nurturance, can be provided by men or women, but it is curious that here Tecmessa will have no part in it. Though regularly used for the protection a father provides his family, the word is often also used for the literal feeding of a child at his mother's breast.[40] Until this moment, moreover, Tecmessa has clearly been the one responsible for Eurysakes' welfare. Later she will be sent offstage to look after him. It would not be impossible, then, for Ajax to mention her role in his upbringing; but that is apparently completely unimportant to Ajax. Instead, he gives the function of *trophē* over entirely to Teucer. Ajax goes on to tell the chorus to tell Teucer to take his son to Telamon and Eriboia, so that he can care for them in their old age (568–70).[41] Again, he makes no mention of Tecmessa. Eurysakes, it seems, is part of the paternal lineage of Telamon in Ajax's eyes; but Tecmessa has no claim on the family line. As a spear-prize, she is no more than an object of exchange in "the traffic in women." She mediates between men (creating a relationship between Ajax and his son) but takes no part — or at least no part worth mentioning — in that relation.

All of this changes once Ajax dies.[42] Ironically, Tecmessa's social status *improves* with Ajax's death. Granted, she is placed in a precarious position, and without the protection of Teucer, she might well fall victim to the fate that she predicts at 496–505: to be enslaved by the Greeks, without protection, without a fatherland. With Ajax dead, however, it becomes clear that Eurysakes will remain Ajax's only male child. As Ajax's instructions to Teucer and Eurysakes make clear, he intends for him to be his heir, and he even wills his trademark shield to the boy (574–76). Winnington-Ingram tentatively suggests that this recognition of Eurysakes "implies perhaps a kind of status for his mother."[43] Indeed, Tecmessa becomes, retroactively as it were, his legitimate wife.[44] Before the catastrophe, Ajax might well have married elsewhere. Had he done so, he would have rendered Eurysakes a *nothos*, which would have conferred a much lower status on Tecmessa.

The pivotal moment for Tecmessa actually comes just before Ajax's death; in Ajax's great final speech at 644–92, he paves the way for her new social position.[45] At 652 he calls her *gunē* (though the deictic, τῆσδε τῆς γυναικός, suggests the translation "woman" rather than "wife"), and says that he pities her "widowed" (*chēra*) among his enemies. A little later, he gives Tecmessa what turn out to be final instructions: σὺ δὲ / ἔσω θεοῖς ἐλθοῦσα διὰ τέλους, γύναι, / εὔχου τελεῖσθαι τοὐμὸν ὧν ἐρᾷ κέαρ ("But you, wife, / going inside, wife, pray to the gods continuously (*dia telous*) / to bring to completion that which my heart desires," 684–86). Regardless of how we read Ajax's intentions here, we must recognize that the speech marks a transitional point in the play. So, too, it marks the beginning of Tecmessa's transformation. Where before Ajax spoke to and about her harshly, here he expresses concern for her future and, simultaneously, addresses her as *gunē*, the standard word for a legitimate wife.[46] The chorus does not immediately pick up on this, waiting until Ajax has actually been found dead to recognize her new status.

Just at the moment that Tecmessa finds Ajax's body, however, the chorus (which still is not quite sure what Tecmessa has found) begins to modify its terminology: τὴν δουρίληπτον δύσμορον νύμφην ὁρῶ / Τέκμησσαν, οἴκτῳ τῷδε συγκεκραμένην ("I see the spear-won, ill-fated *bride*, / Tecmessa, wrapped up in this grief," 894–95). She is still spear-won, but now rather than being a bedmate, Tecmessa is for the first time a *numphē*, a word that always carries bridal connotations.[47] The participle συγκεκραμένην may also suggest a close family tie (cf. *Antigone* 1311). A few lines later, when the chorus has learned for certain that Ajax is dead, it laments briefly. It exclaims over its own loss of a homecoming, and ends, ὦ ταλαίφρων γυνή ("O wretched wife," 903). Again, *gunē* is the standard term for wife,[48] and it is surely significant that the chorus first uses it of Tecmessa here. She begins to be treated as the mother of a *gnēsios* son.

The chorus continues to use terms that imply legitimacy, again calling Tecmessa *gunē* at 940. But this line, seeming to support Tecmessa's new status, deserves a second look: οὐδέν σ' ἀπιστῶ καὶ δὶς οἰμῶξαι, γύναι, / τοιοῦδ' ἀποβλαφθεῖσαν ἀρτίως φίλου ("I don't disbelieve you at all, even as you cry out doubly, woman (wife) / you having been robbed of one so near just now," 940–41). On the one hand, the chorus validates Tecmessa's grief. But the double negative in 940 is curious: Does it have reason to disbelieve her? If not, why does the idea suggest itself to the chorus, and does it emphasize her (perhaps) overstated mourning ("even [*kai*] crying out doubly")?

I do not necessarily mean to deny the validity of Tecmessa's love for Ajax, nor the strength of her emotions at his death. But however affected she may be, she also remains level-headed enough to ensure her own position now that Ajax is gone. At this point Tecmessa is certainly acting the role of the dutiful wife. She rushes, once the body is found, to cover it with her cloak,[49] again using language that attaches her closely to the dead man:

οὐδεὶς ἂν ὅστις καὶ φίλος τλαίη βλέπειν
φυσῶντ' ἄνω πρὸς ῥῖνας ἔκ τε φοινίας
πληγῆς μελανθὲν αἷμ' ἀπ' οἰκείας σφαγῆς.

No one, even one who is *philos*, would endure to see
him spurting the dark blood down from his nostrils, and
from the bloody spring of his self-inflicted wound. (917–19)

Philoi should not see this sight, which Tecmessa already has. By implication, she is closer to Ajax even than his closest friends, perhaps even than Teucer. (Teucer will uncover him at 1003, with Tecmessa offstage.) Moreover, the word that I have translated as "self-inflicted" (*oikeias*) has as its basic meaning "domestic, private." Ajax's wound here is "private" in more than one sense: in that he inflicted it himself, but also in that only Tecmessa is close enough to him to see it. His death has literally become the marker of their mutual bond.

When Tecmessa cries out in grief, therefore, I suggest that the chorus hints — ever so carefully — that this may be an act (940, above). Tecmessa responds to this suggestion with a forceful declaration of the legitimacy of her emotions: σοὶ μὲν δοκεῖν ταῦτ' ἔστ', ἐμοὶ δ' ἄγαν φρονεῖν ("So these things may *appear* to you, but I *feel* them acutely," 942). She is asserting her right to lament. Again, her position is best understood in the context of fifth-century practice. As Alexiou and others have discussed, a series of laws originally attributed to Solon placed restrictions on the extravagance of funerals, and limited the right to mourn a dead person to those in the immediate family. Implicit in this last restriction, Alexiou argues, is that "the right to inherit was directly linked to the right to mourn."[50] Tecmessa's expression of emotional ties, therefore, along with the chorus's tentative support of that expression, establish her status at the crucial moment of Ajax's death.

The chorus is not alone in validating Tecmessa's new position. When Teucer arrives onstage, he asks after Eurysakes. Learning that the boy is alone by the tents, Teucer tells Tecmessa to fetch him. Teucer's instructions include a simile that confirms Tecmessa's place in the relationship between Ajax and his son:

οὐχ ὅσον τάχος
δῆτ' αὐτὸν ἄξεις δεῦρο, μή τις ὡς κενῆς
σκύμνον λεαίνης δυσμενῶν ἀναρπάσῃ;

Will you not bring him here, as quickly as possible,
lest some enemy snatch him away,
[him] like the young of a widowed lion? (985–87)

Not only does the simile imply that Tecmessa is recognized as the child's mother, but if we take *kenēs* as "robbed of her mate,"[51] then attention is drawn to her relationship with Ajax. Ajax's death has made her part of the family. Accordingly, when she returns with the child, Teucer announces the two as ἀνδρὸς τοῦδε παῖς τε καὶ γυνή ("the child and wife of this man," 1169). And although Teucer pays little attention to her, and speaks directly only to Eurysakes (1171–85), Tecmessa offers a lock of hair to the corpse along with Teucer and the child. Similarly, when Teucer is making his stand against Agamemnon, he declares that the three of them stand together (1309). Tecmessa is no longer *merely* an object of exchange between men (though she is always that to some extent); she now functions as an individual with familial ties and rights.

TECMESSA'S SILENCE

Oddly enough, however, Tecmessa's inclusion in Ajax's household does not result in her exercising new rights and authority. We have seen before that women, once married, tend to lose the very subjectivity that their new position seems to confer on them. In Tecmessa's case, this loss of subjectivity takes on an extreme form: from her return with Eurysakes at 1168 until the end of the play, she does not speak a single line. In fact, she is played by a mute actor, and the usual explanation for this extraordinary dramatic maneuver relies on stage convention. Odysseus must resolve the dispute between Agamemnon and Teucer; all three must be onstage, and in speaking roles, at the same time.[52] But this explanation ignores an important feature of Tecmessa's long silence, namely that from her entrance at 1168 until Odysseus's at 1315, the original audience cannot have known that Tecmessa was a silent character.[53] Major characters who leave the stage to return as mute are quite rare, and Tecmessa's silence is unique in several respects.[54] The closest parallel is Alcestis at the end of Euripides' *Alcestis*, though there the other characters onstage give an explicit explanation for her silence.[55] In the *Ajax* no such explanation is proffered; rather, Sophocles creates a dazzling series of entrances and exits that only emphasizes Tecmessa's quiet presence.

Consider the stage actions that make Tecmessa's silence possible and, eventually, necessary. Although earlier in the play Tecmessa had been onstage with her son and Ajax (544), she apparently left the child by the tents while searching for her husband. Thus, when Teucer enters, it seems that he sends Tecmessa to fetch the boy (986).[56] At 1042 Menelaos begins his entrance, and Teucer and Menelaos have their bitter argument. Menelaos leaves at 1160. Almost immediately (1168), Tecmessa and Eurysakes return. Bear in mind that we have no reason to suspect that Tecmessa is a mute character at this point — only she, the boy (too young for a speaking part), and Teucer are onstage with the chorus. Moreover, Teucer announces her entrance just as if she were a speaking character: καὶ μὴν ἐς αὐτὸν καιρὸν οἶδε πλησίοι / πάρεισιν ἀνδρὸς τοῦδε παῖς τε καὶ γυνή ("Look, just at the right time these two are near, / the son and wife of this man," 1168–69). After a brief dedicatory offering, Teucer leaves to set up a tomb (1184). In less than 200 lines, we have seen three exits and two entrances. This is an unusually swift pace for tragedy.

As Teucer leaves, the chorus begins a short song. When it is finished, the audience must expect that Tecmessa will begin to lament her dead husband. She is the only speaking character (so far as we know) left on the stage, and it would certainly be in character and within the bounds of the genre for her to do so. In fact, lament of the dead is a traditional role for women, in real life, in tragedy, and in its epic precursors.[57] Tecmessa has even hinted at such a lament, shortly after finding Ajax's body: ὦ δύσμορ' Αἴας, οἷος ὢν οἴως ἔχεις, / ὡς καὶ παρ' ἐχθροῖς ἄξιος θρήνων τυχεῖν ("Wretched Ajax, that things are such for one such as you, / so that even by your enemies you deserve to be mourned," 923–24). Moreover, the chorus's song seems very like an introduction to just such a lament: after a general introduction to the Trojan War, the chrous members blame the inventor of war for keeping them away from love:

> ἐκεῖνος οὐ στεφάνων οὔ-
> τε βαθειᾶν κυλίκων νεῖ-
> μεν ἐμοὶ τέρψιν ὁμιλεῖν,
> οὔτε γλυκὺν αὐλῶν ὄτοβον δυσ-
> μόρῳ, οὔτ' ἐννυχίαν τέρψιν ἰαύειν·
> ἐρώτων δ' ἐρώτων ἀπέπαυσεν, ὤμοι.

He did not allow me to take part
in the pleasure of the garland

> or of the deep drinking-cup,
> nor allow ill-fated [me] to enjoy the sweet clamor of the
>   flute,
> nor to enjoy the night's pleasures.
> From love, from love he has hindered me. (1199–1205)

Clearly the strophe calls to mind the tragic situation of Tecmessa, deprived of her husband. And in the antistrophe, the chorus specifically laments the loss of Ajax. What would be more natural than for Tecmessa to join in at 1223 with a lament of her own? We have, therefore, every reason to expect some sort of formal lament of Ajax by Tecmessa, and it is little short of astounding that it never happens.

Before Tecmessa can speak, however, Teucer returns (1223). Again, this must have been shocking to the audience. We just saw him leave the stage forty lines earlier. Teucer is at some pains to explain his hasty return:[58] καὶ μὴν ἰδὼν ἔσπευσα τὸν στρατηλάτην / Ἀγαμέμνον' ἡμῖν δεῦρο τόνδ' ὁρμώμενον ("Hello (καὶ μὴν)! Seeing the commander Agamemnon, / as he set out for here, I hurried [back]," 1223–25). Teucer and Agamemnon proceed to dominate the scene with an abusive interchange, in which they dispute Teucer's right to speak for Ajax. Note, however, that it would still be possible for Tecmessa to speak. That possibility is not foreclosed until the entrance of Odysseus at 1315. In short, Tecmessa's silence is unexplained, not remarked on, and thoroughly odd. It does not seem to be the result of dramatic convention so much as it seems that dramatic convention has been marshaled in order to keep her silent.

Such manipulation of dramatic expectations has a point. Tecmessa's surprising silence here mirrors a deeply felt Athenian ambivalence toward women's traditional roles in funerary ritual.[59] Traditionally, women were expected to lead the funeral procession and to lament the dead. But in the sixth and fifth centuries, a series of laws was passed that limited participation in and ostentatious display during funerals. Alexiou points out that many of these limitations seem directed at women and are particularly concerned to curtail the women's lamentation, "which might amount to a social menace, not only indecent but dangerous."[60] Tecmessa's silence exactly parallels, therefore, this ambivalence. On the one hand, we expect her to lament Ajax, to show her closeness to him. On the other hand, by remaining silent, she adheres to the letter of fifth-century law, and makes possible a funeral procession that provides no threat of disruption (unlike, e.g., that of Antigone).[61] She stands exactly at the crux where behavior and birth are to be linked, and she proves her legitimacy by behaving as a woman should.

In this final scene, no character onstage addresses Tecmessa (though

Teucer mentions her several times). As she has gained legitimacy, therefore, she has lost her position as an actor, as a speaking character who takes part in the plot. In place of the Tecmessa who was so bold as to rebuke Ajax (288), we have been given an entirely passive woman whose only importance on-stage is in her presence. We should not underestimate the importance of that presence, of course. Throughout Teucer's arguments with Menelaos and Agamemnon, Tecmessa and Eurysakes combine with Ajax's corpse to form a somber and impressive tableau.[62] They are (now) the concerned parties in the case, the legitimate wife and son of the hero who stand to lose or gain from the treatment of Ajax's body. In a play that has thrown familial categories and ties into considerable confusion, they visually reinforce the idea of the legitimate family as a stable social unit.[63]

As roles of gender are carefully reestablished, moreover, so are those of class. Earlier in the play, Ajax had lamented the fact that the relationships between men were apparently no longer stable:[64]

> ἐπίσταμαι γὰρ ἀρτίως ὅτι
> ὅ τ' ἐχθρὸς ἡμῖν ἐς τοσόνδ' ἐχθαρτέος
> ὡς καὶ φιλήσων αὖθις, ἔς τε τὸν φίλον
> τοσαῦθ' ὑπουργῶν ὠφελεῖν βουλήσομαι,
> ὡς αἰὲν οὐ μενοῦντα.

> For I have just learned that
> my enemy should be hated by me to such an extent
> as one whom I will love later, and that I will want to help a
>   friend
> to such an extent as I would one who will not always remain
>   a friend. (678–82)

And indeed, the actions of Atreidae seem to confirm his verdict. Surprisingly, however, at the end of the play, Odysseus steps forward and comes to the rescue of the dead Ajax. His action confirms Ajax's sense that the old order of things has passed, that the definitions of "friend" and "enemy" have become fluid in this new world. But at the same time, Odysseus's actions restore order both to the scene in the play and to the myth: of course Ajax must be buried if he is to become an Athenian eponymous hero. Here we see the careful working-out of a new democratic aristocracy. Odysseus arrives on-stage and intervenes between Teucer and Agamemnon, who were, moments before, unable to communicate because of their difference in class. Agamemnon, who is certainly under no obligation to do so, gives in to Odysseus's arguments; and most surprising of all, Odysseus offers to help Teucer with the burial. Noble and *nothos* are placed on the same level, and Teucer responds to Odysseus's offer with a gracious refusal, in deference to Ajax's supposed wishes.[65]

Shot through this equalizing camaraderie, however, are reinforcements of class status. Critics have given Odysseus a variety of motives for coming to Teucer's aid, some of which are supported by the text: he recognizes their common mortality,[66] or acts out of "enlightened self-interest"[67] or out of "tolerance and due respect for one's fellows."[68] These are all to some extent correct, but Odysseus cites a more pointed reason for his actions: ὅδ' ἐχθρὸς ἀνήρ, ἀλλὰ γενναῖός ποτ' ἦν ("This man was an enemy, but he was well-born," 1355). For Odysseus, the unity of social class overrules personal enmity, and so in one fell swoop he reestablishes the superiority of birth over circumstances. The other characters respond in kind: Teucer recognizes Odysseus's birth as son of Laertes (1393) and refers to Odysseus as *esthlos*, "noble," for his offer of help (1399). We may be in a new democratic mode, but it is a democracy of nobles. Thus, I would argue, the play carefully negotiates the clash between democratic and aristocratic ideology, glossing over the embarrassing fact that Ajax's son would, in Athenian law, be a *nothos*. Through Odysseus's generous offer, the society of wellborn men is once again secure.[69]

As we see so often in tragedy, however, the establishment of that stable society results in the silencing of the woman who has culturally and biologically made it possible.[70] Indeed, Tecmessa is once again elided, this time by the playwright, and far more thoroughly than she was by Ajax earlier in the play. Though we expect her to mourn for her husband, instead the issue of Ajax's burial becomes a dispute decided entirely between and by men. The question of whether or not to bury Ajax is resolved by Odysseus, Teucer, and Agamemnon; the burial itself is carried out under the direction of Teucer; and as the procession begins, Teucer calls on Eurysakes to help carry the body (1409–11), again reinforcing the paternal line that runs from Ajax to his son. Tecmessa does not speak, and is not addressed or referred to, despite the fact that the exodus is staged as a funeral procession, in which Athenian women regularly took part.[71] Before his death, Ajax told Tecmessa that silence was decoration for a woman (293). Now it seems that the silent Tecmessa has herself become a pure ornament, an entirely passive figure whose presence adds to the pathos of the scene played out onstage. She reflects glory back to the masculine subject: as the heroes decide Ajax's fate, his wife waits, well behaved and silent, mourning him.

Chapter 6   NATURE AND ITS DISCONTENTS IN THE *Oedipus tyrannus*

> *"It's disquieting to reflect that one's dreams never symbolize one's real wishes, but always something Much Worse." She turned the light on and sat up. "If I really wanted to be passionately embraced by Peter, I should dream of something like dentists or gardening. I wonder what are the unthinkable depths of awfulness that can only be expressed by the polite symbol of Peter's embraces. Damn Peter!"*
>
> DOROTHY SAYERS, *Gaudy Night*

Few plays have had such a profound influence on the Western literary tradition as the *Oedipus tyrannus*. Whatever we may think of Freud's theories of child development, few would deny that this play, with its central, hidden facts of incest and parricide, has shaped the way that we moderns define the individual.[1] As a result of that long critical history, it is extraordinarily difficult to interpret the play without the specter of Freud's "Oedipus complex" looming over every scene. At the heart of this difficulty is the fact that Freud offers his reading as representing a transcendental, transhistorical truth: Oedipus is posited as Everyman, his forbidden lusts and angers representative of our own developmental stages. As such, some version of Freud's family drama underlies virtually every critical reading of this play, even those that take issue with it.[2]

Feminist critiques of psychoanalysis, however, have pointed out that Freud's (and Lacan's) subject is male, that even when he is discussing "female" sexuality, it turns out to be a reflection of masculine desires.[3] At the same time, duBois has shown that the Freudian model of sexuality (and especially female sexuality) is not supported by numerous ancient texts.[4] My concern throughout this study, similarly, has been to locate questions of marriage in a specific cultural context. Rather than viewing Oedipus's story as a map to the human psyche, I want to see how his birth from one marriage (that of Laius and Jocasta) and participation in another (that of himself and Jocasta) fit into both mythical paradigms and contemporary views of marriage. It is from these two marriages, I argue, that we come to know Oedipus's identity, that he is "hailed" as a subject. In saying this, however, I am referring not to the inner workings of his psyche, but to his place and function in society, and to his recognition of that place and function.

This chapter, then, is something of a departure. The previous four chapters have been an account of various characters' representations of marriage. We have been concerned less with the function of married life within Athenian society than with the ways in which that society defines and characterizes marriage, and the ways in which those definitions come to play in Sophocles' dramas. In short, we have examined marriage as a socially structured phenomenon, and seen how a subtle understanding of Athenian matrimonial customs informs our reading of Sophocles' tragedies.

In this chapter I intend to look at the other side of the coin. The center of the *Oedipus tyrannus*, the point upon which all else turns, is Oedipus's incestuous relation with his mother. In this drama, however, the *experience* of marriage is never a question. Indeed, no character ever speaks about what marriage has been like for him or her. Instead, the play assumes a basic structure of marriage, and depends on the fact that Oedipus, in marrying his mother, has violated that structure.[5] Rather than search for traces of Athenian ideology of marriage in this play, therefore, I examine the way that this play constitutes marriage as a structuring institution, and particularly as a producer of biological identity. That is, I analyze the process by which Oedipus becomes recognized as "really" the child of Laius and Jocasta. This recognition is crucial to the play, and, despite its necessity, it takes a surprisingly indirect route. The play suggests that, contrary to general expectations about parentage, biological identity is an unstable category, confirmed by processes of displacement.[6]

I use the term "displacement" in a specialized sense, though derived from its use in psychoanalytic theory. In classic psychoanalysis, a traumatic event is "displaced" onto a parallel, though less traumatic, event. So, for example, a man might demonstrate little grief over the death of a close relative, only to break down in uncontrolled hysteria a few weeks later over the loss of a family pet. In such a case, the grief the man feels over the loss of the pet is real and authentic. But it is simultaneously a marker of another, hidden grief that was not expressed earlier.

Similarly, every work of literature contains rifts in logic, gaps that are not filled in. We shall be looking at a specific type of such an occurrence in this text, one that involves careful misdirection. Such an event stands both as an important event in itself, and as a marker, pointing us to some other "displaced" meaning. The answer to one question, for example, is posited and accepted in place of the answer to the question that was asked. On a more physical level, Oedipus has been displaced from his birth family—cast out to die on Mt. Cithaeron—and this act serves, ironically, both as a marker of his "outcast" status and as confirmation of his identity as the son of Laius and Jocasta. Such processes of misdirection fix Oedipus's place on his family tree and in society throughout this play. I do not mean by this that Sophocles intends us to see Oedipus's identity as Laius and Jocasta's child as invalid, culturally produced, and therefore a sham. Oedipus really is who the play says he is. In this play, however, Oedipus's biological identity asserts itself as natural only insofar as it forcibly displaces other forms of identity. It becomes "natural" through a socially accepted process of recollection and subsequent suppression of other, competing possibilities, and through masking the instability inherent in this process.[7]

In important ways, then, this is an abstract reading of the *Oedipus tyrannus*. I am not so concerned with the action of the play itself as with the way that the play interacts with basic social categories. In such an enterprise, we risk failing to encounter the drama as a moment of dramatic production. We gain, however, a vision of the drama as ideology and in concert with ideology. Such a reading shows us how an apparently natural category of human social behavior—such as biological identity—directs our perception even as it is directed by it. The *Oedipus tyrannus* presents marriage as a mediating institution, one that both creates categories of biological identity and allows for the possibility of violating the rules implicit in those identities. As such, marriage both enables and mirrors those processes of displacement that confirm Oedipus's identity. I offer the following, then, in an attempt to break out of the free-floating psychoanalytic questions about individual development that Freud postulates. I approach the drama here as representing a social mechanism, demonstrating the way that we produce both individual identities and interpretive meanings. This chapter, therefore, attempts both to interpret the play (from my own politically and socially invested standpoint), and to imply a critique of Freud's ahistorical reading.

PROBLEMS OF INTERPRETATION

Goodhart begins his challenging article on the *Oedipus tyrannus*, "We are accustomed to believing that we understand Sophocles' treatment of the Oedipus myth."[8] He goes on to show that we do not understand Sophocles' treatment, or rather that our understanding is produced by long familiarity with an accepted interpretation. In fact, the play largely defies analysis because it is self-interpreting. That is, as Vernant points out, "The play is itself constructed as a riddle,"[9] and riddles, especially the sorts of riddle that Oedipus answers, deny a multiplicity of answers. The answer to the sphinx's riddle, for example, reduces an apparent plurality of beings to one: What walks on four legs, and two, and three? Answer: Man, who crawls as a baby, walks as a man, and walks with a cane as an old man.[10] Once we know the answer, it seems obvious; and any apparent disparity of meaning is dispelled.[11]

Similarly, the play sets up its crisis — the need to find the killer of Laius — as two questions rather than one. We spend the play learning not only "Who killed Laius?" but also "Who *is* Oedipus?" And when it finally comes out (as we knew all along that it would) that the answer to both questions is "Oedipus, son of Laius and Jocasta," interpretation stops. The solutions to the play's problems have all come to the surface: It was Oedipus who killed his father and married his mother. He is the cause of the plague, and now that he has revealed himself, civilized structure can be restored. When we accept the play's own interpretation of events in this manner, however, we also accept a certain logic of displacement. The "obvious" answer to the play's questions, like the answer to the riddle above, does not seem to exist in the categories set up by the questions. When asked the sphinx's riddle, presumably, the unsuspecting victim tries to find an animal that walks on two, three, and four legs simultaneously. When the answer is revealed, it fits into the question's categories by introducing an answer that we did not think eligible and, in effect, displaces those categories.

In much the same way, when Oedipus begins his search for the killer of Laius, he does not consider himself a candidate; still less does he imagine that in the process he will discover himself to be Laius's son. Most striking of all, however, the play allows the answer to one question to stand in for the answer to the other. Goodhart's analysis centers on this problem: Is the crucial question "Who killed Laius?" or "Who is Oedipus?" Before the herdsman enters the scene, Oedipus focuses on the first, hoping that he is not the culprit. He pointedly sets up a logical criterion for answering the question:

> ληστὰς ἔφασκες αὐτὸν ἄνδρας ἐννέπειν
> ὥς νιν κατακτείνειαν. εἰ μὲν οὖν ἔτι
> λέξει τὸν αὐτὸν ἀριθμόν, οὐκ ἐγὼ 'κτανον·
> οὐ γὰρ γένοιτ' ἂν εἷς γε τοῖς πολλοῖς ἴσος.

> You said that he said that *highwaymen*
> killed him [Laius]. If therefore he still
> will say the same number, I did not kill him;
> for it would not happen that one is equal to many. (842–45)

Later, he completely ignores this criterion and, moreover, offers no explanation for doing so: "In the interim between his summoning and his arrival, the Corinthian messenger has appeared and shifted the action to the question of Oedipus's origin. . . . And it is to this issue exclusively that the Herdsman's remarks are addressed." [12] With the benefit of hindsight, it is easy to say that the answer to one question is the answer to the other. Oedipus is both the killer and the dead man's son. But it is far from clear how the second question manages, in the course of the drama, to supplant the first.

Both questions center on Oedipus's identity and provide alternative paradigms for establishing that identity. If asked who Oedipus was, we might say, "The son of Laius and Jocasta," or, equally likely, we might say, "That guy who killed his father and married his mother." The first definition depends on a widespread cultural assumption of biological relationship, the second on identity as a matter of deeds. This play problematizes the question of identity — often a crucial question in Athenian legal cases — by making these two paradigms interchangeable. Oedipus does not simply become distracted by the question of his parentage. Rather, he ignores the single criterion to which, up to this point, he has given considerable weight of credibility. He never once asks the herdsman if one or more than one person killed Laius. He apparently accepts the answer to the question "Who am I?" as sufficient answer to the question that has consumed him, "Who killed Laius?" He actively allows his biological identity to displace the question of what he has done. Like the answer to a riddle, the discovery of Oedipus's identity changes the categories that the original question suggested.

Modern critics, moreover, have imitated Oedipus. The following series of statements either overlook or validate his leap in logic: "The great news of the death of Polybus is brought by the Corinthian messenger, and he is able to renew the search, this time not for the murderer of Laius but for the secret of his own birth." [13] "The play therefore moves from the question of who killed Laius to that of who generated Oedipus." [14] "Behind the question that he thinks he is answering (who killed Laius?) can be detected the outlines of another problem (who is Oedipus?)." [15] "Oedipus's fate is such a unity that at the moment of understanding one truth subsumes the other." [16] And finally, "By this time the emphasis of the inquiry has shifted from the identity of Laius's murderer(s) to that of Oedipus's identity, and as Oedipus realizes that he is the son of Laius, he does not need any confirmation of the strong presumption he has already obtained that he is also the killer of Laius." [17] In short, the self-interpretive mode of this play wields a great force over its readers and watchers. Like Oedipus, most critics have accepted that his biological identity is sufficient answer to whatever question the play poses.

We should not presume that virtually all modern critics have simply made a mistake in accepting Oedipus's slip from one question to the next, or, still worse, that Sophocles erred in leaving Oedipus's first question unanswered. On the contrary, the play sets us up to see the two categories of judging Oedipus — by his birth and by his deeds — as interchangeable. We know from the *Odyssey* (11.271ff.) that in an earlier version, Oedipus continued to rule in Thebes even after he discovered who he was and what he had done.[18] There, apparently, his parricide and incest do not make him unfit to rule. But in Sophocles' version, once Oedipus realizes that his marriage has been incestuous, he blinds himself, and tries vigorously to have his earlier curse enacted on himself: ῥιψόν με γῆς ἐκ τῆσδ' ὅσον τάχιστ', ὅπου / θνητῶν φανοῦμαι μηδενὸς προσήγορος ("Throw me out of this earth, as quickly as possible, [so that] wherever / I show my face, [I will be] addressed by no one of mortals," 1436–37).[19] Once he recognizes himself as the son of Laius, he tries to act out the punishments that he decreed for the killer of Laius. Sophocles, then, makes Oedipus confirm his self-recognition as *the* answer to both questions that the play poses. Oedipus's marriage to Jocasta creates a social identity for Oedipus, therefore, that goes far beyond the simple implications of incest. He proclaims, in essence, that as the son of Laius, he is by definition both parricide and regicide.

How, then, does Oedipus's apparently natural and unquestioned self-identification come about? Here it is helpful to recall Althusser's theory of ideology as a producer of subjects. Althusser suggests that ideology creates subjects by an act of *"interpellation* or hailing" the individual. He explains the concept by the analogy of a policeman (or other person) calling out on the street, "Hey, you there!"

> Assuming that the theoretical scene I have imagined takes place in the street, the hailed individual will turn round. By this mere one-hundred-and-eighty-degree physical conversion, he becomes a subject. Why? Because he has recognized that the hail was "really" addressed to him, and that "it was really him who was hailed" (and not someone else). Experience shows that the practical telecommunication of hailing is such that they hardly ever miss their man.[20]

We must note, especially in reference to Oedipus, that this act of "hailing" takes place even before an individual is born. That is, society has certain expectations concerning the identity of a child from the moment of conception (and perhaps even before):

> It is certain in advance that it will bear its Father's Name, and will therefore have an identity and be irreplaceable. Before

its birth the child is always-already a subject, appointed as a subject *in and by the specific familial ideological configuration* in which it is "expected" once it has been conceived.[21]

It would be difficult to imagine a more nearly perfect example of such subjectivity than Oedipus. Long before he was conceived, he was hailed by an oracle as the man he turns out to be:

> χρησμὸς γὰρ ἦλθε Λαΐῳ ποτ᾽ . . .
> ὡς αὐτὸν ἥξοι μοῖρα πρὸς παιδὸς θανεῖν,
> ὅστις γένοιτ᾽ ἐμοῦ τε κἀκείνου πάρα.

> For an oracle came to Laius then . . .
> that it was fated for him to be killed by his child,
> who would be born from me and from him. (711–14)

This form of the oracle is specific to Sophocles' version. In Aeschylus's version of the myth, Laius is warned that he must not have children, if he wishes to save the city.[22] The oracle is proscriptive rather than descriptive. Sophocles, then, has made the oracle unavoidable, creating the appearance that Oedipus-the-subject exists (and must exist) before Oedipus-the-individual does. His "specific familial ideological configuration" takes on the form of inevitability.[23]

In referring to the inevitability of Oedipus's identity, I do not mean to deny his "free will." As Althusser explains, ideology creates a subject who "shall make the gestures and actions of his subjection 'all by himself.'"[24] Oedipus has always-already been Oedipus; what the play shows us is his active discovery of this obvious fact. At the same time, Oedipus's discovery presents itself as inevitable, as *the* answer, most significantly through the social process of naming. Many scholars have pointed out important puns on Oedipus's name.[25] The most crucial, for my purposes, takes place in the exchange between Oedipus and the messenger:

Οι.	τί δ᾽ ἄλγος ἴσχοντ᾽ ἐν χεροῖν με λαμβάνεις;
Αγ.	ποδῶν ἂν ἄρθρα μαρτυρήσειεν τὰ σά.
Οι.	οἴμοι, τί τοῦτ᾽ ἀρχαῖον ἐννέπεις κακόν;
Αγ.	λύω σ᾽ ἔχοντα διατόρους ποδοῖν ἀκμάς.
Οι.	δεινόν γ᾽ ὄνειδος σπαργάνων ἀνειλόμην.
Αγ.	ὥστ᾽ ὠνομάσθης ἐκ τύχης ταύτης ὃς εἶ.

Oe.:	What pain did I have when you took me in your hands?
Me.:	The joints of your foot would show you.
Oe.:	Alas, why do you speak of that old pain?
Me.:	I freed you as you had the tops of your feet pierced through.

Oe.:   I picked up that terrible disgrace from my swaddling-clothes.

Me.:   Thus, who you are, you were named from this chance.

                     (1031–36)

This exchange provides the unavoidable proof that Oedipus *is* the son of Laius, since the messenger, identifying Oedipus by his "swollen feet," can confidently say that this is the baby he saved. At the same time, these swollen feet are directly responsible for *who Oedipus is*, that is, his name is a pun on οἰδέω ("swell") + πούς ("foot"). He does not just discover who he is, then; he discovers who he *always already* has been.[26] And like the solution to a riddle, this identity comes as a flash of insight, unarguable, single, and apparently natural. Such a process is a function of ideology, especially the ideology of naming:

> It is indeed a peculiarity of ideology that it imposes (without appearing to do so, since these are "obviousnesses") obviousnesses as obviousnesses, which we cannot *fail to recognize* and before which we have the inevitable and natural reaction of crying out (aloud or in the "still small voice of conscience"): "That's obvious! That's right! That's true!"[27]

In other words, Oedipus accepts his biological identity as a sufficient answer to the question "Who killed Laius?" because the oracle has functioned as a form of ideology. It has created Oedipus as a subject, and given him the (apparently inevitable) identity of "the man who killed his father and married his mother": "Oedipus discovers he is guilty of parricide and incest . . . less by uncovering certain hitherto obscure empirical facts than by voluntarily appropriating an oracular logic which assumes he has always already been guilty."[28] We have duplicated the production of this identity, however, by ignoring the difficulty that Goodhart carefully points out. To allow Oedipus's biological identity — and subsequent incest — to displace the other questions that the play raises is to accept that "oracular logic" ourselves. If we wish to see beyond the play's self-proclaimed solution, we must step outside of the specific ideology that creates Oedipus's slip in logic. Rather than accept his biological identity as a sort of universal signifier, we must analyze the social structures around marriage that allow that definition of identity to displace all others.

ALWAYS-ALREADY OEDIPUS

Biological identity always presents itself as natural. That is, no culture denies the relationship between a child and his or her parents.[29] In fifth-century Athens, we should remember, this biological identity carried

the full force of law: citizens could only be those who were *biologically* iden-
tifiable as born of two citizens. In every genetic and social understanding of
identity, Oedipus really is the child of Jocasta and Laius. This play forcefully
privileges that biological identity. The entire problem of Oedipus's marriage
with Jocasta is that he really is her son; contrary to his own fears, it would be
of no outstanding consequence if he were to have sex with Merope. At the
same time, however, this play presents Oedipus's birth in competition with
other forms of identification, a process that emphasizes the cultural baggage
that surrounds "natural" identity. And when Oedipus does finally recognize
who he really is (thus displacing the question of who killed Laius), he does
so through a convoluted series of displacements. Biological identity, this play
seems to say, is a cultural fact and potentially unstable.

Oedipus's search for his birth is necessarily convoluted, since that process
creates the dramatic tension that sustains the drama. But *our* understanding
of Oedipus's identity also takes a serpentine path. Everything in this play
depends on our implicit acceptance of Oedipus's parentage, yet Sophocles
suggests a surprising number of possible parents for his hero. In addition to
the obvious surrogate parents, Polybus and Merope (e.g., 774), we see *Tuchē*
("Luck," 1080), the mountain Cithaeron (1089–91, 1451–54), and Bacchus
with some nymphs (1105–09) suggested as possibilities.[30] Tiresias adds yet
another, if only metaphorically: ἥδ' ἡμέρα φύσει σε καὶ διαφθερεῖ ("This
day will give birth to you and will destroy you," 438). And if we accept the
manuscript reading at 873, we may also list *hubris* as a possible parent of
Oedipus.[31]

Going through this list, we are forced to see that the concept of parentage
is not the same in each case, though all contain a certain kind of truth.
Polybus and Merope have been Oedipus's parents in social terms. They have
raised him and, until he is disabused of his error, Oedipus derives his social
identity from them. Even though Polybus and Merope know that Oedipus is
not "really" their son, for example, Oedipus inherits their property: the her-
ald arrives to inform Oedipus that Corinth has pronounced him king (939–
40). *Tuchē* and Mt. Cithaeron are his parents under a strained metaphor: he
survived his exposure thanks to them, so that Oedipus understands them to
have given him life. Bacchus and the nymphs seem a mythological extension
of this metaphor, a divine origin assigned to a mortal of importance whose
"real" origin is not known. "This day" is perhaps the most complex parent of
all. Tiresias means that on this day, Oedipus will discover his true identity
for the first time. But we spectators may be tempted to suggest another meaning, namely, that this day has given Oedipus life because it is one of the days
of the tragic festival, and his play is on the program.

Most importantly, a metaphor of biological parentage defines each of these various surrogate births: of *Tuchē*, for example, Oedipus says, "For I was born (*pephuka*) from her" (1082). All of the "parents" listed above, then, are attempts to replace the horrible truth that we know lurks just offstage, that Laius and Jocasta are Oedipus's "real" parents. This misdirection works, to a point: the very surfeit of alternatives suggests that the identity provided by Laius and Jocasta can be called into question. We have been playing within a broad spectrum of meanings for the idea of giving birth. Once Oedipus's real biological identity is known, however, it must supplant these other playful possibilities. Again, we see the force of biology as a cultural signifier. It becomes *the* answer to the question of Oedipus specifically by displacing all other options.

Although biological identity asserts its own authority in this play, we must bear in mind that in the world of everyday Athens, such identity could be far from secure, at least as it was socially recognized. The possibility of illegitimacy was a constant threat, as Knox points out: "When Tiresias asks Oedipus if he knows who his parents are (415), we are reminded of the vituperation of the law court, where one of the commonest weapons . . . was a suggestion that the adversary was of low, illegitimate, foreign, or even servile birth."[32] This play picks up on the instability of biological identity, and reverses it, by discussing Oedipus's birth in terms entirely typical of the law courts. Oedipus, ironically, is concerned that he will be found of low birth. Almost immediately after learning that Polybus was not his father, he asks the messenger, σὺ δ᾽ ἐμπολήσας ἢ τυχών μ᾽ αὐτῷ δίδως; ("Did you buy me, or, happening on me, give me to him?" 1025). When he is questioning the herdsman later, he asks a similar question: ἢ δοῦλος, ἢ κείνου τις ἐγγενὴς γεγώς; ("Then am I a slave, or someone born legitimately to someone?" 1168). Oedipus even thinks that Jocasta has the same concerns. When she tries to dissuade him from seeking further, he responds: θάρσει· σὺ μὲν γὰρ οὐδ᾽ ἐὰν τρίτης ἐγὼ / μητρὸς φανῶ τρίδουλος, ἐκφανῇ κακή ("Be brave. For even if I turn out to be thrice a slave / from a third-generation mother, you will not turn out to be base-born," 1062–63). It is remarkable that with all the talk of Laius's death, the oracles, and Oedipus's parentage, it never occurs to him that Jocasta might be afraid that he is *legitimate* rather than illegitimate. But, unless we read Oedipus as dissembling in this scene, the possibility never enters his mind. When Jocasta leaves the stage for the last time, Oedipus offers this comment: αὕτη δ᾽ ἴσως, φρονεῖ γὰρ ὡς γυνὴ μέγα, / τὴν δυσγένειαν τὴν ἐμὴν αἰσχύνεται ("But she, perhaps, is proud like a woman / and is ashamed of my low birth," 1078–79). Oedipus fears his low birth when the entire audience is gasping over his high birth. An essential element of the way the play works, therefore, is to take this extraordinary situation — Oedipus's incestuous relations with his mother — and pose it (reversed) in mundane terms. Issues of paternity, citizenship, and family membership are common in the legal arena, so that Sophocles simply borrows the expression of class structure that underlies such contests and puts it in Oedipus's mouth.[33] As a result, we recognize that Oedipus has missed the point completely — it would be far better if Oedipus *were* a slave, and no biological relation to Laius.

In the remarkable inversion of this drama, then, legitimacy is a bigger problem than illegitimacy. Sophocles emphasizes the particular horror of Oedipus's legitimacy through a number of lines that create wild dramatic irony.[34] One especially telling example occurs when Oedipus asks Jocasta what Laius was like. Jocasta replies: μέλας, χνοάζων ἄρτι λευκανθὲς κάρα. / μορφῆς δὲ τῆς σῆς οὐκ ἀπεστάτει πολύ ("Dark, just sprinkling his head with grey, / and in form not far different from yours," 742–43). The beginning of the description is innocent enough, but the second line is devastating. What makes it more effective, though, is the fact that physical similarity is normally considered a positive sign. Hesiod, for example, describes those who live in a just city: τίκτουσιν δὲ γυναῖκες ἐοικότα τέκνα γονεῦσι ("And wives bear children very much like their parents").[35] Oedipus's very physical features mark him, just as they should, as a legitimate child. But as this legitimate child he has committed parricide and incest. The marks of biological identity, then, have been given a twist: in addition to signifying the fidelity of the wife, they also signify the violation of the most basic of rules regarding marriage.

The purpose of legitimacy tests within society, moreover, is to establish difference. *Gnēsioi* children are citizens, eligible to inherit property; *nothoi* are not. When these boundaries are crossed, all social distinctions are threatened. So, in [Demosthenes] 59, Apollodorus argues that if Athens allows a prostitute (Neaira) to be a wife, it will make all Athenian wives into prostitutes.[36] Legitimacy distinguishes one class from another within the city, and one nationality from another outside the city. But Oedipus's legitimacy has the opposite effect — it breaks down difference, and difference on an even more "natural" level than that of class or nationality.[37] Oedipus eliminates distinctions between generations, as any number of lines point out. I cite only one instance here, Tiresias's dire prediction:

φανήσεται δὲ παισὶ τοῖς αὑτοῦ ξυνὼν
ἀδελφὸς αὐτός καὶ πατήρ, κἀξ ἧς ἔφυ
γυναικὸς υἱὸς καὶ πόσις, καὶ τοῦ πατρὸς
ὁμόσπορός τε καὶ φονεύς.

He will turn out, living with his own children,
to be their brother and father, and of the woman from whom
he came, he will be son and husband, of his father,
he will be a sower in the same place, and a murderer.
(457–60)

Oedipus's legitimacy, therefore, has an effect structurally opposite to that which legitimacy is supposed to have. Rather than solidifying identity and naturalizing difference, it eliminates it. This particular biological identity creates a multiplicity of identities, and a tangle of relationships that Oedipus would gladly trade for the simplicity of status as a *nothos*. The unfortunate fact of Oedipus's birth creates a fundamental instability in his identity, so that basic terms of familial relationship become interchangeable. The idea of displaced identity, therefore, is essential to Oedipus's experience. Oedipus's crimes depend on the certainty of his biological identity, and we, insofar as we are horrified at his realization of incest, accept that certainty. We do so, however, in the face of the paradox that his unwitting incest has thrown the whole paradigm into question. He fills too many categories at once.

As much as biological identity tends to displace other constructs of identity, moreover, Oedipus arrives at his "true self" only through a complicated series of displacements. Above, for example, I argue that Oedipus's name literally suggests "who he is." But he has gotten this name in an unconventional way. That is, it is not a name that indicates (as names should) his familial connections. Oedipus should carry his father's name, as Althusser points out (above). Instead, his name emphasizes his lack of family: "He is a 'child of chance' in the grimmest possible way: he has his name from chance." [38] It is ironic, then, that the name Oedipus bears eventually confirms that he "really is" the child of Laius. Indeed, Oedipus arrives at this conclusion (as we do) only through his own physical removal from his family. His personal displacement and attending circumstances confirm his place in society. [39]

Oedipus's displaced questions of identity, moreover, have plagued him all his life. Significantly, whenever he has asked who he is, he has been answered with misdirection. Oedipus tells the chorus that, accused of being "illegitimate" (πλαστός, 780), he questioned his "parents" about his birth. They do not, at least in Oedipus's account, exactly deny the charge; rather, they take offense at the one who said it (784), which Oedipus says pleases him. Nonetheless, he goes then to the oracle, who also evades the question, and instead tells Oedipus what we already know about him:

ὡς μητρὶ μὲν χρείη με μειχθῆναι, γένος δ'
ἄτλητον ἀνθρώποισι δηλώσοιμ' ὁρᾶν,
φονεὺς δ' ἐσοίμην τοῦ φυτεύσαντος πατρός.

NATURE AND ITS DISCONTENTS IN THE *Oedipus tyrannus*

> [He said] that it was necessary for me to sleep with my
> mother, and
> that I would bring to light a race unbearable to see,
> and that I would be the murderer of the father who sowed
> me. (791–93)

In answer to the question "Who are my parents," the oracle replies, "You will sleep with your mother and kill your father." Just as the herdsman's revelation that Oedipus is Laius's son becomes sufficient proof that Oedipus killed Laius, then, the fact that Oedipus will kill his father becomes sufficient answer to the question "Who am I?" At least, Oedipus acts as if he then knows who his father and mother are: he leaves Corinth in order to avoid fulfilling Apollo's prediction. The oracle predicts Oedipus's future actions as if that were his identity, an act of displacement. Oedipus reacts, unsuccessfully, in kind: as Pucci notes, "By running away from his home in Corinth . . . he authenticates Polybus and Merope as his own legitimate parents." [40] By removing himself from Corinth, however, he also begins the journey during which (and by which) he will confirm the oracle.

Later in the play, Oedipus learns that in fact he is not Polybus's son, and again we find confusion and misdirection. When the messenger first tells him that he need not fear Merope, we hear a somewhat evasive dialogue as Oedipus comes to realize that he does not belong to the family he has always known as his own:

Αγ.	ὁθούνεκ' ἦν σοι Πόλυβος οὐδὲν ἐν γένει.
Οι.	πῶς εἶπας; οὐ γὰρ Πόλυβος ἐξέφυσέ με;
Αγ.	οὐ μᾶλλον οὐδὲν τοῦδε τἀνδρός, ἀλλ' ἴσον.
Οι.	καὶ πῶς ὁ φύσας ἐξ ἴσου τῷ μηδενί;
Αγ.	ἀλλ' οὔ σ' ἐγείνατ' οὔτ' ἐκεῖνος οὔτ' ἐγώ.
Οι.	ἀλλ' ἀντὶ τοῦ δὴ παῖδά μ' ὠνομάζετο;

Me.:	After all, Polybus was nothing to you in race.
Oe.:	What do you mean? Did not Polybus beget me?
Me.:	No more than me, but equally (with me).
Oe.:	And how is the one who begot me equal to this nobody?
Me.:	Because he did not beget you, any more than I did.
Oe.:	But then why did he call me his son? (1016–21)

As with many passages in this play, the messenger's answers border on riddles. Rather than saying, "No, Polybus did not sire you," he says, "He no more sired you than I did." This bit of rhetorical showmanship has a point. Oedipus's identity is at stake, and just as when he asked the oracle about it earlier in his life, he is answered indirectly and evasively. The type of answer he keeps receiving serves to underscore the potential instability of his own familial ties.

Perhaps most important is line 1021: "Why then, did he call me his child?" The question reminds us again of the procedures used in law courts to establish legal identity. A father would be expected to introduce his legitimate children to his phratry, and if no member of the phratry objected at that time, this introduction became legal evidence for the child's family membership and citizenship.[41] Oedipus's question, then, is not idle. The fact that Polybus called him his child is fairly compelling evidence that he *was* Polybus's child. Moreover, the word I have translated "called" (*ōnomazeto*) more literally means "named." Polybus's "naming" Oedipus his child, therefore, is an act that should establish Oedipus's legal and social identity.[42] In fact, Laius performed the exact opposite of Polybus's "naming" when he cast his son, unnamed, out into the wilds. And as we have already seen, it is the fact that Oedipus *was* cast out in this way that gave him his "real" name of Swell-foot (see line 1032, and above). Polybus's naming, which followed normal Athenian rules for establishing social identity, has been overruled in Oedipus's life. Oedipus's "real" name, then, points out the very instability of familial relationships that rituals of naming try to circumvent.

Nonetheless, once Oedipus learns who he really is, the play forces him (and us) to accept this fact as final. As Oedipus himself says, οὐκ ἂν γένοιτο τοῦθ', ὅπως ἐγὼ λαβὼν / σημεῖα τοιαῦτ' οὐ φανῶ τοὐμὸν γένος ("It could not happen, that I, grasping / such signs as these, should not show forth my birth," 1058–59). The apparent inevitability that pervades this play makes it quite possible for us to overlook just how unusual a statement this is. Establishing paternity (if not maternity) is always a problem, as Telemachos makes clear at *Odyssey* 1.215–16: μήτηρ μέν τ' ἐμέ φησι τοῦ ἔμμεναι, αὐτὰρ ἐγώ γε / οὐκ οἶδ'· οὐ γάρ πώ τις ἑὸν γόνον αὐτὸς ἀνέγνω ("My mother says that I am his [Odysseus's] son, but I for my part / do not know. For no one fully knows his own birth").[43] Oedipus, it seems, is the only man in all of ancient Greece who has absolutely no questions about his father's identity. For Oedipus, discovering his parentage takes on the guise of inevitability through several media: the oracle, Tiresias's predictions, the riddle of his own name. Each of these creators of identity works through a principle of displacement. The oracle and Tiresias refuse to tell Oedipus who his parents are, saying instead that he will sleep with his mother and kill his father. His name confirms his identity as the legitimate son of Laius but also emphasizes that he was cast out from his family at birth. For Oedipus, identity is confirmed by misdirection and lack of familial connections. When those familial connections are discovered, and confirmed by Oedipus-the-subject, they have the effect opposite from what is expected. Rather than creating difference and establishing identity, Oedipus's identity of displacement breaks down difference on the most basic level.

Toward the end of the play, Oedipus suggests one more metaphorical parent: ὦ γάμοι γάμοι, / ἐφύσαθ' ἡμᾶς ("Marriage, marriage, / you begot me," 1403–4). Oedipus is literally correct. Marriage did give birth to him. But he is even more correct in that marriage has created Oedipus-the-subject. His legitimacy, through a tangle of displacements, makes him (biologically) the person he is. At the same time, his current marriage to Jocasta both confirms the person he is (in the terms of the oracle, i.e., incest) and denies that he can be defined under the biological paradigm. He is Jocasta's son, but also her husband, and also the father of her children. In the end, his identity is little more than this series of displacements. "Who are my parents?" he asked. "You will marry your mother," is the self-fulfilling, almost autonomous response.

SUPERNATURAL MARRIAGES

As we have seen in previous chapters, Athenian tragedy (like many of the representations of Athenian culture) naturalizes marriage. It describes marriage with a series of metaphors from the wild and agricultural spheres in order to make the cultural bond between husband and wife appear straightforward, normal, and analogous to other processes of civilization. The *Oedipus tyrannus* does the same, but with a twist. It uses these same naturalizing images to describe the patently "unnatural" marriage of Oedipus and Jocasta. But the play does more than simply create this juxtaposition. A number of descriptive passages suggest that, as with Oedipus discovering his identity, this marriage should have spontaneously discovered and denounced its own perversity. These conventional images serve here to denaturalize the institution of marriage, to expose the mechanisms by which culture defines itself.

Early on, the play suggests that something is wrong with Oedipus's marriage through descriptions of the plague, which manifests itself as an interruption of fertility on all levels. The chorus of suppliants says,

> φθίνουσα μὲν κάλυξιν ἐγκάρποις χθονός
> φθίνουσα δ' ἀγέλαις βουνόμοις, τόκοισί τε
> ἀγόνοις γυναικῶν.

> [The city is] wasting away with the fruit-bearing crops of earth,
> wasting away with herds of grazing oxen,
> with the unborn children of women.[44] (25–27)

The assumption behind this description is an association with which we are familiar: often Athenian literature equates the fertility of the land with the fertility of women.[45] Such images naturalize the production of children, and woman's role in the *polis*. Here, however, fertility has stopped on both a human and an agricultural level. For all who know the myth of Oedipus, the perversion of fertility described above has an obvious (we might even say biological) cause: Oedipus's marriage to his mother, Jocasta.[46] Such an "unnatural" marriage (especially one between the rulers of Thebes) results in the disruption of everything that marriage represents to the community.[47]

Surprisingly, then, the *Oedipus tyrannus* presents Oedipus's marriage in the same naturalizing terms that we see elsewhere. The play contains an unusually high number of images of women as harbors and plowed fields, both common in descriptions of *parthenoi* as they undergo marriage.[48] In some instances, these images appear to have no sexual connotations at all: Oedipus is several times characterized as a helmsman, piloting the "ship of state."[49] Elsewhere, however, this civilizing image is specifically a metaphor for his marriage. Tiresias, for example, says:

> βοῆς δὲ τῆς σῆς ποῖος οὐκ ἔσται †λιμήν†
> ποῖος Κιθαιρὼν οὐχὶ σύμφωνος τάχα,
> ὅταν καταίσθῃ τὸν ὑμέναιον, ὃν δόμοις
> ἄνορμον εἰσέπλευσας, εὐπλοίας τυχών;

> What harbor will there not be for your cries,
> What Mt. Cithaeron will not cry in response quickly,
> when you perceive the wedding, which
> you steered, harborless, into the house, happening on good
>   sailing? (420–23)

Though the syntax here is unusually complex, the notion of a marriage being represented by the image of a ship sailing into safe harbor is a fairly common one.[50] The image also clearly suggests the sexual act of penetration. Oedipus's fateful marriage, then, takes on the same aspect that any normal marriage would, rendering the act of intercourse with the civilized and civilizing images of sailing. Here, however, we should note that it is the wedding that is sailed into the house, and that the same wedding is marked "harborless." This marriage, it seems, is neither safe nor normal.

The play uses the same image, moreover, to suggest that this marriage *should* discover its own perversity. Tiresias says that the *limēn* itself will be a "harbor of cries" (line 420). The text is difficult here, and Lloyd-Jones and Wilson suggest that λιμήν be replaced by 'λικών, although they admit that this introduces a "metrical anomaly."[51] If, however, we take λιμήν, in keeping with the nautical imagery of the stanza, as metaphor for Jocasta's womb, then the lines suggest another interpretation.[52] Oedipus's marriage and intercourse with Jocasta seem to be a harbor, a place of safety. Instead, it is an echo chamber of cries — as it will become once Oedipus recognizes his identity. Similarly, Cithaeron, the mountain where Oedipus was abandoned, becomes associated in Oedipus's mind with his birth (cf. lines 1451–54). Looking into the future of this play, Tiresias suggests that Oedipus's birth and marriage will cry out of their own accord. The image of a harbor, like Oedipus himself, partakes in self-recognition.

The same sort of variation is put on an even more common image of marriage, that of the plowed field. Again, this image occurs in the play with unusual frequency.[53] In an early ironic passage, Oedipus describes his link to Laius in these terms, saying that he is ἔχων δὲ λέκτρα καὶ γυναῖχ' ὁμόσπορον ("holding his same-sowed bed and wife," 260).[54] When Oedipus recounts what the oracle told him, the father that he is destined to kill is modified by the adjective *phuteusas* ("having planted," 793).[55] Later, Oedipus uses the same adjective to describe Polybus and Merope (*phuteusantes*, "having planted," 1007, 1012). After Oedipus knows his identity, the metaphor is used more often and more explicitly, as in lines 1255–57:

> φοιτᾷ γὰρ ἡμᾶς ἔγχος ἐξαιτῶν πορεῖν,
> γυναῖκά τ' οὐ γυναῖκα, μητρῴαν δ' ὅπου
> κίχοι διπλῆν ἄρουραν οὗ τε καὶ τέκνων.

> He rushed in, asking me to provide a sword,
> that he might meet with his wife, no wife,
> and maternal double field where he also begot children.[56]

The idea of sowing a field creates an image of sex and reproduction that is in accord with the world of agriculture. The image is highly ironic here, a suggestion of naturalness just at the point when Oedipus has fully realized how "unnatural" his marriage has been.

Similar to Tiresias's treatment of the harbor image, moreover, is the chorus's suggestion that the agricultural model of marriage should have spontaneously recognized Oedipus's perversion. In fact, the chorus combines the two images, and states:

> ἰὼ κλεινὸν Οἰδίπου κάρα,
> ᾧ μέγας λιμὴν
> αὐτὸς ἤρκεσεν
> παιδὶ καὶ πατρὶ

θαλαμηπόλῳ πεσεῖν,
πῶς ποτε πῶς ποθ' αἱ πατρῷ-
αί σ' ἄλοκες φέρειν, τάλας,
σῖγ' ἐδυνάθησαν ἐς τοσόνδε;

Look, the famous head of Oedipus,
for whom a great harbor
itself was sufficient,
for both son and father
to fall in as chamber-attendant;[57]
how then, how then were the paternal
furrows able to bear you, alas,
silent for so long? (1207–13)

DuBois suggests that Oedipus's frequent use of these metaphors weakens the impact of the incest in the play: "He committed incest—but he was only a plow that plowed where it had been planted. He is refusing her humanity. . . . She is a furrow cut into the earth."[58] This interpretation, however, overlooks the fact that these same images anthropomorphize the furrows. The chorus asks how Jocasta's "furrows" could bear her son's "plough" in silence. On the surface, it is an odd question. We would hardly expect "furrows" to react to a plough. That is the point. In the same way, Jocasta's body does not react to incest with instinctive knowledge. These naturalizing images come head up against the realization that the incest taboo is not a natural fact, is not recognized by Jocasta's vagina spontaneously. The chorus's complaint does not lessen the horror of incest. Rather, it emphasizes that horror by coupling it with the realization that this boundary is not a permanent, self-defined, natural fixture.

Still more important, however, is the process of self-recognition that these images suggest. The chorus expects that incest will be self-proclaiming, in much the same way that this play suggests that biological identity will be self-proclaiming. In the end, however, the agricultural metaphors for marriage proclaim only their inadequacy to describe marriage as a cultural phenomenon. Oedipus's act of incest disrupts the cultural production of marriage just as it disrupts the paradigm of biological identity. In the face of Oedipus's unnatural marriage, neither paradigm sufficiently explains the facts at hand. The incest taboo ceases to operate if a man can marry his mother, and biological identity cannot describe the man who is both father and brother to his offspring. The agricultural metaphors for marriage imply an ordered process of civilized and civilizing fertility. Oedipus's fertility denies that process and the categories that it establishes.

JOCASTA : OEDIPUS :: EXCESS : IDENTITY

Few critics have much to say about Jocasta, and it is easy to relegate her to the status of a plot device.[59] Despite Whitman's assertion of Jocasta's "charm," she has few scenes in which she commands our undivided attention.[60] She does not tell us, as Deianeira does, what her life has been like. She does not describe either her marriage to Laius or her life with Oedipus. We know nothing of how she felt when she allowed her child to be exposed, or when she learned that her first husband had died, or when she married Oedipus shortly thereafter. Her experience is masked in the text, overshadowed by Oedipus and protected from public view.[61] Nonetheless, she is important: she is, after all, the relationship center that creates Oedipus as the person he is. And if we cannot recover "her" experience (because Sophocles does not represent it), we can look at the way she serves as a link between key characters, and thereby creates a social identity for others.

I have focused above on the nature of biological identity as a displacing and displaced construct. Jocasta embodies that process of displacement. She fulfills the traditional role of woman-as-other, in that she does not establish an identity for herself so much as she serves as a creator of identities for the men around her.[62] That is, Oedipus obtains his biological identity through her and, as we shall see, also realizes that identity because of Jocasta's pronouncements. Moreover, the male characters in the play try to establish relationships with one another through Jocasta, often invoking the links that have been created by her marriage. In this respect, her marriage in and of itself mirrors the process of displacement: Oedipus is confirmed as king, for example, because he has married the queen, a state that replaces and masks his status as the heir apparent. Such attempted social identities, as we might expect, become superfluous when Jocasta's "real" relationships to Oedipus and Laius become clear. Once again, biological identity displaces other, competing social forms of identity. Most important of all, then, Jocasta's marriage mirrors the process of displacement in that it creates relationships — and categories of relationships — beyond and outside of those that the characters seek.

Before Jocasta arrives on the scene, Creon and Oedipus recognize and validate a relationship to one another through her. At line 551, Oedipus warns Creon that he will receive no special treatment although he is *suggenēs*. The word suggests that the two are tied by blood (as they are, though they do not realize this yet) and indicates the strength of Oedipus's marriage bond with Jocasta. Similarly, Creon emphasizes his relation to Oedipus as he begins his defense: τί δῆτ'; ἀδελφὴν τὴν ἐμὴν γήμας ἔχεις; ("What? Are you not married to my sister?" 577) He then goes on to argue that as the brother-in-law of the king, he enjoys all the benefits with none of the responsibility of royalty (583ff.). His relationship to Oedipus, which he currently believes to be a simple marriage-tie through Jocasta, creates an unofficial political identity as well.

Even more important, however, is the purely social link that Jocasta creates between Laius and Oedipus. This link exists in both political and personal terms. When Oedipus is beginning the manhunt, he says:

> νῦν δ' ἐπεὶ κυρῶ τ' ἐγὼ
> ἔχων μὲν ἀρχάς, ἃς ἐκεῖνος εἶχε πρίν,
> ἔχων δὲ λέκτρα καὶ γυναῖχ' ὁμόσπορον,
> κοινῶν τε παίδων κοίν' ἄν, εἰ κείνῳ γένος
> μὴ 'δυστύχησεν, ἦν ἂν ἐκπεφυκότα —
> νῦν δ' ἐς τὸ κείνου κρᾶτ' ἐνήλαθ' ἡ τύχη.

Now since I am ruler,
holding the kingship, which he held before,
and holding the bed and same-sowed wife,
and there would be a bond of common children, if for him
his race had not been cursed,
but now, this misfortune has fallen on his head. (258–63)

In Oedipus's speech, holding Laius's rule and holding his former wife are parallel. Jocasta, then, has functioned similarly to an *epiklēros*. Her husband having died without children, she provided a stable center for the *oikos* until it could be successfully transferred to another man. True, Jocasta is not Laius' daughter, but here she functions as if she were: rather than returning to her own father's household, she transfers Laius's political power (and bloodline), keeping his *oikos* intact. Marriage to the queen, as we have seen several times before, is one of the signs of "being the king," of ruling over the *polis*, and it is this legacy that Jocasta transfers to the stranger who comes to town.[63] Jocasta and Oedipus fail to realize, however, that she has also transferred her husband's property according to the more usual method, by providing a male heir. The problem, then, is not that Jocasta (like Clytemnestra) has transferred the *oikos* to an enemy or outsider, but that she has transferred it in too many ways to a too-near relative. Oedipus's political legitimacy, then, has been overconfirmed: he cannot both inherit and marry into the kingdom.[64]

Perhaps even more remarkable, however, is the way in which Oedipus tries to establish his *personal* relation to Laius. In the passage just cited, he suggests that, if only Laius's *genos* were not ill-fortuned, they might have been related through the bond of common children. Oedipus seems aware of the tenuous political identity that he has acquired by marrying Jocasta, and he wants to create a stronger relationship, if only by hypothetical proclamation. Ironically, Laius's *genos* is cursed in a way different from that which Oedipus supposes. He did have a child, and Oedipus and Laius do indeed share the link of children from the same wife. Jocasta's role as mediator, then, is literally overdetermined. She creates a "cultural" relation at the same time that she embodies a "natural" one. And that "natural" relationship between Laius and Oedipus is the problem, the very thing that will displace the tenuous cultural tie that Oedipus distrusts. The bond of common children carries a hidden threat of being too close, of destroying difference altogether (as we saw earlier). Jocasta becomes a sort of hyper-woman, creating too many links, facilitating too many relationships between men.[65]

Jocasta's speeches, moreover, are analogous to her position. Consistently when she tries to mediate, to smooth things over, she ends up creating an excess of information, just as with Oedipus she creates an excess of relationships. The most obvious example is her attempt to calm Oedipus about the oracle. She offers the oracle she and Laius heard — that he would be killed by his own offspring — as proof that oracles are meaningless. For, she says, Laius was killed by robbers at a crossroads (711–25). This last detail, seemingly inconsequential, catches Oedipus's attention, and he begins at this point to suspect that he is the regicide. In many of Jocasta's speeches we see such elements of excess, and such excess is part of the topos of women as other.[66] For even as they create links between men, women remain in some sense radically outside; they leave a residue — of information, of relationships — that does not dissolve. Significantly, the details that Jocasta first brings to Oedipus's attention — for example, that Laius was killed by *several* people — remain unresolved.[67] Jocasta may be telling Oedipus too much, but even when he follows her clues and accepts the awful truth, what she has said remains outside of his interpretation, unintegrated into the "meaning" of the play.

Ironically, Jocasta brings up the issue of dreams in one of these moments of excess (980–83, above). Since Freud's compelling reading of the dream, classical scholars have been hard put to interpret it differently.[68] But critics do not seem to have noticed the oddity of Jocasta bringing up the idea of dreams at all. Oedipus has not mentioned, and never does mention, a dream of sleeping with his mother; he only fears a prophecy that he will do so. Kamerbeek, following Jebb, simply points out that dreams in the ancient world were considered prophetic.[69] But it hardly follows that since one form of (apparently quite common) prognostication often proves meaningless, Oedipus should disregard the oracles of Apollo. Grene is troubled enough by this easy equivalence that he translates lines 981–82 (πολλοὶ γὰρ ἤδη κἀν ὀνείρασιν βροτῶν / μητρὶ ξυνηυνάσθησαν) as follows: "Before this, in dreams, too, *as well as oracles,* / many a man has lain with his own mother."[70] The italicized phrase is quite a lot to pull out of the *kai* ("also") in line 981. The translator has to strain, in other words, in order to make Jocasta's words fit the context.

Commentators have largely ignored this strain. But the difficulty persists, and it is worth asking ourselves why Jocasta brings up the issue of dreams at this point in the play. From her point of view, it is just another example of the failure of predictions: πρόνοια δ' ἐστὶν οὐδενὸς σαφής ("No one has clear foresight," 978). But why does Sophocles introduce the idea? The idea of a dream, as opposed to an oracle, is important for two reasons. First, it places the question of incest within the realm of Oedipus's experience. Many people, Jocasta says (perhaps even Oedipus?), have had this dream. Unlike the idea that Oedipus is fated to sleep with his mother, Jocasta's speech suggests that he himself might have already committed incest, if only in his mind. Even Jocasta's mention of the dream makes it seem like an event that has already happened. Unlike the phrasing of the oracle, which puts all such action in the future (e.g., 994–96), Jocasta speaks in the past tense, of men *having slept* (*suneunasthēsan*, 982) with their mothers. Jocasta's switch to the medium of dreams, then, brings us a step closer to Oedipus's final realization: for him, this dream is literally true. She plants the image of that action in our minds, and confronts the men in the audience with the horror that what for them is just a dream (signifying something other than what it represents) is for Oedipus actual incest. She does so, however, through an act of displacement: Oedipus's fear of oracles is displaced into the more common realm of dream interpretation, and, moreover, in a speech that is meant to dispel Oedipus's identification with the oracle. Jocasta's attempts to mediate, to redirect harmful signification, end instead in too much signification, and even more positive identification.[71]

Second, unlike the oracle, the dream brings up the issue of signification itself. The oracle says that Oedipus will do two things: sleep with his mother and kill his father. Though it is possible that the oracle may not come true, it need not be interpreted. It presents its meaning as clear. The dream, on the other hand, is not so simple. In ancient Greek (as in modern) methods of dream interpretation, dreams suggest symbolic, not literal, meaning. In particular we should consider Hippias's dream in Herodotus 6.107:[72] Hippias dreams of sleeping with his mother and concludes that he is fated to recapture his power in Athens and die there comfortably in old age. From Hippias's dream, as well as Artemidorus's dream analysis, it is clear that an Athenian who dreamed that he had sex with his mother would not leap to the conclusion that he in fact had done so or would do so.[73] On the contrary, such a dream indicated one of a variety of political meanings: Hippias's interpretation (above) probably is based on the traditional equation of motherhood with the generative powers of the earth, so that his act of sex with his mother foretells political and economic prosperity.

Herodotus does not tell us Hippias's reasoning for interpreting the dream as he does, but this interpretation seems confirmed by the story's end: Hippias, after disembarking at Marathon, coughs, and in the process loses a tooth, which he is unable to find. He then decides to give up, declaring that the land is not his, and that his tooth possesses the only part of the earth that he ever will. In a Freudian system, this second interpretation makes little sense. But if we bear in mind the equation of mother with earth, and the fact that teeth are sometimes equated with semen (cf. the story of the dragon's teeth at Thebes), it becomes clearer. Hippias's dream of having sex with his mother has come true: his tooth (semen) has penetrated the earth (mother).[74] And since this event is of no account, he understands that the dream also did not predict the important event that he had hoped it would. Hippias's dream does not, therefore, signify that he will sleep with his mother. It signifies something else, though in this case, nothing of importance.

I do not mean to suggest that Jocasta's speech is a specific reference to Hippias's dream in Herodotus. Hippias's two interpretations of the same dream, however, can be taken as typical. Dreams in ancient systems of interpretation never produce straightforward meaning. They create meaning by a process of symbolic substitution. Jocasta wants to discourage the very act of interpreting that dream. Having brought her very suggestive dream up, she argues, ἀλλὰ ταῦθ' ὅτῳ / παρ' οὐδέν ἐστι, ῥᾷστα τὸν βίον φέρει ("But for whomever these things / count as nothing, that one bears his life most easily," 982–83). But by raising the issue of such dreams, which she says "many men" have had, she cannot help but invoke the structure of dream interpretation, in which one image signifies another, apparently unrelated, event. As we have already seen, such a structure of signification holds true for Oedipus: the swelling of his feet, for example, assures that he *is* the son of Jocasta, and the fact of his incest somehow assures that he *is* a parricide.[75] This dream of many anonymous men, then, is "intimately related to the shocking and terrible story of the myth"[76] — not because it represents a universal and transhistorical truth, but because it invokes the logic of displacement that confirms Oedipus's birth.

Such is the nature of Jocasta's mediation between men, and of her role in confirming Oedipus's "true" identity. Although this play is extraordinary in the emphasis it places on misdirection in the process of signification, it also suggests that this misdirection is the special province of women. Jocasta is the unspoken center of all the problematic relations in this play: Oedipus and Creon, Oedipus and Laius, Oedipus and his offspring. As a mediator between households, her role is always overdetermined, always potentially doubled (if not duplicitous).[77] Little wonder, then, that so much of Jocasta's speech seems to embody displacement. Possessed of no stable identity of her own, Jocasta creates identities for others through a disturbing process of displacement and oversignification.[78]

ONE MORE MARRIAGE?

We still do not know what Jocasta's experience of marriage was. Even her final speech is primarily a declaration of future silence: ἰοὺ ἰού, δύστηνε· τοῦτο γάρ σ' ἔχω / μόνον προσειπεῖν, ἄλλο δ' οὔποθ' ὕστερον ("Alas, alas, wretch; for I am able to address you only thus, / but [will call you] nothing else ever again," 1071–72). Like Heracles at the end of the *Trachiniae*, however, Oedipus provides a glimpse into what men might think of a woman's experience of marriage. The play expresses his suffering in terms that call to mind the position of a *parthenos*. The most important passage is a speech by Creon, who has good reason to emasculate Oedipus; he is trying to establish his own power over the former king. On finding the now-blind Oedipus outside, Creon admonishes him as follows:

ἀλλ' εἰ τὰ θνητῶν μὴ καταισχύνεσθ' ἔτι
γένεθλα, τὴν γοῦν πάντα βόσκουσαν φλόγα
αἰδεῖσθ' ἄνακτος Ἡλίου, τοιόνδ' ἄγος
ἀκάλυπτον οὕτω δεικνύναι, τὸ μήτε γῆ
μήτ' ὄμβρος ἱερὸς μήτε φῶς προσδέξεται.
ἀλλ' ὡς τάχιστ' ἐς οἶκον ἐσκομίζετε.

But if you are not yet ashamed before the race of men,
have respect for the flame of King Helios,
which nourishes everything, [be ashamed] to show such
    pollution
uncovered, which neither the earth
nor the holy rain, nor the light will accept favorably,
but you, escort him into the house as quickly as possible.
(1424–29)

Creon is clearly establishing a position of control in this speech. He wishes to contain the pollution that Oedipus has come to represent, and indeed, at the end of the play, he will lead Oedipus indoors.[79] Oedipus, by contrast, seeks to be thrown outward (e.g., lines 1436–37). Creon's admonition, then, is an assertion of his power.

At the same time, Creon prescribes conditions for Oedipus that are typically the lot of young women. Clytemnestra, for example, complains because Electra will not remain indoors:

> ἀνειμένη μέν, ὡς ἔοικας, αὖ στρέφῃ.
> οὐ γὰρ πάρεστ᾽ Αἴγισθος, ὅς σ᾽ ἐπεῖχ᾽ ἀεὶ
> μή τοι θυραίαν γ᾽ οὖσαν αἰσχύνειν φίλους.

> Let loose again, as it seems, you wander around,
> for Aegisthus is not present, who holds you in check always
> lest, being out of doors, you shame family and friends.
> (Electra 516–18)

Parthenoi, as we have seen, are not supposed to be loose and out of doors, because being so invites the possibility of inappropriate contact with men outside the family. As in Creon's speech, then, Clytemnestra sees Electra's being out of doors as something that brings shame. Electra's shame is localized—she only hurts those with whom she has ties of *philia*—whereas Oedipus is a source of disgrace on a universal scale. Oedipus is not, moreover, in danger of inappropriate sexual contact—at least, not any more. Structurally, however, the speeches come from a similar impulse. Oedipus, like a young unmarried woman, is not fit for public eyes.

We might not make the connection between Oedipus and the *parthenos*, however, if not for two other details in Creon's speech. First, the cosmos that Oedipus risks offending is specifically the cosmos of fertility: the nourishing sun, holy rain, and the earth. The passage recalls fragment 44 of Aeschylus, a passage that unites the concept of marriage with agricultural fertility:

> ἐρᾷ μὲν ἁγνὸς οὐρανὸς τρῶσαι χθόνα,
> ἔρως δὲ γαῖαν λαμβάνει γάμου τυχεῖν·
> ὄμβρος δ᾽ ἀπ᾽ εὐνάεντος οὐρανοῦ πεσὼν
> ἔκυσε γαῖαν· ἡ δὲ τίκτεται βροτοῖς
> μήλων τε βοσκὰς καὶ βίον Δημήτριον
> δένδρων τ᾽ ὀπώραν· ἐκ νοτίζοντος γάμου
> τελεῖθ᾽ ὅσ᾽ ἔστι· τῶν δ᾽ ἐγὼ παραίτιος.[80]

> The pure heaven desires to wound the ground,
> desire for marriage seizes the earth;
> the rains falling from the mating sky
> impregnate the earth. The earth gives birth
> to flocks of sheep and livelihood of Demeter [grain]
> and blooming of trees for mortals. From this raining wedding
> everything that is comes to completion; and of all this I have
> a part.

We see here the same elements: the earth, the rain, and the concept of nourishment (note the echo of βοσκάς in βόσκουσαν, 1425) — that is, those things which Aeschylus defines as the realm of Aphrodite, particularly the Aphrodite who oversees legitimate marriage. Oedipus is not just a source of pollution, then; he endangers marriage as it is represented on a cosmic scale. His being out of doors may be more parallel to the position of an unruly *parthenos* than it appears at first. What is more, Oedipus is found to be a disgrace particularly because his face is *akaluptos* (1427). The adjective is rare — LSJ lists only this line for the fifth century. It seems likely that the use of the word here is meant to call to mind the *anakaluptēria* of a young bride.[81] Creon portrays Oedipus's fall, then, in terms that make him a parody of marriage.

I do not mean to suggest that we should read the *Oedipus tyrannus* as a modern drama of sexuality and identity in which the truth of Oedipus's character is revealed in this final scene. In the first place, I am not arguing that Creon and Oedipus actually get married. Rather, the play uses, and perverts, the imagery of a wedding to demonstrate how completely Oedipus has disrupted the process of fertility. His *anakaluptēria*, the moment that commonly represents the ritual of marriage,[82] is not a sign of marital bliss, but of the risks corrupting fertility altogether. Obviously, such a representation tells us little about the position of real brides in real weddings; Oedipus's state is meant as an inversion of norms, and his suffering is part of that inversion. In the second place, we should read Oedipus the bride not in terms of some ancient notion of sexuality, but in terms of gender. Both Heracles and Ajax, in the moments before their deaths, describe their moments of failure in gendered terms: Heracles says that he cries out "like a *parthenos*" (*Trachiniae* 1071), and Ajax says he has been "made female" (*Ajax* 651). Similarly here, when Oedipus is no longer in control of his own life, when he is asking to be exiled (and cannot even attain that for himself), his experience is written in feminizing terms. Men in Greek tragedy live the woman's role as one of suffering and lack of control.[83]

Oedipus asks Creon for exile; instead, Creon leads him into the house. With Oedipus just described in terms that call to mind the realm of Aphrodite and the social position of a *parthenos*, I suggest that we see their entrance through the doors as a parody of a wedding. Given the tendency we have seen for Greek brides to describe their marriages in terms of exile, Oedipus's new role might be an adequate substitute for the punishment he requests. In any case, his shift in gender roles (and social standing) is Oedipus's final displacement in this tragedy. Oedipus's role as a *parthenos*, however, is important in another way. It signals Oedipus's function in the final scene of this play. Like Jocasta, he is now in the role of a wife, creating identity for others through his own mediation. If Athenian inheritance laws were in full effect, the kingdom of Thebes would fall to one of Oedipus's sons. Instead, it appears that Creon will rule Thebes from this moment on. By leading Oedipus into the house, he obtains the kingdom in much the same way that Oedipus did—by "marrying" the former owner. This mock wedding not only establishes Creon's dominant position, it also confirms his right to rule.[84]

At the same time, Oedipus concerns himself with the identity—biological and social—that his marriage has created for his daughters. Oedipus recognizes that his daughters will be unable to marry because of their relation(s) to him:

> ἀλλ' ἡνίκ' ἂν δὴ πρὸς γάμων ἥκητ' ἀκμάς,
> τίς οὗτος ἔσται, τίς παραρρίψει, τέκνα,
> τοιαῦτ' ὀνείδη λαμβάνειν, ἃ †τοῖς ἐμοῖς†
> γονεῦσιν ἔσται σφῷν θ' ὁμοῦ δηλήματα
> . . . κᾆτα τίς γαμεῖ;
> οὐκ ἔστιν οὐδείς, ὦ τέκν', ἀλλὰ δηλαδὴ
> χέρσους φθαρῆναι κἀγάμους ὑμᾶς χρεών.

> But when you have reached the perfection that leads to
>   marriage
> who will there be, who will take the chance, children,
> to seize such a reproach, which to my
> offspring, and to the offspring of them likewise will be a
>   bane,
> . . . and then who will marry [you]?
> There is no one, children, but clearly
> it is necessary for you to die, unirrigated and unmarried.
>   (1492–1502)

His doubled marriage will be balanced by lack of marriage in his daughters. Their biological identity, which carries its own element of displacement (they are both sisters and daughters to Oedipus, lines 1497–99) eliminates any chance of future change of social identity through marriage.[85]

It is an extraordinary situation. Oedipus responds, however, in a very ordinary way. He transfers *kurieia* of his daughters to the senior male in the family, Creon.

> ὦ παῖ Μενοικέως, ἀλλ' ἐπεὶ μόνος πατὴρ
> ταύταιν λέλειψαι, νὼ γάρ, ὢ 'φυτεύσαμεν,
> ὀλώλαμεν δύ' ὄντε, μή σφε, πάτερ, ἴδῃς
> πτωχὰς ἀνάνδρους ἐγγενεῖς ἀλωμένας,
> μηδ' ἐξισώσῃς τάσδε τοῖς ἐμοῖς κακοῖς.

Son of Menoikeos, since you alone are left as father
to these two, since we two who sowed them
are gone, both of us, do not, as their father, watch them
wandering, husbandless kinswomen, beggars,
do not equate these two with my evils. (1503–7)

Earlier Oedipus has told Creon that he need not worry about his sons (1459–61). It is only the young women who need a guardian. In asking that Creon take charge of them, moreover, Oedipus addresses him by his genealogy — an attempt to create for the daughters a legitimate surrogate family. Finally, in making this transfer, Oedipus asks specifically that Creon not allow the young women to remain unmarried. This has all the markings of the familiar situation of the *epiklēros*. The *epiklēros* becomes the charge of her nearest paternal male relative, who is responsible for her welfare, and specifically for overseeing her marriage. Oedipus's speech represents a common legal transaction, a cultural exchange of women that can legally remove them from Oedipus's disastrous branch of the family.

Part of the purpose of the institution of the *epiklēros*, however, is that she preserves her father's bloodline. Her "natural" genealogy is preserved in this cultural exchange. If Oedipus's marriage is not to become a curse for his daughters, that cannot happen here. He asks, therefore, that the link between him and his daughters be broken: "Do not equate these two with my evils" (1507). His request, insofar as it is successful, is ambivalent at best. The audience can recognize a return to order in the recognition of the epiklerate. But at the same time, the effect of Oedipus's transfer of his daughters is to question the biological identification of family membership.[86] The play does not resolve this tension: Oedipus's last words are to ask Creon *not* to take his daughters away: μηδαμῶς ταύτας γ' ἕλῃ μου ("In no way take them from me," 1522). His "natural" affection for his daughters struggles with the cultural identity that he tries to create for them.

The very end of the play carries the same ambivalence. On the one hand, we expect that Oedipus will be exiled once he is revealed as the killer of Laius. Because the punishment of exile was pronounced by Oedipus himself, however, Creon must refuse the pronouncement in order to establish his own ascendancy. *His* final lines demonstrate this concern: πάντα μὴ βούλου κρατεῖν· / καὶ γὰρ ἁκράτησας οὔ σοι τῷ βίῳ ξυνέσπετο ("Do not wish to rule over everything. / For that which you ruled does not follow your [remaining?] life," 1522–23).[87] Creon refuses to honor Oedipus's request to exile him (see especially 1518), therefore, and in so doing establishes himself as the head of the household (and state). His pious control seems to indicate a return to order. But the simultaneous result is that the murderer of Laius, this Oedipus who has become a perversion of fertility on every level, remains within the *oikos*. His blood ties remain symbolically within the house.[88]

It is worth remembering here the difficulty inherent in establishing identity in the Athenian legal system. In order to prove oneself a citizen in fifth-century Athens, one had to prove that both father and mother were citizens. The former could be, in some cases, difficult; the latter appears never to have been easy. As we saw in Chapter 1, the process of establishing a woman's identity could only rely on a series of recollections of public events during which no citizen stepped forward to deny her citizenship: the marriage ceremony, the introduction of sons into the phratry, the marriage of daughters to citizen men, and the like. The very notion of Athenian citizenship depended on a stable biological identity; that biological identity proved itself, over and over again, impossible to establish with certainty.

Oedipus can transfer his daughters to the son of Menoikeos, but they remain "his" daughters. It seems unlikely that Creon will be able to transfer them to husbands. Their social identity, like Oedipus's, is confirmed by a series of failed displacements, and ultimately rests in their biological link to their father. And that is exactly how ideology—how the production of the subject—works. Against the background of unsuccessful "cultural" productions, it presents itself as "natural," and thus displaces other possible identities. But here, the "natural" relationship is that which is specifically unnatural, a product of excess and a disrupter of difference. The play allows us, if only momentarily and with much effort, to see that even biological identity is potentially unstable, is subject to political and cultural manipulation.

The *Oedipus tyrannus* presents, in this reading, a complex and subtle critique of Athens's insistence on biological citizenship. Oedipus really is the man who killed his father and married his mother. His daughters really are his daughters. But we are unhappy because the play's confirmation of these facts—Oedipus's continued presence in the *oikos*—has now displaced our dramatic and social expectations. The small wrench that we feel as the play fails to achieve closure mirrors the process by which we have seen Oedipus discover who he is. Thus we are afforded a glimpse—perhaps no more—of the workings of ideology. But that perspective does not allow us to escape the world of constructed subjects; like the characters in the play, we have no choice but to leave Oedipus, securely identified, within the house of Laius.

Epilogue　　　EXIT TO SILENCE

> *What would you infer from this? The woman is gone*
> *again, without speaking a word, either good or bad.*

CHORUS OF *Antigone* (speaking of Eurydice)

A hallmark of Sophoclean tragedy is the exit to silence. In several of Sophocles' extant plays, a principal character — often a woman — leaves the stage about two-thirds of the way through the drama. A messenger appears shortly and announces what the audience must surely have been expecting: that the missing character has committed suicide. Reactions to this death then drive the remainder of the play. In each of these cases, we have, directly or indirectly, the exiting character's last words. It will be instructive to consider how these women sum up their lives.

Three of the principal women in this study see their deaths explicitly in terms of their marriages. Loraux suggests that women in tragedy are "wives in their deaths . . . because only their deaths belong to them, and in them they bring their marriages to fulfillment."[1] But, as we have seen, each of the plays treated here has expressed a lack of fulfillment in marriage, even at the moment of death. These plays deny the construction of marriage as a *telos* for the woman. This is not to say that marriage, or death, is not a *telos*. Both are *telē* in fifth-century perception. Electra, for example, clearly does regard marriage as a goal in her life, something from which Aegisthus blocks her. And Oedipus regards the fact that his daughters will be unable to marry as a failure. He instructs Creon, μή σφε, πάτερ, ἴδης / πτωχὰς ἀνάνδρους ἐγγενεῖς ἀλωμένας ("Do not, as their father, watch [i.e., idly] them wandering, husbandless kinswomen, beggars," 1505–6).[2] But the death scenes in Sophocles' plays suggest that women — contrary even to their own expectations — might not have experienced marriage as a fulfillment. Once Sophoclean women are married, as in the case of Deianeira, they find that the marriage itself was not an end. When they die, they do so with a sense of longing for the *process* of marriage (especially continued love-making) that death interrupts.

Antigone, for example, denies fulfillment of any sort. As has been so often noted, Antigone's death is a marriage. But in line after line, Antigone insists that her death represents a lack of marriage:

> ἄλεκτρον, ἀνυμέναιον, οὔτε του γάμου
> μέρος λαχοῦσαν οὔτε παιδείου τροφῆς,
> ἀλλ' ὧδ' ἐρῆμος πρὸς φίλων ἡ δύσμορος
> ζῶσ' ἐς θανόντων ἔρχομαι κατασκαφάς.

> Unbedded, without wedding song, having no share of
>   marriage,
> nor of the nurturing of children,
> but thus, deserted by *philoi*, wretched,
> still living I go to the caves of the dead.[3] (*Antigone* 917–20)

As I discussed earlier, this reverses the usual import of the marriage-as-death theme, which is generally taken as representing the woman's transformation: "Death is a natural metaphor for marriage because, in the course of the wedding procession, the young girl renounces herself."[4] For Antigone, such a death emphasizes only that her life is without proper completion.

As does Electra, moreover, Antigone compares her plight to that of Niobe. Implicit in the reference to Niobe is, of course, Antigone's loss of opportunity to bear children. But unlike Electra, Antigone makes no mention of children — hers or Niobe's. Instead, she emphasizes Niobe's open-ended suffering (χιών τ' οὐδαμὰ λείπει, "The ice-water [i.e., her tears] never ends," 830). Antigone shares in this lack of closure: ᾇ με δαί- / μων ὁμοιοτάταν κατευνάζει ("A *daimon* puts me to sleep just like her," 832–33). The chorus misinterprets Antigone's comparison, hinting that she is preening by comparing herself to an immortal; but for Antigone, the point of the comparison is not that she is *isotheos*, ("godlike"), but rather that she will experience suffering without end. As she walks to her bridal thalamos, then, her experience is entirely one of lack and loss.

One passage from the play might seem to contradict this characterization, the chorus's comment on the death of Haemon and Antigone: κεῖται δὲ νεκρὸς περὶ νεκρῷ, τὰ νυμφικὰ / τέλη λαχὼν δείλαιος ἔν γ' Ἅιδου δόμοις ("Corpse lies on corpse, and the wretch comes upon his / marital completion in the house of Hades," 1240–41). But the subject of these lines is

Haemon, not Antigone.[5] Haemon might have enjoyed a "bridal *telos*" in his death, though in what sense is never made clear. By then Antigone was already dead, and she died without experiencing that completion. Or, if she did experience some sort of marital completion, the text does not describe it.

What of the women who do successfully marry? Deianeira has her husband, and has borne children. Hyllus, her son, is apparently a young man at the time of the play. Yet Deianeira clearly does not see her marriage, and particularly her role as a child-bearer, as finished. Early on she complains about Heracles' long absences in terms of producing children:

> κἀφύσαμεν δὴ παῖδας, οὓς κεῖνός ποτε,
> γῄτης ὅπως ἄρουραν ἔκτοπον λαβών,
> σπείρων μόνον προσεῖδε κἀξαμῶν ἅπαξ.

> And we have borne children, whom he sees then,
> like a farmer visiting an outlying field,
> only once, during sowing and reaping. (*Trachiniae* 31–33)

We might overlook this passage, if Deianeira did not suggest the possibility of producing more children just before she died. As I discussed in Chapter 2, she complains before she stabs herself of τὰς ἄπαιδας ἐς τὸ λοιπὸν οὐσίας ("the house having no children in the future," 911). Her final words, moreover, emphasize that her end is not, for her, a completion:

> ὦ λέχη τε καὶ νυμφεῖ᾽ ἐμά,
> τὸ λοιπὸν ἤδη χαίρεθ᾽, ὡς ἔμ᾽ οὔποτε
> δέξεσθ᾽ ἔτ᾽ ἐν κοίταισι ταῖσδ᾽ εὐνάτριαν.

> Bed, and my marital chamber,
> for the rest, goodbye already, since no longer
> will you receive me as a bedmate in these intercourses.
> (920–22)

If all were well, she seems to suggest, then she and Heracles would continue to have intercourse, and perhaps even produce more children together. The nurse who describes this scene calls Deianeira's end a *telos* (917); but Deianeira experiences it, however unlikely her desire may seem, as a longing for what will never be again.[6]

Jocasta, oddly enough, dies in a way that reminds us of Deianeira. In a sense, Jocasta's problem is that she has been fulfilled overmuch, that she has produced children with both her husband and her son. Yet her last on-stage words sound a little like Deianeira's final words: ἰοὺ ἰού, δύστηνε· τοῦτο γάρ σ᾽ ἔχω / μόνον προσειπεῖν, ἄλλο δ᾽ οὔποθ᾽ ὕστερον ("Alas, alas, wretch; for I am able to address you only thus, / but [will call you] nothing else ever again," (*Oedipus tyrannus* 1071–72). Her regret, too, is over the loss of future opportunity. Even as she recognizes that she can only call Oedipus "wretched," she regrets she will never be able to call him such again.

Jocasta's actual death scene also reads like a variation on Deianeira's. We are told that Jocasta, like Deianeira, γοᾶτο δ᾽ εὐνάς ("groaned over her bed," 1249). Jocasta laments her bed because of what has happened there, rather than because of what will not in the future, but the language is much the same. Even more striking, she laments her former marriage to Laius in the same terms that Deianeira used to lament the loss of Heracles (in indirect speech reported by the messenger):

ἵετ᾽ εὐθὺ πρὸς τὰ νυμφικὰ
λέχη . . .
καλεῖ τὸν ἤδη Λάιον πάλαι νεκρόν,
μνήμην παλαιῶν σπερμάτων ἔχουσ᾽, ὑφ᾽ ὧν
θάνοι μὲν αὐτός.

She went straight to her marriage bed . . .
she called Laius, already long dead,
holding the memory of the long-ago children [literally
   "seeds"], by whom
he [Laius] died. (1242–47)

Jocasta perhaps remembers her children because, as the next phrase tells us, Oedipus is the one who killed Laius (1246–47). But the fact that she remembers the children "long ago" suggests that she is thinking not of recent events, but of having given birth. In any case, in the same moment that Jocasta regrets the unfortunate outcome of her first marriage, her language and actions suggest that she also regrets the early termination of that marriage.

Like Deianeira, moreover, Jocasta cries out when she remembers her previous love-making. Here, too, we see the importance of the messenger-narrator's role in relating this scene. We cannot tell if the comment that Laius's corpse is "already an old corpse" came from Jocasta's mouth or is a comment of the nurse. The former seems unlikely, given Jocasta's emotional state. The latter possibility makes better sense. The nurse, in narrating this event, does not understand why Jocasta should regret now the loss of something that has long been over, and expresses her confusion by emphasizing that Laius is long dead. But for us, Jocasta's death scene, like Deianeira's, expresses a sense of open-endedness to her (legitimate) marriage that continues even to the close of her life.

A particularly interesting feature of the portrayals of these last two women is the strangeness of their last thoughts. It seems odd, to say the least, that two mature women who have borne several children would view their deaths expressly as a loss of opportunity to bear more. I suggest, therefore, that Deianeira and Jocasta provide here a confusing excess of meaning as a direct result of the unfulfilled nature of their marriages. It is most strange that Jocasta should look back, fondly as it seems, to having given birth to Oedipus. She does so because that was the one moment in her life when her role was central, when her actions were meaningful and culturally important. As such, these women demonstrate neatly the concept of women as "other," as being outside of the purview of the masculine world of the play. At the end of their lives, they can only look back to that moment when they had a place, a valued role. Their place at the end of their lives, then, is out of context and out of time. Their concerns do not make sense; their experience, insofar as the plays express it, is incomprehensible.

I have written a good deal about tragedy's reluctance to describe the transformation that marriage represents. Deianeira, in fact, implies that the chorus will not understand what she has gone through till its members, too, are wives (*Trachiniae* 143–49). Similarly, those deaths that take place on the "marriage bed" are not only offstage but hidden even from the narrator. In the *Trachiniae*, the nurse who has been watching Deianeira tells us that she dashed off just at the crucial moment:

> λύει τὸν αὑτῆς πέπλον, ᾧ χρυσήλατος
> προὔκειτο μαστῶν περονίς, ἐκ δ᾽ ἐλώπισεν
> πλευρὰν ἅπασαν ὠλένην τ᾽ εὐώνυμον.
> κἀγὼ δρομαία βᾶσ᾽, ὅσονπερ ἔσθενον,
> τῷ παιδὶ φράζω τῆς τεχνωμένης τάδε.

> She loosened her robe, on which a gold-plated
> buckle lay on her breast, and she uncovered her
> whole side and her left arm,
> and I went running, as fast as I could
> and I told her child that she was contriving these things.
> (924–28)

The *Oedipus tyrannus* uses the same narrative technique: the messenger is on the verge of telling us about Jocasta's death when he announces that he does not know what happened next, for at that moment Oedipus burst in and commanded his attention (1249–54). We must recognize this as a Sophoclean technique. Just at the moment that these women express a sense of incompleteness in their marriages, the play literally makes the description of their deaths (which take place on the marriage bed) incomplete.

Such an understanding is helpful in reading a curious comparison made by Electra, who remains standing (though silenced) at the end of her drama.

For Electra, as I argue, the fact of being unmarried is a continual state of being, a state that she actively pursues and maintains as a reproach to Clytemnestra and Aegisthus. She makes her state of perpetual liminality all the more marked, however, by comparing herself to both Procne and Niobe:

ἀλλ' ἐμέ γ' ἁ στονόεσσ' ἄραρεν φρένας
ἃ Ἴτυν αἰὲν Ἴτυν ολοφύρεται,
ὄρνις ἀτυζομένα, Διὸς ἄγγελος.
ἰὼ παντλάμων Νιόβα, σὲ δ' ἔγωγε νέμω θεόν,
ἅτ' ἐν τάφῳ πετραίῳ,
αἰαῖ, δακρύεις.

But the mourning one is pleasing to my mind,
she who continually laments, "Itys, Itys,"
the distraught bird, messenger of Zeus.
All-suffering Niobe, you I consider divine,
you who pour tears,
alas, in a rocky grave. (*Electra* 147–52)

The immediate point of comparison is between Electra's unrelenting lament for her father, and Procne and Niobe's paradigmatic mourning for their dead children. But Electra's dedication to her father, as I have argued, is part and parcel of her unmarried state. Here, she implicitly compares her lifelong dedication to her father to its structural opposite, marriage and childbirth.

Electra, then, figures a lack of children as a loss of them. The comparison calls to mind the *telos* that Electra will never experience, the bearing of children.[7] And indeed, Electra later blames Aegisthus explicitly for keeping her from producing offspring who would be potential heirs to Agamemnon's estate (964–66). The comparison also reminds us, however, that bearing children is not an end in itself. It, too, can lead to the sort of open-ended lamentation in which Electra engages. Lack of children is only comparable to loss of children insofar as both imply a lack of closure, a fundamental unfulfillment in a woman's life. In the course of the play, Electra never will experience what Procne and Niobe have. But if she did, the image suggests, she might be no more satisfied.

Ajax also dies two-thirds of the way through his drama, and it is instructive to note how his death differs from those of Deianeira, Jocasta, and Antigone. First and foremost, his is an onstage suicide (unique in extant Greek tragedy); it takes on a public aspect from the beginning. In other ways, too, his is a masculine and heroic death. Just before he dies, he has a soliloquy (also rare), and since we get to hear all of his last speech directly, there is no danger of our vision being obscured, of his final words being rendered incomplete. And unlike the women I have been discussing, he does not lament the loss of future intercourse with his spouse. Instead, he asks Zeus to see to it that Teucer will overlook his proper burial, asks the Furies to avenge his death, asks Helios to tell his parents of his death, then takes his leave of the sun and earth (815–65). In short, he is concerned with his heroic *kleos*. Insofar as he is concerned about his death, he speaks not in terms of what he is losing, but in terms of how it will, or should, affect others. He spares no word for his spouse.

Interestingly, however, Ajax's death also leaves his wife in a position similar to that of Antigone, Deianeira, and Jocasta. Tecmessa's case is paradoxical because her marriage literally is not recognized as a marriage, and Ajax does not recognize her as a wife until after his death. She accomplishes this *telos*, then, only when it is guaranteed that her married life will be empty of a husband, when she will be bereft. As I have pointed out at length, moreover, this chapter of her life becomes a silent one.[8] For the last third of the play she does not speak, and is spoken to only rarely, and then primarily in conjunction with her (and, more importantly, Ajax's) son. What kind of fulfillment this is, we can only guess; but in any case, her story ceases to be her own once her marriage is recognized, and her primary function becomes one of creating pathos for her now-dead husband. Hers is also an exit to silence.

I would like to close this study by examining a character in the *Antigone* whose entire role consists of silence, the unhappy Eurydice. As Creon's spouse and Haemon's mother, she is conspicuously absent throughout the play—sequestered indoors, we presume, like a good Athenian wife. She enters suddenly at line 1183, asks the chorus to tell her of Haemon's death, and leaves the stage again, without comment, at 1243. A few minutes later, a messenger relates the details of her death to a grieving Creon. Her death scene is vexed with textual difficulties, but a few points are clear. Her suicide is, as often, figured as a sacrifice, taking place before an altar (*bomia*, 1301). More importantly for my purposes, as she kills herself she regrets the death of not one but two sons: Haemon, and Megareus, dead long ago.

Eurydice's lament has long troubled scholars. The text as Lloyd-Jones/Wilson prints it runs thus:

κωκύσασα μὲν
τοῦ πρὶν θανόντος Μεγαρέως κενὸν λέχος,
αὖθις δὲ τοῦδε, λοίσθιον δὲ σοὶ κακὰς
πράξεις ἐφυμνήσασα τῷ παιδοκτόνῳ.

> Lamenting first,
> the empty marriage bed of Megareus who died before,
> and then of this one (i.e., Haemon), and last reciting
> your base deeds as a child-killer. (1303–5)

The textual difficulty lies in the second line, with the words *kenon lechos* ("empty marriage bed"). The words make sense when applied to Haemon, less so when applied to Megareus. The manuscripts all read *kleinon* ("famous") in 1304 rather than *kenon* ("empty"), but that seems to fit the situation even less well. A number of variants have been suggested, all bringing with them some difficulties.[9] I take Lloyd-Jones and Wilson's text as correct; if the situation does not quite fit Megareus, it is an appropriate course of thought for Eurydice. It is not only her sons' marriage beds that are empty, but hers as well. Earlier she was described as *pammētōr* (1282) of Haemon, a word that in other contexts means "mother of all."[10] Here it is usually taken to mean "the very mother," or "the mother, indeed," of Haemon. If, as the word seems to imply, she found a kind of fulfillment in the role of mother, that role is now empty. Little wonder, then, that she sees the deaths of her sons in terms of empty marriage beds: her marriage, too, has become pointless, an open rift without closure.

But even more important than Eurydice's lament is her silence. When she first leaves the stage, the chorus does not know quite what to make of it. (It is not, evidently, well-schooled in Sophoclean poetics.) The terms it uses are revealing: οὐκ οἶδ'· ἐμοὶ δ' οὖν ἥ τ' ἄγαν σιγὴ βαρὺ / δοκεῖ προσεῖναι χἠ μάτην πολλὴ βοή ("I don't know. It seems to me that this over-heavy silence / goes beyond even a lot of pointless shouting," 1251–52). I suggest that one of the reasons women leave the stage silently in these Sophoclean dramas is that their silence is the correlative of their unresolved marriages. Silence cannot be resolved; it is unbounded. We cannot be sure of what the character has chosen not to say. It matches perfectly, then, the state that we have repeatedly seen for women in marriage. Their social identities are always open to question, because they are not figured as subjects in themselves but are defined, always, in relation to a man. In other words, because women in fifth-century Athens were supposed to be silent, to be kept out of public view, to be removed from a position of subjectivity, they became, in the Athenian imagination, ciphers: unbounded, unresolved, dangerous. The wives in Sophocles' plays embody the paradox of that unbounded position: the men onstage do not know what they are going to do next, because the women do not tell them. And in that moment of not telling, the women enact their position as always unresolved, always left longing. Eurydice's silence is ominous; but what it portends is not just her death, but her lament for marriage beds that will, from now on, be empty.

In a series of articles, Roberts argues that the final lines of Sophoclean plays usually leave some loose ends and point to various unfinished story-lines.[11] Sophocles' dramas, she suggests, resist the closure that an ending implies. For the women of Sophocles' plays, marriage also fails to be a *telos* in the full sense of the word. It may be an end; it may even be their death. But at the moment of death, these women express a regret for lost opportunity and a continued longing for the intimacy and childbirth that can no longer be. Even the description of these women's deaths is often incomplete, interrupted by a character-narrator's shift of attention. Sophocles' dramas represent women's marriages as a state of perpetual and unfulfilled longing. The heroine's exit to silence is both a result and an emblem of this representation.

NOTES

INTRODUCTION

1. I rely largely on Althusser 1971 for my understanding of ideology and the subject. Althusser's formulations have been variously modified by later Marxist scholars, generally on the ground that Althusser does not allow enough for individual consciousness. See, e.g., Zizek 1989, ch. 1; Smith 1988. A useful discussion of Marxist approaches to literature can be found in Rose 1992, introduction.

2. Althusser 1971, 174.

3. Ibid., 181–83.

4. Unless otherwise noted, all references to Sophocles will be taken from the OCT text of Lloyd-Jones and Wilson (1990a). Translations are my own, and are as literal as possible.

5. Althusser's classic (and still useful) definition of ideology. See Althusser 1977, 162.

6. Zizek 1989, 45.

7. Althusser (1971, 165) emphasizes that ideology (as he defines it) has its basis in material culture. See also Williams 1978, 55–71.

8. See Scafuro 1994.

9. Marriage as such is ill-defined in Athenian society; betrothal was clearly delineated, and a transfer of the woman's *kurios* took place, but as for marriage per se, it is well to remember Vernant's statement, "Marriage is first and foremost a state of fact, the fact being συνοικεῖν" (Vernant 1980, 47).

10. See, for example, Williams 1978 and Macherey 1978. Seaford 1994 is an unusually comprehensive attempt to understand Greek tragedy in terms of Athenian cult practice. See esp. chs. 6, 8–10 there.

11. See, e.g., Katz 1994; Rabinowitz 1993; Zeitlin 1990a; Foley 1981; Gould 1980. Gomme 1925 presents an early formulation of the problem.

12. Such a generic force may well be at work: Seaford (1994, 361–62) points out that tragedy tends to focus on the destruction of the family, even when the epic source-material does not.

13. See Katz 1994; Zeitlin 1992; Foley 1992 and 1981; Bergren 1992.

14. Zeitlin 1990b.

15. Seaford 1994, 345–47.

16. Ibid., 351, 384.

17. For a full-scale discussion of this legislation, see Patterson 1981. Boegehold (1994) argues persuasively that Pericles' law was a codification of prevalent public attitudes, as a growing number of citizens began to compete for limited land-inheritances.

18. See especially Patterson 1990, 61.

19. See Scafuro 1994, 156–57.

20. See, e.g., Lysias 1, and Euripides' *Ion* and *Hippolytus*. It must be admitted that none of our legal speeches is exactly contemporary with Sophocles; the earliest comes from the last years of the fifth century, and some that I discuss below belong to the middle of the fourth. Nonetheless, events in the fifth century (such as the affair concerning Pericles' sons) indicate similar legal concerns.

21. Sutton 1981, esp. 212–13. More recently, see Petersen 1997, 44–49.

22. Such concern is also present in Xenophon's *Oikonomikos*, as Sutton (1981, 224) points out.

23. See, for example, Sappho 96, and duBois's discussion (1988, 26–27).

24. See duBois 1988, 65–68. Obviously, these are not hard and fast lines. One can easily find examples of women as unploughed fields in tragedy (e.g., Aeschylus's *Agamemnon* 1387–92). Ideologies do not change overnight. As with any cultural phenomenon, we are speaking here of a matter of degrees.

25. It appears, for example, that Euripides' first version of the *Hippolytus* was booed off the stage, probably because the character of Phaedra was too forward. See Barrett, 1964, 11–15.

26. See Seaford 1986, passim; also Redfield 1982. Seaford 1994 explores the question of why tragedy so often perverts familiar rituals; on marriage, see especially ch. 6 and 8.

27. This is not to say that marriage is not a rite of passage for men. But men, typically, have other rites to mark their passage into the world of adults — ceremonies in the context of hunting and war, for example. Women lack such other ceremonies; for them, therefore, marriage is of prime importance. See Chapter 1 for further discussion.

28. See, e.g., Case 1988, 7, cited, with a useful discussion, in Rabinowitz 1993, 1–3. Seaford (1994, 311), suggests that the function of maenadism was specifically to express and contain the threat that female sexuality posed to marriage and to the *polis*.

29. Hexter and Selden 1992, xiv.

30. On Aeschylus, see Zeitlin 1992 (*Suppliants*) and 1978 (*Oresteia*); duBois 1988,

140–47 (*Suppliants*). On Euripides, see Rabinowitz 1993; Loraux 1993, ch. 5 (*Ion*); Rabinowitz 1986 and 1987 (*Hippolytus*); Foley 1992 (*Alcestis* and *Helen*) and 1982a (*Iphigenia at Aulis*); Powell 1990 (several essays on various plays).

31. Segal has done extensive work on marriage in Sophocles, focusing mainly on the *Trachiniae*. See Segal 1992 and 1975.

32. E.g., *Agamemnon* 1387–92, and frag. 44. I discuss both of these in more depth in Chapter 1.

33. See duBois 1988, 65. A famous example is Creon's line 569 in the *Antigone*.

34. See duBois 1988, 130–66.

35. For the association of Phaedra's use of the tablet with her own sexuality, see Rabinowitz 1993, 166–69; 1987, 134.

36. As duBois (1988, 161) points out. This episode receives more detailed treatment in Chapter 2.

37. There is virtually no marriage material in the *Philoctetes*; what there is in the *Oedipus at Colonus* is not central to the play, and in any case largely duplicates the concepts I discuss in the *Antigone* and *Oedipus tyrannus*.

38. Though such caveats are common, it is typical to ignore them once made. Reed 1995 is especially good on the masculine aspect of myths about strong women (see esp. 332–33).

39. D. Konstan suggests in correspondence that "law and poetry are both encoded in texts, but they represent different discourses," which sums up the relation nicely. Althusser would say that these different texts possess different "modalities of material existence" (Althusser 1971, 166).

CHAPTER 1

1. It appears that the state of matrimony (unlike the *engyēsis*) was not legally defined—which makes it quite difficult to determine exactly what constituted legitimate marriage beyond the fact of *sunoikein*. See Vernant 1980, 47ff.; Just 1989, 43–45.

2. I have assembled this brief account from useful summaries in several modern works, most notably Ogden 1996, 83–87; Rehm 1994, 11–21; Oakley and Sinos 1993; Garland 1990, 217–25; Just 1989, 40–76; Sutton 1981, 150–59; Flaceliere 1959, 80–87. References to the appropriate ancient sources can be found in their notes. Needless to say, we are not nearly as sure about these proceedings as my account might suggest. Our sources range from interpretations of fifth-century vase paintings to the questionable and late accounts given in Pausanias. A useful discussion of Athenian myths about marriage (including several of the texts treated in what follows) appears in Tyrrell and Brown 1991, 99–132. Oakley and Sinos 1993 is the first work to attempt a reconstruction of the complete wedding ceremony from evidence of pottery, and is particularly helpful.

3. Boegehold (1994) argues that Pericles' legislation probably reflected current practice in the law courts. It may not, therefore, have been as radical a change in practice as is sometimes assumed.

4. Patterson 1990, 61. See also Seaford 1994, 214–16.

5. The definitive work is Patterson 1981. It is not entirely clear when living with a non-Athenian became illegal in itself. Pericles' legislation of 451/50 discouraged such arrangements, but does not seem to have prohibited them (Patterson 1990, 62). Scafuro (1994, 156–57) and Patterson (1994, 207) argue that the marriage itself is not illegal, but only the attempt to pass off one's spouse as a citizen.

6. All references to Demosthenes are taken from the OCT edition of W. Rennie (1921 [vol. 2] and 1931 [vol. 3]). See Patterson 1994 for an illuminating discussion of the issues in this case.

7. Patterson (1994, 207–8) points out that Apollodorus never proves that the daughter, Phano, is an alien. Her status is assumed from the fact of her two divorces. In addition, the speaker does not mention Neaira's two sons, or question their entry into Stephanus's phratry. It is possible that their status as citizens was more easily verified.

8. Typical of Athenian court cases; see Scafuro 1994.

9. On the myth of autochthony, see Loraux 1993, 37–71. Patterson (1987) provides an important response (she is responding to the original publication of Loraux in French), emphasizing women's valued position in the household and the city.

10. Sealey 1990, 21ff. Women could be "introduced" to the phratry, but were not listed as members in it. "The proper inference is that women were not so enrolled" (24). See also Cole 1984, 235–36.

11. See also Gould 1980, 50ff; Foley 1982b, passim.

12. Sealey 1990, 14. Cf also Patterson 1987, 52; Gould 1980, 44.

13. Patterson 1987, 63 and passim. Patterson (1994, 200–203) also argues for an understanding of Athenian women as citizens.

14. Scafuro 1994.

15. On which the best discussion is Patterson's appendix in Patterson 1990, 70–73.

16. Similarly, Ciron's son in Isaeus 8.18–20 offers circumstantial evidence that his mother was, in fact, married to his father: a wedding feast is cited, as is the fact that Ciron's sons were all introduced to the phratry, and that no objection was made at that time, etc. See Cole 1984, 236, for an argument that the gamēlia, or wedding feast, served the purpose of publicly recognizing the new bride as a legitimate citizen wife.

17. Scafuro 1994, 172.

18. Patterson 1987, passim; and Sealey 1990, 44: "The language of the law spoke of the women themselves as becoming owners by inheritance."

19. Patterson 1990, 55.

20. A number of scholars trace this suspicion back to the myths of archaic Greece, and specifically the story of Pandora. See, e.g., Loraux 1993, 37–71; Bergren 1983; Pucci 1977, 82–126. Zeitlin 1990a and 1981 are brilliant discussions of female mimesis and its role on the Athenian stage.

21. Vernant (1983) roams over a full range of texts for his examples, many of which are not from the fifth century. The summary here only sketches the main points of his argument; more concrete examples will follow.

22. Jameson (1990, 98, 105–6) points out that very few actual fifth-century Athenian houses had hearths. As Jameson notes, however, the hearth continues to play an

important role in literary houses. Its poetic existence outlives its actual existence. We need not, therefore, deny the hearth's importance to Athenian ideology.

23. Vernant 1983, 133.

24. Ibid., 132; emphasis mine.

25. Gould 1980, 46.

26. See Zizek 1989, 24–25, for a discussion of the relational nature of all identities.

27. Exceptions include Euripides' *Ion* and, as I argue, Sophocles' *Ajax*.

28. Seaford 1994, 217–19; Sealey 1990, 25ff.; Goldhill 1986, 72; Lacey 1968, ch. 5; Wolff 1944, 46ff. For the concept in Western society in general, see Rubin 1975. See below for further clarification of the exact terms of the transaction.

29. Found in various fragments of Menander, e.g., *Dyskolos* 842ff. A full list of citations can be found in Gould 1980, 53. We should note with Patterson (1990, 56 n. 64), however, that this formula is not found outside Menander and may not be authentic for the fifth century.

30. The marriage also contains elements of a less formal arrangement; see below on abduction marriages, and Chapter 2.

31. See Rubin 1975; Sedgwick 1985; Just 1989, 46–47. Humphreys (1986) shows that matrikin often play an important role as witnesses in legal cases, so that women quite literally create important links between men of different families.

32. See Sedgwick 1985, chs. 1–2; Rubin 1975, passim.

33. The structure persists in modern Hollywood cinema: see, e.g., *Tin Men, Tango and Cash, Tequila Sunrise, Lethal Weapon 2, Face/Off*, or any of a number of other "buddy movies."

34. For full-scale treatments, see Rabinowitz 1993, and Wohl 1998. I discuss the workings of homosocial desire in the *Trachiniae* at length in the next chapter.

35. Rabinowitz 1993, 1986, and 1987.

36. All references to Euripides are from the OCT edition of Diggle (1981, 1984).

37. Rabinowitz 1993, 166–69; 1987, 135. Rabinowitz's analysis is bolstered by a Lacanian model of paternity/law/language as an expression of authority.

38. See, for example, Euripides' *Alcestis* 533ff. (cited in Patterson 1987, 56; see the full discussion in Rehm 1994, 92). Also see Vernant 1983, 133 and passim. It is important to remember that it is exactly this sort of infiltration that legal speeches (e.g., [Demosthenes] 59) are trying to prevent.

39. Wolff 1944, 48ff.

40. Gould 1980, 43.

41. Wolff 1944, 53. See also Garland 1990, 237: "So we should probably think of a married woman not so much as alienated from her natal home as entrusted to her marital one."

42. Garland (1990, 217) points out that Sparta had a similar institution; such a woman there would be called a *patrouchos*.

43. The most-often cited version of this law is in Plutarch's *Solon* 20.2–4. Good discussions of the position of *epiklēroi* can be found in Sealey 1990, 29–30; MacDow-

ell 1978, 95–98; Just 1989, 95–98; Lacey 1968, 139–45. For a full citation of all the sources, see Broadbent 1968, 203ff. Patterson (1994, 212 n. 9) argues that we should see such women as "real heirs," though most scholars see them as merely transferring the inheritance to a male owner.

44. For example, see Andocides 1.117–23.

45. Vernant 1983, 142ff.

46. Ibid., 133. See also MacDowell 1989, 15: "Normally the term *oikos*, when it refers to persons, refers to the line of descent from father to son through successive generations."

47. I borrow the phrase from Gould 1980, 43. See also Just 1989, 76.

48. Isaeus 3.64. In a particularly acute analysis, Patterson (1990, 73) argues that such a possibility may be the unstated background of this speech.

49. MacDowell (1978, 96) argues that a woman would not be considered an *epiklēros* if she had already borne a son, but does not provide the source for this argument. Just (1989, 96–97) expresses doubt about this suggestion.

50. An exception may be Euripides' *Ion:* see Loraux 1993, 184–236.

51. See the analysis in duBois 1988, 141. For a full treatment, see Zeitlin 1992.

52. The myth of Mestra provides a particularly telling example, as I argue in a forthcoming paper.

53. Redfield 1982, 188. Redfield here draws on terminology developed by Lévi-Strauss.

54. Foxhall 1989, 43.

55. In Euripides' *Helen*, Menelaus must undergo a false death in order to maintain his marriage to Helen and rescue her from Egypt; here, as in the *Antigone*, his marriage-as-death seems modeled on the more typically female trope.

56. See Cole 1984, 233–37.

57. It is disputed when this phase of life became part of a formal, state institution; our earliest solid evidence dates from the fourth century. Winkler 1990b compiles all the evidence.

58. See Cole 1984, 243.

59. Redfield 1982, 187. For some of the symbolic trappings of this rite of passage, and its civic importance, see Burkert 1966, passim; Seaford 1987, 106.

60. Though *kurios* is a fifth-century term, the abstract form (*kurieia*) does not appear until the second century B.C.E. See LSJ ad loc.

61. See Garland 1990, 214.

62. As Patterson (1987, 56) points out.

63. See Dougherty 1993, ch. 4, for a discussion of the way that narratives of marriage are mapped onto narratives of colonization, in which Greek men resolve differences with indigenous populations by marrying these foreign women.

64. King (1983) discusses marriage as an attempt by Greek male culture to control the physiological changes that women undergo. See Dean-Jones 1992 for a sophisticated analysis of the way the medical texts construct masculine and feminine desire differently.

65. See duBois 1988, 39–64. Examples include Sappho 94; Aeschylus frag. 44; in

the *Theogony*, Gaia mates with Ouranos, 132ff. Patterson (1987, 56–57) argues that this imagery valorizes women. See Aeschylus *Agamemnon* 1387–92 for a reversal of this imagery.

66. See duBois 1988, 65–85. Seaford 1987, 106, has a useful and concise summary of typical wedding imagery. A good discussion can also be found in Goldhill 1986, 207ff.

67. DuBois 1988, 65.

68. See ibid., 43.

69. The most important work done with this imagery remains Stigers's (1981) article on Sappho. See also Seaford 1987, 111. His n. 58 gives a list of relevant passages in tragedy, including *Euripides Bacchae* 468; *Phoenician Women* 337, 1366; *Iphigenia at Aulis* 698; *Trojan Women* 676; *Alcestis* 994; etc. See also Gould 1980, 53; Sourvinou-Inwood 1987, 138; Seaford 1986, 51–53; King 1983, 111. I discuss Sophocles' *Trachiniae* 536 in Chapter 2. Note also that this imagery is not used exclusively for women. Men are also "yoked" by marriage. Only women, however, are wild animals who must be tamed.

70. See Dougherty 1993, ch. 4, for the use of this motif in narratives of colonization.

71. This is exactly the structure that Ortner argues has been used by virtually every culture to insure masculine superiority: man is to culture what woman is to nature (Ortner 1974, passim).

72. A more prosaic account of this idea can be seen in Xenophon's *Oikonomikos*. For a reading of this text that emphasizes the affection between husband and wife, see Scaife 1995.

73. Lysias 1.6ff.

74. Ajax expresses a similar doubt about his son: "If he truly is my son, from the father's side" (Sophocles *Ajax* 547).

75. This passage receives a fuller treatment below.

76. Though Walker (1983, 81) argues that this must have been more an ideal than a practical reality, much in this picture is no doubt correct. A good example of such an account is still Pomeroy's (1975, chs. 5, 6). Garland (1990, 199–241) gives a balanced view of both negative and positive elements of marriage.

77. Foxhall 1989, 25ff.

78. In general, see Schaps 1979 for women's economic rights and powers.

79. Foxhall 1989, 38. She also notes that Plato's *Laws* 6.774c advises against large dowries for women, as it leads to too powerful a voice for them. The law code at Gortyn grants even greater economic rights to the woman on divorce; see Lefkowitz and Fant 1992, 55–58.

80. D. Konstan points out in correspondence that in New Comedy, the father can intervene if the marriage is going badly — e.g., *Epitrepontes, Stichus, Menaechmi*. Similarly, in Terence's *Hecyra*, the bride returns to her own home when she thinks she is pregnant by a man other than her husband. The husband's family (the husband is away) assumes that *they* have injured her in some way, and endeavor to persuade her to return to their house.

81. As McManus (1990, 229) points out.

82. See the discussion of a fragment from Sophocles' *Tereus*, below.

83. This is in part due to the tendency in tragedy, as Seaford puts it, for "the negative to prevail." Seaford 1987, 107 and passim.

84. Text is that of Radt 1977 (= 524 Nauck).

85. Presumably the speaker refers not to a dowry, but to a *hedna*, or bride-price, a practice that seems to disappear from use in the fifth century.

86. Patterson 1990, 61. It is not entirely clear whether marriage to a non-Athenian was actually illegal in Pericles' time, but, as Patterson points out, if it were not, it would leave an awkward gap in the laws, since children of such a union would be able to inherit family property but not citizenship.

87. The topic is treated most helpfully in Seaford 1987, which gives an extensive list of the most common images and cites numerous instances of each. See also duBois 1988, passim. Dougherty 1993, ch. 4, is particularly useful for agricultural metaphors.

88. On the general topic, see Rehm 1994.

89. See Foley 1982a for a full investigation of Euripides' version. Seaford 1987, 125ff.; Armstrong and Ratchford 1985, 9–12; and Cunningham 1984, passim, all show that Aeschylus's version also describes Iphigenia's sacrifice in terms reminiscent of marriage.

90. See Seaford 1987, 120ff.

91. Ibid., 127–28.

92. See ibid., 114. Seaford here summarizes Lebeck. For a full-scale treatment of the Danaids' experience of marriage, see Zeitlin 1992.

93. Loraux 1987, 23.

94. As Redfield (1982, 181) does: "The joys of marriage are undramatic. . . . We should therefore not be surprised to find that marriage in Greek drama . . . is always something broken and in crisis: this fact tells us little about Greek culture."

95. See, for example, Peek 1988 [1955], nos. 658, 1162, 1238, 1551, 1553, 1989 (cited in Seaford 1987, 106 n. 11).

96. Seaford 1987, 108; Burkert 1983, 62–63.

97. See Rabinowitz 1993, esp. 31–99.

98. Arthur 1977, 12–13.

99. Rehm (1994) sets out to use the set of imagery as a "fulcrum" (9) to analyze various aspects of Greek tragedy; but he does not put forth an interpretation of the imagery as a whole. Rabinowitz (1993) is an exception: in 31–99, she analyzes the way in which Euripidean heroines who sacrifice themselves enable the continuation of the state.

100. Prose texts provide an exception: Ischomachus in Xenophon's *Oikonomikos* believes that his wife's transformation is successful, and portrays her as a willing subject within the household. Among Athenian tragedies, only Euripides' *Alcestis* shows the process from beginning to end, and the success of the marriage there is open to debate. See esp. O'Higgins 1993.

101. For a full discussion, see Seaford 1986, passim.

102. Even in the *Alcestis*, once Alcestis returns from the underworld to restart her marriage, she is bound to silence for the remainder of the play. Foley (1992, 148) suggests that those plays that do present marriage as successful do so in the context of *remarriage*.

103. Seaford 1986, 58.

104. The exception, of course, is when the transformation ends in death. Cf. Loraux 1987, 28. Even so, their fulfillment becomes masculinized: "When young girls die, or when, as we have seen, wives die, there are no words able to denote the glory of a woman that do not belong to the knowledge of male renown. And glory always makes the blood of women flow" (ibid., 48).

105. Dean-Jones (1992, 75) points out that mastery over sexual impulses was a sign of manhood, and that "it was an axiom of society that women had a greater appetite for sex and less self-control than men."

106. Text is the OCT edition of D. Page (1972).

107. Zeitlin 1978.

108. McManus 1990, 232. A particularly illuminating example of such anthropological work is Winkler 1990a.

109. Reed (1995) is more forthright than most on these issues, responding in part to Winkler 1990a. Petersen (1997) attempts to read female subjectivity from vases, but does so largely by glossing over the problems of male authorship.

110. For a full-scale discussion in terms of Lacanian psychology, see Irigaray 1985a.

111. Sutton disagrees with this interpretation: "[This position] is not . . . associated exclusively with sexual leading off, and cannot be regarded as a survival of a primitive practice of marriage by capture" (1981, 182). Sourvinou-Inwood (1987, 139) sees evidence of mock abduction within the wedding ceremony on other vases.

112. Sourvinou-Inwood 1987, passim.

113. Ibid., 147.

114. Keuls 1984, 295.

115. Deianeira's crossing of the river on the back of Nessus is, of course, complicated. It will receive a full treatment below.

116. Jenkins 1983, 140–41.

117. Evans-Grubbs 1989. Evans-Grubbs's focus is Roman law, but she traces the patterns of behavior back to archaic Greece.

118. Ibid., 62.

119. Sutton 1981, 212–13. Sourvinou-Inwood sees a similar element of consent in the vases portraying erotic pursuits (1987, 140ff.).

120. Sutton 1981, 184. Of course, what the groom intends in his iconographic glance is largely a matter of interpretation.

121. Ibid., 214–15.

122. McManus 1990, 231.

123. Myself included. McManus (1990) seems simply to assume that brides would be, so that she (ironically) is reinscribing the ideology that she discusses. It is equally valid, and possibly more productive, to assume that "we have evidence here for an alternative erotic paradigm," as D. Konstan suggests to me in correspondence.

124. Redfield 1982, 191–92. See also Sutton 1981, 165, 185; Oakley and Sinos (1993) are generally more optimistic about the bride's experience than I am (see Ormand 1996b).

125. As Althusser points out, ideology works so that subjects "work by themselves" (1971, 182). Dean-Jones (1992, 82) remarks: "The functional model of female sexual appetite rationalized and integrated the cultural belief that women were constantly desirous of intercourse with the societal need for obedient and chaste wives who were always ready to produce heirs and citizens."

126. Evans-Grubbs 1989, 63.

127. The most recent treatment is Perkins 1996. See also Faraone 1990, 238; Richardson 1974, ad line 213. I am grateful to N. Evans for first pointing this out to me.

128. Text is Richardson 1974.

129. Faraone 1990, 243.

130. See also ibid., 238 on the myth of Atalanta. There, Faraone argues, accepting the apple is a way to "display her consent to the seduction which is always implicit in marriage."

131. Text is that of Perrin 1914.

132. A euphemism for sex. The legal texts are quite reluctant to name the sexual act.

133. Faraone 1990, 231, 236ff.

134. Just 1989, 95–98.

135. Text is that of Forster 1927.

136. Isaeus 3.6; a similar imputation at Demosthenes 40.8ff.; [Demosthenes] 59.13.

137. See Patterson 1994, 210.

138. "L'acquittement prononcé fait Hypermestre un 'sujet de droit'; elle peut se lier elle-même à l'homme qu'elle prefêre. . . . Le mariage d'Hypermestre n'a pas en vue la production d'enfants dont la legitimite devrait être affirmée" (Detienne 1988, 172).

139. Text is that of Radt 1985.

140. See the particularly keen discussion in Zeitlin 1992, 230–31.

141. Seaford 1987, 110–11.

142. I have, in this rapid survey, largely ignored the evidence of comic texts. Even plays such as the *Lysistrata*, however, prove surprisingly conservative when it comes to the function of female desire: women's desire in the *Lysistrata* is held up as a display of female incompetence, and as evidence of men's right to rule. See Foley 1982b, passim.

143. See Reed 1995.

CHAPTER 2

1. For a summary of Deianeira's focus on her marriage, see Kraus 1991, 79–88.

2. Segal 1992 (reprinted in Segal 1995, ch. 3) presents a useful reading of all these marriages as perversions of the normal order, both of marriage and of the larger uni-

verse. For a Freudian reading of the sexual imagery that runs throughout this play, see Wender 1974.

3. I follow here the argument of Sedgwick 1985, chs. 1 and 2.

4. See Rubin 1975. Rubin's work is a recasting of Lévi-Strauss 1969, which, unlike the work of Rubin, Irigaray, et al., assumes that such a system of relationships is proper and natural.

5. This understanding of male-male relations is closely allied, of course, to Girard's theory of mimetic desire. Sedgwick freely acknowledges her use of Girard 1972; for a brief overview and useful examples of mimetic desire, see Girard 1990, 89–108.

6. See especially the excellent discussion of Sedgwick 1985, 1–5.

7. Wohl (1998) analyzes this play in similar terms and has independently reached many of the same conclusions that I do. I am grateful to Professor Wohl for allowing me to see her excellent discussion of this play before publication.

8. Seaford 1986, 58.

9. I prefer this reading (with Kamerbeek and Easterling) over ὄτλον, printed by Lloyd-Jones and Wilson 1990a and by Dawe. See the sensible comments by Easterling 1982, ad loc.

10. Wender (1974, 5) suggests that Achelous is "simply a fearful young girl's fantasy of adult sex." This goes too far in the other direction; the remarkable thing about the passage is the juxtaposition of a genuinely fantastic creature with Deianeira's relatively typical reaction.

11. A vexed line; some read θατὴρ ("watcher") for μάτηρ (see Easterling 1982, ad loc.).

12. Wohl (1998, 21–22) discusses these lines as creating for Deianeira an impossible subjectivity, a male fantasy of female space in which she (as subject) neither sees nor is seen.

13. Seaford 1986, 53. He discusses as a parallel, for example, Euripedes' *Iphigenia at Aulis* 1083–88. Of course, one of the effects of the image is to reinforce the traditional view of the bride as an animal that must be tamed: see Gould 1980, 53.

14. Deianeira refers to the battle at line 26 as a τέλος, a word often used of weddings (see Seaford 1986, 54).

15. Armstrong 1986, 101. The observations that follow are all Armstrong's. Segal (1992, 86) also comments on this as a perversion of the normal wedding procession.

16. Armstrong 1986, 101. For complaint of this sort of separation from paternal family, see Chapter 1.

17. Seaford 1986, 54–55. He also points to the fear for one's husband that Deianeira suggests every married woman must feel, 144–50 (discussed below). See also Segal 1992, 73–74.

18. Loraux 1987, 25. Seaford (1986, 58) makes a similar observation.

19. I agree with Seaford (1986) that this is the correct reading here, contra Lloyd-Jones and Wilson (1990a), who follow Nauck's suggestion of ἐρῆμοι (which would then modify the altars, rather than Deianeira).

20. Seaford 1986, 57–58.

21. Ibid., 58.

22. Cited in Chapter 1.

23. She is, to my knowledge, the only woman in tragedy to refer to herself in this manner.

24. See Vernant 1983, 133 and 139ff.

25. Segal (1981, 45) takes Deianeira's marginality in these lines as fact, and suggests that "she is a field that stands at the edge of the cultivated and domesticated land, at the point of contact with the wild." I suggest instead that Deianeira believes that she should be central, and resents that Heracles treats her as marginal. There is little to suggest that, in the time frame of the play, Deianeira is "at the point of contact with the wild."

26. I print the text as given in Lloyd-Jones and Wilson (1990a), which is virtually that of Seaford (1986, 50). Seaford proves without question that Dawe (1984) is wrong to delete 144–46; Easterling (1982) also prints 144–46.

27. See especially Seaford 1987, 111; Segal 1981, 84, also has a useful discussion of the image as a transformation from innocence to experience.

28. Wohl (1998, 47–49) provides a keen reading of this passage. She sees in it a particular female subjectivity, located in a lyric rather than a tragic mode.

29. Seaford 1986, 55.

30. See Winnington-Ingram 1982, 239: "Patient of her husband's neglect, tolerant of his amours, submissive and devoted, a mother of children, she has all the merits a wife should have by the strictest standards of fifth century convention."

31. Wohl 1998, ch. 3, shows persuasively that Deianeira creates a subjectivity for Iole that mirrors her own.

32. Rabinowitz (1992, 45) finds Iole a doublet of Deianeira, so that "two stages of women's lives are represented simultaneously." Segal (1992, 67–68, 71–75) makes a similar finding. Segal sees the "marriage" of Heracles and Iole as a perverted version of that of Heracles and Deianeira, since in the former case Heracles resorts to violence rather than an orderly exchange. I see both exchanges as variant modes within the same system.

33. See especially Evans-Grubbs 1989; Jenkins 1983.

34. Wender 1974, 5. Again we see the interesting inversion of Deianeira's marriage: Deianeira's "labor pangs" are caused by Heracles' absence rather than his presence.

35. Segal 1977, 115, lists several such parallels.

36. See Seaford 1987, 111.

37. Text from Radt 1977.

38. Segal 1992, 71–75.

39. Wohl (1998, 26–29) points out that this economic language renders Iole an object of "commodity exchange" rather than the gift exchange that Lichas has earlier indicated. As such, these lines also serve to disavow Deianeira's status as an equal partner in gift-giving with Heracles.

40. Which, as various people have commented, seems to be basically true. Heracles' service to Omphale is confirmed by Hyllus, lines 69–70. Lichas lies by omis-

sion, not commission: Scodel 1984, 35, provides a useful discussion. Winnington-Ingram 1980, 332–33, gives the fullest attempt to resolve the different versions into a single coherent sequence of events. See also Parlavantaza-Friederich 1969, 26–29. Halleran (1986) suggests that Lichas's lies render him an untrustworthy narrator throughout.

41. Scodel 1984, 35.

42. Winnington-Ingram (1980, 333) suggests something similar: "The lost sources may have linked the quarrel and the drunkenness with Heracles' lustful demand for Iole." We might also simply say that the two stories express the same "paradigmatic order" — see Peradotto 1977 for the concept and a useful explanation of the limits of such analysis.

43. Kamerbeek (1970, ad loc.) points out that *phutosporos* is a *hapax* in Sophocles. It serves, of course, to remind us of the frequent agricultural metaphors that bolster the idea of marriage as a transaction between men.

44. Again, this part of Lichas's story seems true, since it is the only reason ever given for Heracles' service to Omphale, which is confirmed by Hyllus (above).

45. I am reminded of Herodotus's statement (1.5) that, while stealing women is wrong, it is foolish to make a fuss about it afterward. Women are used as an excuse for wars, but, Herodotus implies, there is a deeper enmity at work.

46. Noted by Segal (1975, 44).

47. Wohl (1998, 8) reaches the same conclusion: "Instead of redeeming his temporary servitude to Omphale, the capture of Iole evokes and repeats that episode."

48. As Stigers (1981) argues, men's poetry typically describes the male lover as powerful in the face of the love object, but helpless before *Erōs*. In my analysis, Heracles also fits this pattern.

49. Ironically, in this particular case, Heracles' dominance becomes a threat to civilization itself, as he takes on the role of city-destroyer. Sorum 1978, 63ff., provides a good discussion of this ambiguity in Heracles' character, echoed in Segal 1992, 71–75.

50. Dawe (1984) places a loss of two half-lines here, but I do not see that it is necessary.

51. Wohl (1998, 38–41) argues that Deianeira also attributes to Iole an active, desiring subjectivity (cf. especially lines 443–44). This curious ascription further supports Deianeira's insecurity, and her failure to realize that her (and Iole's) desires have no force in this situation.

52. Wohl (1998, 26) shows that Deianeira initially sees herself as a subject in gift exchange with Heracles. She explicitly sends him the poisoned robe in exchange for Iole. Iole's status as "cargo" (see above), however, puts this relation in an ambivalent position.

53. Though at 631 she speaks of her desire for him, she does so only to express the fear that her desire will not be reciprocated. Here as elsewhere, she desires to be desired.

54. Segal 1981, 88, echoed in Segal 1992, 80, though less forcefully. Segal also suggests (1992, 89) that she is closer to Penelope than to Medea or Clytemnestra.

Wohl (1998, ch. 3), however, has pointed out that Deianeira does see herself as actively exchanging gifts with Heracles. In some ways, then, Deianeira does claim a subjectivity. I agree with Wohl's acute observations here, but maintain that Deianeira figures herself more as object than as subject in erotic relations.

55. Wohl (1998, 8) points out that Heracles uses language to describe Deianeira's robe that recalls Clytemnestra's nets in the *Agamemnon* (cf. *Trachiniae* 1051–52, *Agamemnon* 1382, 1580). I would point out, however, that this is Heracles' view of Deianeira, not her own.

56. DuBois 1979, 41.

57. See Sedgwick 1985, 56ff.

58. See duBois 1988, 151–56, for a lucid analysis of the *Trachiniae*; 130–66, on women as tablets in general.

59. The discrepancy between the two oracles is nicely pointed out and discussed in Lawrence 1978, 291ff. See also Bowman 1996.

60. Segal (1975, 48) points out the parallel with 156–57.

61. Henderson 1975, 146. See also duBois 1988, 130–66; Rabinowitz 1986b, 134. Other ancient parallels include Aristophanes' *Lysistrata* 151; Artemidorus *Oneirocritica* 2.45: Ἔτι καὶ πινακὶς γυναῖκα σημαίνει διὰ τὸ τύπους παντοδαποὺς γραμμάτων ἐπιδέχεσθαι. "τύπους" δὲ ἐν τῇ συνηθείᾳ καὶ τὰ τέκνα καλοῦμεν. ("And the tablet signifies a woman, because tablets receive every sort of imprint of letters. So we also call children 'imprints' in customary speech.")

62. Rabinowitz (1986b, 134) argues that Phaedra's *deltos* represents her vagina: she inscribes both with the (false) accusation of rape.

63. DuBois 1988, 162.

64. Ibid., 154.

65. One might think in particular of Socrates' complaint about the written word in Plato's *Phaedrus*: ὅταν δὲ ἅπαξ γραφῇ, κυλινδεῖται μὲν πανταχοῦ πᾶς λόγος ὁμοίως παρὰ τοῖς ἐπαίουσιν, ὡς δ' αὕτως παρ' οἷς οὐδὲν προσήκει, καὶ οὐκ ἐπίσταται λέγειν οἷς δεῖ γε καὶ μή ("But when once you write it down, each argument rolls around everywhere, going likewise to those who can hear and to those for whom it is inappropriate; and it does not know to whom it should speak and to whom it should not," 275d–e).

66. DuBois 1988, 161.

67. I am grateful to David Halperin for this observation.

68. Noted by Sorum (1978, 67).

69. Rabinowitz (1987) demonstrates a similar pattern of resolution in the *Hippolytus*.

70. Lloyd-Jones and Wilson (1990a) bracket the line. I believe that it is genuine.

71. I would like to note here a particularly apt typographical error of Kamerbeek (1970). At line 879 he states: "There are perhaps more miserable ways of dying than by the word" (for "word" read "sword," I presume).

72. Wohl 1998, 36.

73. Hyllus is speaking, of course, but he is reporting his father's cries in indirect

speech, and there is no reason to suppose that Heracles referred to the marriage in some other way.

74. Sedgwick speaks in another context of the fact that "a stable relation to a woman is impossible in the context of male transactive circulation" (1985, 53).

75. Segal (1992, 84) argues that in the course of the play, Heracles plays every part in a wedding: that of husband, bride, and finally (in regard to Iole and Hyllus) father of the bride.

76. An interesting inclusion, since Hera's complaint against Heracles is a result of a situation analogous to Deianeira's. Zeus slept with Alcmene to produce Heracles, and Hera resents this infidelity.

77. Deianeira is here included in the generalized masculine plural of *kakous*, so she is *grammatically* indistinguishable from Heracles' former enemies as well. I am grateful to Peter Rose for this observation.

78. Reinhardt 1979, 59. It is also worth noting that the poison itself is personified as a monster: see Sorum 1978, 59–60, for a list of examples.

79. Segal (1992, 69) points out that Hyllus comes of age in this scene, and is called *anēr* (1238) instead of *pais*. Wohl (1998, 11–16) discusses Hyllus's maturation at some length, and notes that his willingness to separate from his mother becomes a test of his legitimacy.

80. See, for example, Arthur 1982.

81. The move is structurally close to that of Apollo in Aeschylus's *Eumenides* 657ff.

82. McCall 1972, 159; Sorum 1978, 67.

83. DuBois 1979, 39–40. Segal (1992) echoes this idea several times.

84. Sorum 1978, 68. See also Segal 1977, 152ff.; 1981, 102; 1992, 90–91.

85. Wohl (1998, especially ch. 3) also argues that this marriage reestablishes the social order of masculinity.

86. Of course, if one believes that the text paves the way for Heracles' apotheosis, the father-son relationship is celebrated on a divine level as well. I am not concerned with this issue, but I do believe that the apotheosis is assumed by the play. For a recent and thorough treatment of this problem, see Holt 1989.

87. Foley 1981, 159; Segal 1981, 107–8.

88. Again, see Wohl 1998, 11–16.

89. Seaford 1986, 57. Segal (1992) expands on this idea. See also Ormand 1993, and the fine response by Pozzi (1994). Pozzi analyzes the ways in which Heracles and Deianeira change places (especially in terms of gender) at some length.

90. Segal 1992, 89. Zeitlin (1990a, 72) points out that "at those moments when the male finds himself in a condition of weakness, he too becomes acutely aware that he has a body—and then perceives himself, at the limits of pain, to be most like a woman."

91. *Pace* (Rehm 1994, 82–83), who finds the end of the play considerably more positive in tone. He argues that the audience would find reassurance in the double ritual of Hyllus's marriage and Heracles' funeral.

1. See Woodard 1966, 125. Woodard's analysis is one of the few articles that do not focus on Orestes. Kitzinger (1991, esp. 319–23), expanding on Woodard, shows that much of Electra's speech is undercut by Orestes' actions. Her most effective moments, when she is mourning her (supposedly) dead brother, must necessarily ring hollow for the audience, which knows that Orestes is still alive. Thus Electra's one action in the play (continuous mourning) makes her seem a liar.

2. E.g., Kitzinger 1991; Seaford 1985; Segal 1966; Woodard 1966; Whitman 1951. Most of the literature on the play is concerned with the issue of Orestes' culpability in the matricide: Segal 1981, 461 nn. 1, 2, 3, provides a useful summary.

3. Segal 1966, 539. I quote Segal (as Woodard, below) only *exempli gratia*. I could add Linforth (1963, 118: "Here and always she is moved by the essential instincts of a woman"), or any number of other critics.

4. Woodard 1966, 143. See also Kitzinger 1991, 308.

5. Kitzinger 1991; Seaford 1985.

6. I am indebted here to Juffras 1991 and Kitzinger 1991.

7. Sorum 1982 provides an excellent brief discussion of the changing role of the *oikos* within the *polis* in the second half of the fifth century. Her argument underlies much of what follows.

8. Kamerbeek 1974, introduction, 2. Segal (1981, 261; 1966, 494) also notes the pun.

9. An interesting parallel, especially in the light of the fact that Electra was (in some way) Orestes' nurse as a child—see line 1147. See also the useful remarks of Sorum 1982, 208.

10. I follow all recent editors of Sophocles in printing Meineke's τεκέων rather than τοκέων here.

11. See Seaford 1987, 125; Armstrong and Ratchford 1985; Cunningham 1984.

12. The *Oedipus tyrannus* presents us, then, with a variation on the topos. In Oedipus's daughters' case, their very proximity to their father's table prevents their marriage, since he has undergone pollution (1492ff.). Electra suffers from no such stigma.

13. See, e.g., Xenophon's *Symposium* 8.3.

14. See Seaford 1985, 319.

15. Segal 1981, 261. See also Burkert 1985, 70.

16. Seaford 1985, 319. Seaford (1994, 211) points out that tragedy often portrays brides who are torn between their natal and marital families. See also Seaford 1990a.

17. Seaford 1985, 320.

18. On Artemis's connections with virginity, marriage, and childbirth, see King 1983.

19. Burkert 1985, 150. Seaford (1994, 308–11) argues that maenadism is defined by women's return to such a state of potential sexuality.

20. See Callimachus's *Hymn to Artemis* 6.

21. Sorum 1982, 208. Vernant (1983, 137) also points out that Electra nurses Orestes, and suggests that she is, therefore, a Hestia figure.

22. Cf. also Seaford 1985, 322: "She associates herself by her oath [1238–42] with the fearless, homicidal, extra-mural, permanent (ἀεί) virginity of Artemis."

23. Vernant 1983, 133.

24. In a similar way, Seaford (1985, 320) notes that the rituals of mourning in this household are "perverted by both sides into a weapon in a conflict within the kinship group."

25. Winnington-Ingram 1980, 233. Certainly lines 289–92 support such a reading, if we can trust Electra's report of Clytemnestra's speech.

26. Cf. also line 312.

27. Cf. Lefkowitz 1986, 44ff., for myriad examples: Persephone, Europa, Io, etc.

28. Redfield (1982, 190) points out that the moment of being a *korē* is one of considerable social power for women: "The equivalent [to the *kouros*] moment of perfection for the woman is the moment of marriage. . . . The *korē* thus, like the *kouros*, represents a person not naturalistically but in the form of an archetype — in the woman's case, as the perfect *agalma* which is the bride." This active liminality also fits in nicely with Artemis's erotically charged virginity.

29. Winnington-Ingram (1980, 233) suggests that in lines 783ff., Clytemnestra portrays her daughter as a Fury. It is also worth noting that the Furies are eternal virgins (cf. Aeschylus's *Eumenides* 68–70), much like Electra.

30. Segal (1981, 261–62) notes several other similarities between Clytemnestra and Electra. Cf. also Winnington-Ingram 1980, 246.

31. Vernant 1983, 137.

32. Segal 1981, 256.

33. The suggestion is not unique to Sophocles. Euripides' *Electra* presents us with a Clytemnestra and an Aegisthus who already have two children. I am now convinced that Euripides' *Electra* was produced before Sophocles': see Bremer 1991.

34. Winnington-Ingram 1980, 231–32. In 1996, Naomi Finkelstein presented a fine paper at the annual meeting of the American Philological Assocation, in which she suggested that depictions of Furies on pottery often signify sexual transgression.

35. After my manuscript had already gone to press, I found that Bowman (1997, esp. 138–44) had anticipated my discussion of Clytemnestra's dream in several respects. Her article is particularly lucid on the way in which this dream writes Clytemnestra out of the seat of power.

36. Devereux (1976, 250) calls the dream's dramatic function "negligible." Devereux's analysis of this dream remains the most thorough and, despite some questionable methods, is often quite perceptive. His catalogue of Near Eastern parallels definitively establishes this dream as one of a Mediterranean-Near Eastern topos.

37. Ibid., 250, emphases in the original.

38. For Devereux's parallels, see ibid., 229–30.

39. Ibid., 232.

40. A recent compelling reading of the narrative structure of the dream in Herodotus is Pelling 1996.

41. For the two concepts, see Peradotto 1977.

42. I agree with Kells's (1973, 419) reading of ὁμιλίαν: "Surely sexual intercourse

is meant." See also Kamerbeek 1974, ad loc. Devereux (1976, 248) does not think that ὁμιλίαν designates coitus here, but his argument is based on the assumption that the sort of repetition for which I am arguing cannot exist in this dream. A similar doubling of the event occurs in Astyages' dream in Herodotus, however; see Pelling 1996.

43. This passage is one of the texts that Vernant (1983, 135) uses to demonstrate the myth of Hestia.

44. Devereux 1976, 244. Cf. also Scodel 1984, 80: "The dream presents an Orestes who is his father's son only."

45. Vernant 1983, 133 (quoted above).

46. Juffras 1991. Juffras's work informs much of the following section, though she does not link Electra's newfound activism to her position as an epikléros.

47. Such is the reasoning of Linforth (1963, 103).

48. Segal (1981, 258) suggests that the word here could mean "nearest of kin" (i.e., to Clytemnestra and Aegisthus). Kells (1973, ad loc.) seems to see only this meaning. Kamerbeek (1974, ad loc.) has a useful discussion, and sees this meaning as possible.

49. See Chapter 1.

50. This resemblance has been noted in various ways and in various parts of the text by several scholars. Cf. Winnington-Ingram 1980, 246; Segal 1981, 285 (quoted below).

51. The importance Athenians placed on keeping women out of the public eye has been demonstrated so often as to be commonplace. See Pomeroy 1975, esp. ch. 5. The most frequently cited text for this idea is Pericles' funeral oration, Thucydides 2.45. For the public aspect of the praise Electra seeks, see Juffras 1991, 103.

52. Juffras 1991, 103–4.

53. Segal 1981, 285.

54. Gould 1980, 55.

55. Segal 1966, 503.

56. For a useful discussion of Orestes' silencing of Electra, see Kitzinger 1991.

57. Woodard 1966, 125.

58. There is another level of irony here: Aegisthus thinks that Electra is referring to Orestes' death, rather than to his killing of Clytemnestra.

59. See especially Woodard 1966.

60. Juffras (1991, 105) assigns this motivation to both Orestes and Electra. Cf., however, Sorum 1982.

61. Sorum 1982, 210.

62. Kitzinger (1991, 302) argues that Electra's loss of effective speech here is "at the very heart of the tragedy." The following paragraphs are much indebted to Kitzinger's article.

63. Linforth 1963, 111. See also Reinhardt 1979, 161, where Electra is "yet happy once more to be within the bounds of her femininity."

64. Segal 1966, 529.

65. See Calder 1963, 215–16.

66. Marriage is, of course, a telos. See Seaford 1987, 114.

67. This, I take it, is the point of Segal (1966 530–31): "It also serves as a reminder of Electra's initial condition of physical unfulfillment and the waste of her capacities for creating life."

68. As witnessed by the multitude of scholarly articles that focus on Orestes, his return, his mock death, and most of all, his "future" after the drama ends.

CHAPTER 4

1. The bibliography on the *Antigone* is exceptionally large, and I cannot claim to have read it all. Hester 1971 is a useful summary of scholarship up to that time, and the bibliography in Oudemans and Lardinois 1987 covers the next fifteen years. Steiner 1984 is an engaging study of the postclassical life of the play.

2. Exceptions are Rehm 1994, 59–71; Seaford 1990a; Jost 1983.

3. Hester 1971, App. A (48–53), lists the works that "approximate the view . . . that the *Antigone* shows the clash between a good principle (represented by Antigone) and an evil principle (represented by Creon)" (11). Fewer articles take the opposite view — that Antigone is a dangerous rebel in a time of military crisis, and that Creon is a good ruler who makes an honest mistake. But such interpretations (a list can be found in Hester 1971, App. B) focus on the same issues and use the same categories of meaning as the interpretations that favor Antigone. Some recent critics have taken issue with this entire approach, notably Oudemans and Lardinois (1987) and Sourvinou-Inwood (1989a).

4. Fowler (1981, 15–16) calls Haemon's death over Antigone's corpse "shamelessly erotic."

5. Recognized by Rehm (1994), throughout his chapter on the *Antigone*.

6. The scholium on the *Antigone* at the end of ms. L says that in Euripides' treatment, Antigone was caught "through the love of Haemon." Cited in Fowler 1969, 145. See also Roussel 1922, 79–81.

7. See, e.g., the chart in Segal 1981, 186.

8. Patterson (1990) argues that Pericles' law of 451/50 redefined civic membership in terms of familial membership. Sorum 1982, 202, has a brief but useful discussion of the changing role of the household within the city during Sophocles' era. See also Rehm 1994, esp. 70–71.

9. Konstan (1996) argues that, though the abstract noun *philia* can be applied to any affective relation, the word *philos* is not normally applied to kin or fellow citizens, but means "friend" in a restrictive sense. If Konstan is correct, Creon's use of the word here is directed specifically at Haemon's affection toward his father.

10. See, e.g., Segal 1981, 186; Nussbaum 1986, 54–56; Goldhill 1986, ch. 4 passim; Reinhardt 1979, 78; Neuberg 1990, 71ff.; Winnington-Ingram 1980, 129; also noted by Rehm (1994, 60), though Rehm goes on to recognize the personal aspects of Creon's views.

11. Rehm (1994, 63) notes that Creon is legally the *kurios* of both Haemon and Antigone, and suggests that when Creon declares, "Let her [Antigone] marry someone in Hades" (lines 653–54), he is acting in this capacity.

12. We see further evidence for this attitude in Creon's near-total disregard for Eurydice until quite late in the play.

13. Demosthenes *De falsa legatione* 246–47. Calder (1968) argues forcefully, if not always convincingly, that the fifth-century Athenian audience would have sided with Creon in this play. A more successful pro-Creon reading is Sourvinou-Inwood 1989a.

14. Isaeus 3.17.

15. D. Konstan points out in correspondence that "this is no longer family at all." So it would seem—but we should remember that the Hestia myth defines the *oikos* in exactly this way (see Vernant 1983, passim).

16. I follow Konstan (1996) in defining *philos* here as "friend," distinct from kin relations.

17. Text is the OCT of Solmsen 1990 (first printed 1970).

18. The line also supports the traditional figure of woman as ploughed field. See duBois 1988, 65–85.

19. Neuberg (1990, 73) suggests that "the entire scene between Creon and Haemon implicitly involves the replaceability of the spouse."

20. E.g., Heracles in the *Trachiniae*. Cf. Stigers 1981, passim, for a discussion of this topos in lyric poetry.

21. Rabinowitz (1993) explores this theme at length in the plays of Euripides. Jay (1985) argues that one of the basic purposes of sacrifice in many patrilineal societies is officially to enlist children in the order of men. I argue that this is what Creon attempts here, using the bride as a sacrifice (as often: Seaford 1987, 110ff.).

22. The following examples are all pointed out in Segal 1981, 183–86. Sorum (1982, 205) also notes Antigone's emphasis on maternal relations. See also Knox 1964, 79.

23. Segal 1981, 183.

24. Ibid., 173; Oudemans and Lardinois 1987, 167.

25. See Sourvinou-Inwood 1989a, passim, for an interesting discussion of such use of language, which she describes as a "zooming device" (156).

26. Sourvinou-Inwood 1989a, esp. 141, 148. See also Linforth 1961, 222.

27. Segal 1981, 165.

28. See also *Works and Days* 618–94 for Hesiod's comments on the disadvantages of making one's living from sailing.

29. I do not mean to deny that the ode carries ambiguous overtones. The adjective *deinos* is neutral at best, and man's inability to control death (361–62) puts an obvious limit on his powers. I merely point out that compared to Hesiod, who sees these developments as straightforwardly negative, Sophocles' version is quite optimistic.

30. Pucci 1977, 82.

31. See ibid., 105–15.

32. As Foley (1981, 146) points out. See also Bergren 1983.

33. See Seaford 1987, 106, for a summary of common wedding imagery. Segal

(1981, 153) points out that "the metaphors embedded in Creon's language echo the themes of the Ode on Man: sailing, yoking, trading."

34. As is Antigone, lines 477–78. For a list of passages in which the verb *zeugnumi* is used to describe a wedding, see Seaford 1987, 111 n. 58.

35. Goheen 1951, 39. Similar is Eurydice's complete absence from the play until line 1261.

36. Kamerbeek (1978, ad loc.) claims that τίς ἀνδρῶν need not be gender-specific, but cf. Lloyd-Jones and Wilson 1990b, ad loc. Though unnecessarily snide in their treatment of Kamerbeek, they argue persuasively for an ironic reading of the words.

37. For this line I borrow the felicitous translation of E. Wyckoff (1954).

38. See Stigers 1981 for a good discussion of this theme in lyric poetry and numerous examples.

39. Text is that of Campbell 1967.

40. Sourvinou-Inwood 1987, 138. Segal (1981, 155; 1964, 56) also calls attention to the hunting metaphor at work here. Segal is concerned primarily with demonstrating that the image associates Antigone with nature, rather than culture.

41. Seaford 1987, 108.

42. Von Fritz (1934, 28) suggests that the chorus is wrong. Few scholars have followed von Fritz's thesis, that Haemon feels only a legal obligation to Antigone, and not love.

43. For discussion of the problematic use of *philos* in these lines, see Konstan 1996, 89–92.

44. Seaford 1990a also notes the parallel between Antigone and Electra on this point.

45. See my Chapter 3 for Electra's *anchisteia* in a similar context.

46. Again, see Vernant 1983, 133, 142ff., for this construct. Vernant points out that in the case of an *epiklēros*, the *man* becomes the substituted element in a marriage, and this will also be relevant to what follows. See also Neuberg 1990, 66–67.

47. E.g., Neuberg 1990, 68; Hester 1971, 34.

48. So Redfield 1982, 187. See also Foley 1994, 104; Burkert 1983, 62–63, on the *proteleia*.

49. Several good examples of this theme found on gravestones are translated in Lefkowitz and Fant 1992, 6–7. See also Lattimore 1942, 189–92.

50. Seaford 1994, 351.

51. Jost (1983, 135) lists lines 88, 220, 524–25, and 650 as hints early in the play of Antigone's eventual marriage to death. I confine myself here to discussing only those lines in Antigone's death scene proper.

52. Kamerbeek (1978, ad 804) states, "It is clear that θάλαμος is used because 'bridal chamber' is its special meaning."

53. Segal 1981, 179ff. See also Seaford 1990a, 88–89.

54. Though, as Seaford points out, she is distinct from Kore in that her marriage is a form of endogamy that destroys her family (1994, 384).

55. Reinhardt 1979, 81.

56. See Knox 1964, 114; Oudemans and Lardinois 1987, 190; Seaford 1990a, 79.

57. Seaford 1990a, 78.

58. Winnington-Ingram (1980, 140–42) makes this point forcefully.

59. Neuberg 1990, 75–76. See also Fowler 1981, 14.

60. A full discussion of the textual battles can be found in Lloyd-Jones and Wilson 1990b, ad loc. No recent editors besides Brown (1986) have argued against the lines' authenticity. Neuberg (1990, 54–63) summarizes the arguments marshaled against the passage. Neuberg 1990 and Murnaghan 1986 are the best recent interpretations of the lines, and what follows is largely dependent on them.

61. Murnaghan 1986, 195.

62. See Neuberg 1990, 66–67.

63. Murnaghan 1986, 198.

64. As a number of critics have argued. See, e.g., Neuberg 1990, 59.

65. Fowler 1969, 149.

66. Murnaghan 1986, 206–7. Recently, however, Foley has argued convincingly that it makes perfect sense for Antigone to reject a hypothetical husband and children in order to bury a real (if dead) brother (Martin Classical Lectures, Oberlin College 1994). She goes on to suggest that Greek society proscribed specific situations in which it was considered ethically correct for a woman to act outside of civic law; and that Antigone's situation here is one such: she is the last relative available to bury her brother.

67. Murnaghan 1986, 203.

68. See my Chapter 1; Pucci 1977, 96–101; Bergren 1992, 260: "What makes marriage possible makes its certainty impossible."

69. Neuberg 1990, 72–73.

70. Rehm (1994, 183 n. 23) suggests that the fulfilled rites may be those of Haemon or Antigone, since the noun "corpse" is grammatically neuter and allows for this possibility. But the subject of the immediately preceding sentence is Haemon, which would make an unannounced, ambiguous change of subject awkward; and in any case, Antigone has already had her "wedding rites."

71. Fowler 1981, 15–16; Scodel 1984, 51. Rehm 1994, 65, is good on the erotic overtones of Haemon's death.

72. Seaford 1987, 107.

73. Segal 1981, 185. Segal relies heavily on Freudian symbolism. It is perhaps as relevant that Haemon has gone to Antigone's *domos* (in Hades) as that the cave is a representative of the womb.

74. I assign line 572 to Ismene. I admit that I do so in a state of *aporia*. Those who are interested in the problem should see Lloyd-Jones and Wilson 1990a, ad loc.; Kamerbeek 1978, ad loc.; Dawe 1973, ad loc.; Oudemans and Lardinois 1987, 174; Hester 1971, 30 (and n. 1); and Linforth 1961, 209–10.

75. Noted also by Fowler (1981, 15).

76. Seaford (1994, 214) points out that Antigone laments both her own endogamy and her brother's exogamy (lines 863–71), thus bracketing the range of possible dangers in marriage.

77. Oudemans and Lardinois (1987, esp. 118–59) take a similar approach, though on a much broader level. See also Seaford 1990a.

78. The most recent full treatment of the ode is Sourvinou-Inwood 1989b. Seaford 1990a has some pertinent and useful comments, especially concerning the Danae episode.

79. See, e.g., Oudemans and Lardinois 1987, 145–51; Segal 1981, 182; Winnington-Ingram 1980, 110–16; Goheen 1951, 64.

80. Seaford 1990a, 77; Sourvinou-Inwood 1989b. See also Oudemans and Lardinois 1987, 147.

81. Sourvinou-Inwood (1989b, 143–45) contrasts Danae's "good" passive stance with Antigone's "bad" active one.

82. See especially Seaford 1994, 301–11; Winnington-Ingram 1980, 104.

83. Sourvinou-Inwood 1989b, 149–51. See also Winnington-Ingram 1980, 102. Winnington-Ingram sees *mania* (broadly speaking) as the glue that holds this ode together.

84. Sourvinou-Inwood (1989b, 155–59) points out that the ode does not actually tell us who blinded the children, and that in some versions Cleopatra herself does the deed. Such ambiguity, if we accept it, opens up another line of interpretation, namely that Cleopatra represents the dangerous side of Antigone-the-wife.

85. E.g., Winnington-Ingram 1980, 106–7. Winnington-Ingram demonstrates caution here, however, and states, "The point is not to be pressed."

86. As Nussbaum (1986, 78) points out.

87. So Seaford 1990a, 87.

88. Sourvinou-Inwood (1989b, 156) suggests that Cleopatra's wild traits "are ascribed to her girlhood, and, of course, all Greek parthenoi were symbolically wild." If we take these traits as signifying her status as a *parthenos*, then this is another parallel with Antigone.

89. As Winnington-Ingram (1980, 106) points out.

90. For a full discussion of Creusa's paradoxical role, see Loraux 1993, ch. 5.

91. For this as a theme throughout the ode, see Oudemans and Lardinois 1987, 149.

CHAPTER 5

1. An earlier version of this chapter, with somewhat different emphases, appeared in *AJP* 1996 as "Silent by Convention? Sophocles' Tekmessa." My thanks to The Johns Hopkins University Press for permission to reprint portions of that article.

2. Patterson 1990, 61.

3. My understanding of class politics in this play is much indebted to Rose's analysis of the *Philoctetes*, now in Rose 1992 (ch. 5).

4. March 1993 discusses the importance of Ajax as an Athenian hero at length. See especially 3–4, 25.

5. Rose (1995) points out that the chorus in this play consists of Athenian sailors, and he calls attention to several intriguing parallels with Periclean Athens throughout.

6. See Loraux 1993, 37–71 (esp. 46), 111–43. Interestingly, Athenians are only called Erechtheids in poetic discourse (46).

7. Loraux 1993, 46 n. 40.

8. Poe (1986, 23–26) sees the second half of the play as comic. He follows Knox (1966), who argues that with Ajax, "a heroic age has passed away" (31), and that the quarrel serves to mark this new, smaller era.

9. Winnington-Ingram (1980, 65) suggests that the controversy is "quite irrelevant to the tragic situation."

10. See Kamerbeek 1953, ad loc. March (1993, 5) suggests that this genealogy appeared in Aeschylus's version of the Ajax myth.

11. See, e.g., Poe 1986, 26–29; Knox 1966, 31; Winnington-Ingram 1980, 62–65.

12. The fullest work on *nothoi* is Ogden 1996. I largely follow Patterson 1990 in my understanding of the social category. For many years, the term *nothos* has been (mis)translated "bastard." As Patterson shows, being a *nothos* has nothing to do with the marital status of one's parents, but everything to do with their relative social status.

13. See the discussion in Seaford 1994, 207–8; Patterson 1990, 51; Wolff 1944, 89–90.

14. Despite the archaic tone of the play, scholars have seen a number of probable references to the fifth century. At 668, Ajax calls the Atreidae *archontes*, which Knox (1966, 55) argues is an oblique reference to the fifth-century political system. At 1100, Teucer asks Menelaos by what right he is *stratēgos*, and in the lines that follow, "Sophocles exploits fifth-century Athenian prejudice against Sparta to increase his audience's sympathy for Teucer (and Ajax) against Menelaos" (Stanford 1981, ad 1102; cf. Whitman 1951, 78). Some scholars have seen references to the hero cult of Ajax in the final third of the play. See especially Heinrichs 1993 and Burian 1972. For the general technique, see Sourvinou-Inwood 1989a. Rose 1995 is the most sophisticated attempt to read the play against a fifth-century background. Rose sees the play, in part, as a working-out of the problematic of imperialism.

15. See Boegehold 1994.

16. Patterson 1990, 61.

17. For Pericles' ancestry, see Herodotus 6.124–34. H. Foley has recently argued (1994, 146–50) that the *Homeric Hymn to Demeter* explores the emerging conflict between the older practice of exogamy and the movement toward a closed community through endogamy. I believe Sophocles to be doing something similar in the *Ajax*.

18. Patterson (1990, 49) speaks of the "fluidity" of marriage in the Homeric texts, and argues that Briseis was apparently eligible to produce *gnēsioi* sons for Achilles (see *Iliad* 19.287–99).

19. We see a similar argument anticipated by Theseus at *Hippolytus* 962–63.

20. Stanford (1981, ad loc.) suggests that line 1263 may be an interpolation, though he concludes that it is probably a rhetorical flourish.

21. Patterson 1990, 62–63.

22. Taplin (1979) is a notable exception; he suggests (129) that "critics have made too much" of Tecmessa's speech here.

23. As virtually every commentator notices: see Poe 1986, 44–47; Easterling 1984, 5; Scodel 1984, 16; Reinhardt 1979, 21; Winnington-Ingram 1980, 32; Sicherl 1977, 74, 89; Knox 1966, 42–43; Moore (1977, 55–56) reads affection behind this surliness (especially in the "deception speech"), and is followed by Segal (1981, 114) and March (1993, 15–19). The question of Ajax's affection for Tecmessa depends, of course, on how one reads the "deception speech" (lines 644–92). I have no desire to add to the ongoing debate on this passage. Interested readers should see, in addition to the works listed above in this note: Rose 1995, 76–79; Seaford 1994, 392–402; Crane 1990; Stevens 1986; Taplin 1979; Wigodsky 1962.

24. I have translated both instances of the word *gunē* here as "woman," though, of course, it can also mean "wife." Since I later argue that, in the early part of the play, Tecmessa is never addressed as "wife," this instance is problematic. We should remember, however, that these words are spoken in private by Ajax, and only made public by Tecmessa (who has a vested interest in being called "wife"). See further below.

25. It is not entirely clear from the Greek whether ἀεὶ δ' ὑμνούμενα means that Ajax was always saying this, or if the sentiment is a bit of proverbial wisdom. The phrasing suggests the latter, and several commentators have found similar gnomic utterances elsewhere. See Kamerbeek 1953; Stanford 1981, ad loc. By Aristotle's time, Sophocles' formulation had become proverbial, even if it was not so in the fifth century: Aristotle quotes the passage at *Politics* 1260a29.

26. Poe 1986, 45.

27. Easterling (1984) points out this difference throughout; see also Kirkwood 1965, 59.

28. Rose (1995, 64) makes this connection.

29. Significantly, this is true despite the social standing of her parents: Tecmessa makes it clear that she comes from a free and wealthy (though foreign) father, 487–88. She is thus exactly parallel to Hesione.

30. Kamerbeek (1953, ad 485), for example, tells us that her speech cannot be analyzed in logical fashion because "it is not in accordance with her position to express herself with the clarity of the hero; secondly, her motives are purely emotional." Similarly, Stanford (1981, ad loc.) declares that her speech is "intensely and vibrantly personal." Easterling (1984), by contrast, recognizes the strong rhetorical aspect of Tecmessa's speech.

31. Winnington-Ingram 1980, 29; Easterling 1984, 4.

32. Noted, as Poe (1986) says, "by every commentator including the scholiast" (45). Poe provides a useful summary of scholarship on the scene (45–49). Rose (1995, 64) points out that her speech is also parallel to Briseis's lament of Patroclus. Both roles are models for her.

33. Stanford 1981, ad loc.

34. Kamerbeek 1953, ad loc.

35. The ambiguity has led to textual difficulty. See Kamerbeek 1953, ad loc.; and Stanford 1981, ad loc.

36. Pointed out by Reinhardt (1979, 21).

37. This has not kept critics from presuming that he does pity her: see the summary by Poe (1986, 44–45).

38. Kamerbeek 1953, ad loc.; Stanford 1981, ad loc. Stanford (p. xxxiii) thinks that this redeems his character: "Ajax' harsh rejection of his wife's powerful appeal is immediately balanced by the love he shows for his infant son."

39. March (1993, 15) sees "a massive tenderness for both Tecmessa and Eurysakes" in lines 558–59. Peter Rose has suggested in correspondence that the lines also include indications of "tenderness" for Tecmessa. I maintain that Ajax's concern for his son indicates little about his feelings for Tecmessa.

40. See, for example, Sophocles' *Electra* 1143 (used of Electra, where the point is that she, not Clytemnestra, nurtured the baby Orestes).

41. This suggestion may also have served to confirm Eurysakes' status. Patterson (1990, 51) points out that according to Plutarch, *nothoi* were not required to care for their parents (Solon 22.4). Ajax's order, therefore, may be the equivalent of naming Eurysakes a *gnēsios*.

42. Interestingly, Taplin (1979) argues that Ajax dies in order to protect Tecmessa and Eurysakes, though not in the ways that I suggest.

43. Winnington-Ingram 1980, 30 n. 57.

44. We might see a parallel in the *Odyssey*. As Patterson (1990, 48) points out, Menelaos's son Megapenthes fits the description of a *nothos* (born to Menelaos by a *doulē*), but he is Menelaos's *only* son, and he receives treatment "at least the equal of Menelaos's legitimate daughter, Hermione" (cf. *Odyssey* 4.1–14).

45. I wish to avoid adding to the endless debate on Ajax's intent during this speech. I merely state that, whatever Ajax plans for himself, and whatever his motives, he implicitly grants Tecmessa an improved status in the course of the speech.

46. March (1993, 19) ably argues that Ajax's pity for Tecmessa here is genuine; see also Easterling 1984, 5.

47. Stanford 1981, ad loc.

48. See, for example, *Trachiniae* 147–48, where Deianeira speaks of marriage: ἀντὶ παρθένου γυνὴ / κληθῇ ("Instead of 'maiden,' you will be called 'wife'"). Only Ajax has called her *gunē* so far, and the only example early in the play is line 292 (discussed above).

49. Davies (1973) argues that a fifth-century pot shows Tecmessa covering the dead Ajax, which would indicate that this action is part of an earlier literary tradition. March (1993, 6) suggests that this pot refers specifically to Aeschylus's version of the myth.

50. Alexiou 1974, 14–23 (quotation from 20). See further discussion below.

51. So Lloyd-Jones and Wilson 1990b, ad loc.; Stanford 1981, ad loc.; Kamerbeek 1953, ad loc.

52. So Pickard-Cambridge 1968, 140.

53. Taplin (1977, 284) states: "Very occasionally a major character in Greek tragedy will make a completely silent appearance, e.g. Tecmessa at S. *Aj.* 1168ff., Alcestis at E. *Alc.* 1008ff., Orestes and Pylades at *IT* 1222–28; but all these are clearly indicated

and explained in the text." This is true of the *Alcestis* and the *Iphigenia among the Taurians*, but Tecmessa's silence is neither indicated nor explained.

54. Pickard-Cambridge (1968, 138–48) summarizes the distribution of roles in all our extant plays. Aside from the *Alcestis*, the closest parallels to the situation in the *Ajax* are as follows: in Sophocles' *Oedipus at Colonus* it appears that Ismene must be played by a mute actor from 1098 to 1555, though she speaks again later. Unlike the scene in the *Ajax*, however, Ismene is onstage with three speaking actors throughout this passage; there is no possibility that she could speak. This is also perhaps the most problematic of extant tragedies in regard to assignation of parts. In Euripides' *Hecuba*, the serving-woman's second entrance (955) must be played by a mute; hers is not a major role. In the *Iphigenia among the Taurians*, the herdsman is played by a mute, if onstage, for the brief scene at 456–70; likewise Orestes and Pylades for 1222–33. Neither of these compares to the extended silence of Tecmessa. In the *Ion*, Xouthos simply never returns to the stage; as Pickard-Cambridge notes, we are prepared for this nonentrance by lines 1130–31. Kamerbeek (1953, ad 1168) suggests that the end of Euripides' *Andromache* may be parallel (though that is based on the disputed presence of Andromache).

In rather a different class is Pylades' silence in the final scene of Euripides' *Orestes*. That silence is emphasized by Menelaos's question to him (which, as Apollo's imminent entrance confirms, he cannot answer) at line 1591. In this respect, the play resembles the *Ajax*. But as Nisetich (1986) shows, the purpose of this pointed silence is metatheatrical. It indicates that the play is returning to the familiar storyline portrayed by Aeschylus, and recalls Pylades' traditional role as Orestes' taciturn companion. Tecmessa has no such literary history by which to explain her surprising silence.

55. For an interesting discussion of Euripides' use of the mute actor here, see O'Higgins 1993, 93–95.

56. The assignation of the first half of line 985 is disputed; but most editors give it to the chorus. See Stanford 1981, ad loc. In any case, Teucer's command in 986 must be addressed to Tecmessa, as lines 1168–69 show.

57. For a useful discussion of women's roles in ancient Greek lament, see Alexiou 1974, 4–23. For lament in tragedy, see Foley 1993; Holst-Warhaft 1992, 127–70.

58. Taplin (1978, 149) speaks of "the tense flurry of movement which opens up the next act."

59. As I argued in an earlier article: Ormand 1996a, 57–62.

60. Alexiou 1974, 21. This legislation has received fuller treatment, though most of it in agreement with Alexiou, in Foley 1993, 103–8; Holst-Warhaft 1992, 99–126.

61. Segal (1995, ch. 5), reads the *Antigone* in terms of the conflict between private, female mourning and the state-regulated *epitaphios*. In that play, he argues, the death of Haemon results in uncontrolled (private) mourning by Eurydice and Creon, foiling the apparent closure of the play.

62. See Heinrichs 1993 and Burian 1972 on the tableau as a reference to the contemporary Athenian hero-cult of Ajax.

63. Segal (1981, 127) calls Ajax's body a focal point "for a rite of supplication, a juridical debate, and . . . a renewal of family ties."

64. Knox 1966, 39.

65. Rose 1995, 77 speaks of Teucer's new standing here as "the democratization of an aristocratic ideal."

66. So Scodel 1984, 20.

67. Knox 1966, 57.

68. Poe 1986, 98.

69. Here again I am strongly influenced by Rose's reading of the *Philoctetes*. See Rose 1992, 327: "He has turned their most powerful grounds for endorsing an egalitarian society based on persuasion and education into a ringing affirmation of the old hierarchies, which, in the midst of democracy's demise, were asserting their claims to power on new ideological foundations." I would suggest that Sophocles' expression of desire for an aristocratic rule of the democracy exists even in his earlier works.

70. The most obvious parallel is the silent Alcestis at the end of Euripides' *Alcestis*. For a persuasive reading of her silence as a curtailing of her desires, see O'Higgins 1993.

71. This is particularly true in tragedy. See Foley 1993, passim; Holst-Warhaft 1992, 127–70.

CHAPTER 6

1. For a recent defense of a Freudian reading of the play, see Segal 1995, ch. 7.

2. Such as Vernant and Vidal-Niquet's "Oedipus without the Complex," in Vernant 1981.

3. See esp. de Lauretis 1990; Irigaray 1985.

4. DuBois 1988.

5. Lévi-Strauss (1969, 25) suggests that the taboo against incest is *the* founding step of culture, the one near-universal organizing principle that structures society.

6. On revising this chapter I find that I have been anticipated in some ways by Pucci 1992. Pucci's complex and thoughtful work is based on a combination of Lacanian theory and the Derridean notion of the supplement. As such, he is concerned to show that the fabrication of an authoritative father for Oedipus, that is, a "law of the father," is necessarily due to a series of displacements and transgressions of that law. I am more concerned with the way the play problematizes the authority of "natural" parentage, and use the terminology of Marxist literary criticism. I am, nonetheless, much indebted to Pucci.

7. Pucci (1992, 134) notes, "To give things meaning and significance involves repressing and transgressing." We should be reminded here of the difficulties, sketched earlier, in proving Athenian citizenship, esp. if the subject in question is a woman.

8. Goodhart 1978, 55. I owe much of my reading of this play to this article.

9. Vernant 1981, 96.

10. The sphinx's riddle does not appear in Sophocles' play, of course. Knox believes (following Earle) that line 130 refers to it. See Knox 1957, 237, n. 31, for a dis-

cussion of the riddle's familiarity in antiquity. Pucci (1992, 66–76) provides the fullest reading of the riddle in relation to Oedipus's name.

11. A modern riddle that operates on the same principle is: Q: What is black and white and re(a)d all over? A: The newspaper. The apparent tricolor scheme of the unknown object is resolved into a simple page of print, once we recognize that the word heard as "red" is spelled "read," and does not represent a third, problematic color. Even more appropriate to the Oedipus myth: Q: Sisters and brothers I have none, but that man's father is my dad's son. Who is that man? A: The son of the speaker, who is, naturally, his (own) father's son.

12. Goodhart 1978, 56. I wish to make it clear that I do not support Ahl's view (Ahl 1991, passim), i.e., that this shift of questions constitutes evidence that Oedipus is innocent. I agree with Whitlock-Blundell (1992) that if this is Sophocles' point, he has surely been oversubtle about it. Rather, I wish to explore the process of self-recognition in this play, and this leap of logic is both typical and crucial to the process. See also Pucci 1992, 106 and 200 n. 4.

13. Knox 1957, 29.

14. Benardete 1966, 107.

15. Vernant 1981, 91.

16. Scodel 1984, 62.

17. Pucci 1992, 200 n. 4.

18. See Dawe 1982, 1.

19. See also lines 1449–54, 1518–23.

20. Althusser 1971, 174.

21. Ibid., 176; emphasis added.

22. Aeschylus's *Septem* 746–49, 750–52. See Kamerbeek 1967, 6; and also Knox 1957, 206 n. 77.

23. My concept of ideology in this play seems very close to Pucci's notion of the *telos*-narrative (Pucci 1992, 16–17).

24. Althusser 1971, 182. See Knox 1957, ch. 1, passim, for Oedipus as a man of self-motivated action.

25. See, e.g., Pucci 1992, esp. ch. 5; Goldhill 1986, 217ff.; Knox 1957, 184.

26. Pucci (1992, 68–78) discusses Oedipus's identity as a function of the different possible meanings of his name, either "swell-foot" (as here), or "know-foot," i.e., the solver of the sphinx's riddle.

27. Althusser 1971, 172.

28. Goodhart 1978, 67.

29. Although certain exceptional cases sometimes challenge this paradigm; see Konstan 1994.

30. All noted by Pucci 1992; see especially his ch. 1. For Pucci, these alternative parents represent the "narrative of *tuchē*," in which the Lacanian Father is confirmed, paradoxically, by his absence.

31. For a full discussion of the problem, see Lloyd-Jones and Wilson 1990b, ad loc.; and Dawe 1982, ad loc. Lloyd-Jones and Wilson argue for the manuscript reading (contra Dawe), but in such a way that their argument supports Dawe. In the face of

such confusion, I still accept the manuscript reading (which Lloyd-Jones and Wilson 1990a prints), but I do so uneasily.

32. Knox 1957, 85.

33. Ibid.

34. See Vernant 1981, 90–91, for a good discussion of the specific type of irony characteristic of this play.

35. *Works and Days* 235.

36. [Demosthenes] 59.114. See Chapter 1 for a discussion.

37. See Segal 1981, 213–14, for Oedipus as a destroyer of difference. See also Zeitlin 1990b, 148, for Thebes as plagued by the inability to differentiate.

38. Segal 1981, 212.

39. Similarly, Pucci (1992) argues that Oedipus confirms the "law of the father" by "doubling" the father's absence (136, with many echoes).

40. Pucci 1992, 108–9.

41. See, for example, Isaeus 8.18–20. Obviously citizenship could be falsified in this system — phratry members might not object to the introduction of illegitimate children for any number of personal or political reasons. Nonetheless, such evidence is often introduced in inheritance disputes, so it must have carried some weight. See also Humphreys' discussion of Demosthenes 57 (Humphreys 1986, 62).

42. Recall the emphasis that Althusser places on naming for the creation of a subject, above. Althusser 1971, 176.

43. Text is that of Stanford (1965).

44. See also lines 171–73, 182–85.

45. See duBois 1988, 39–85; Patterson 1986, 56–57.

46. As Knox (1957, 114) suggests. See also Pucci 1992, 91–94, 147–50.

47. Oudemans and Lardinois 1987, 49; and see their pp. 1–10 for an argument that the ancient Greek cosmology was "interconnected."

48. See my Chapter 1, and Seaford 1987, 106. See also duBois 1988, 39–85, for an analysis of the application of the images of field and furrow to women in general.

49. Knox 1957, 112–13, lists lines 4–5, 103–4, 694–96, 922–23.

50. See Seaford 1987, 124, for the suggestion that the bride's unveiling in ancient Greece "may have been associated with a nautical image." Seaford cites, in addition to this passage, Aeschylus's *Agamemnon* 690–92, 1178–81; Euripides's *Iphigenia among the Taurians* 370–71, *Trojan Women* 569–70.

51. Lloyd-Jones and Wilson 1990b, ad loc., following a suggestion of Blaydes ('λικών for Ἑλικών, with the initial ε dropped due to crasis).

52. Dawe (1973, ad loc.) suggests that λιμήν might stand as a metaphor for marriage.

53. See Knox 1957, 113–16, for a discussion of Oedipus as a plowman.

54. See Pucci 1992, 80–82, for an enlightening discussion of these lines.

55. Pucci (1992, 111) points out that this is actually an important specification: if Oedipus had understood it (which he cannot, at this point), he would not have feared the possibility of killing Polybus.

56. See also lines 1485, 1497–98.

57. My translation here differs from others'. The word *thalamēpolos* normally means "chambermaid," and here is in apposition to *paidi* and *patri*. It indicates, I believe, an erotic servility on the part of both Laius and Oedipus. I resist making it into a metonymy for the wedding chamber, therefore (as, e.g., Fagles has done), in order to bring this out.

58. DuBois 1988, 78. Loraux (1986, 50–52) discusses these lines in a different vein.

59. Winnington-Ingram (1982, 239) describes Jocasta as a "feminine role," and says, "There is nothing intellectual about her." For Pucci (1992, 51), she is a "figure of chance," but of relatively little interest in his father-oriented reading. See, however, Loraux 1986 for a challenging reading of her impact, and the ways that the text elides her role.

60. Whitman 1951, 132: "Jocasta exercises a curious charm over the reader of the play."

61. Loraux 1986 is one of the few full-scale treatments of Jocasta in the play. Even for Loraux, however, Jocasta serves more as a function in the text than as a person: see esp. 41–42.

62. For this as a traditional role for women, see esp. Irigaray 1985a, 134–36.

63. Compare, for example, Aegisthus in Sophocles' *Electra*, esp. lines 266–74.

64. Knox 1957, 57.

65. Loraux (1986, 48–49) emphasizes Jocasta's doubleness, and insists that this doubling is real, not metaphorical.

66. See Irigaray 1985a, passim. Other examples, though I have not discussed them in precisely these terms, are Antigone's speech at *Antigone* 904–20 (her position is consistent with her actions there, but creates an excess of distinctions that critics have not had an easy time with) and Deianeira at *Trachiniae* 911 (she figures her loss of future children as a lack of children altogether).

67. See Goodhart 1978, passim, esp. 60.

68. Freud 1935, 290. Cf. Segal 1995, ch. 7; Vernant 1981, 63–81.

69. Kamerbeek 1967, ad loc. See also Knox 1957, 178.

70. Emphasis added. Grene (1991, 52) follows Jebb's note (1887–96, ad loc.) in this translation. Pucci (1992, 94–98) supports this translation.

71. Pucci (1992, 97) suggests that Jocasta's recommendation — that we live "at random" — is an indication of promiscuity on all levels.

72. Vernant (1981, 85) discusses this dream in relation to Oedipus.

73. See Artemidorus 1.79, translated in Winkler 1990a, 213–15. Though this work is late, Artemidorus's interpretations of dreams are in several places consistent with Hippias's.

74. DuBois (1988, 71–72) comes to the same conclusion.

75. See Goodhart 1978, passim.

76. Freud 1935, 290.

77. See Chapter 1.

78. Pucci 1992, esp. 167–68.

79. *Pace* Calder (1962). See now Pucci 1992, 171–73.

80. Text is that of Radt (1985). I discuss this passage in another context in Chapter 1.

81. This is a further parallel with the end of the *Trachiniae*. See my Chapter 2, and Seaford 1986, 57.

82. It is often used as iconographic code in pottery to let the viewer know that the scene depicted belongs to some phase of a wedding. See Oakley and Sinos 1993, 7, 23.

83. See Zeitlin 1990a, 72.

84. In the *Oedipus at Colonus*, of course, Creon and Polyneices will both try again to lead Oedipus back to Thebes: in that play the old blind man has become a talisman of power.

85. Again, in the *Oedipus at Colonus* we find that the daughters have remained unmarried so that they could tend to their father. Cf. especially lines 747–52 there.

86. Significantly, Creon is a maternal relative to the daughters, and would not normally be called on to be *kurios* unless no paternal relatives remained.

87. These may in fact be the final words of the play. Most modern editors reject the final seven-line speech of the chorus as spurious. For a full discussion of the problem, see Lloyd-Jones and Wilson 1990b, ad loc.; and Dawe 1982, ad loc.

88. See Loraux 1986, esp. 37: "Pas de sortie, l'histoire d'Oedipe se clôt sur elle-même" ("There is no exit; the story of Oedipus closes in on itself").

EPILOGUE

1. Loraux 1987, 28.

2. Exactly Antigone's fate in the *Oedipus at Colonus*.

3. See also line 876.

4. Loraux 1987, 37.

5. *Pace* Rehm (1994, 183 n. 23).

6. Kraus (1991, passim) argues that the characters in this play continually declare closure, only to have the "end of the story" reevaluated in the next scene. This patterns fits nicely with my argument here.

7. See King 1983, 121, for childbirth as important to a woman's completed status.

8. In addition to Chapter 5 above, see Ormand 1996a.

9. Most notably, some scholars have preferred Bothe's suggestion of *lachos* ("fate") in place of *lechos* ("marriage bed"). For a full discussion of the problem, see Lloyd-Jones and Wilson 1990b, ad loc.; and Kamerbeek 1978, ad loc.

10. It is an epithet of the Earth in [Aeschylus's] *Prometheus Bound* 90.

11. See Roberts 1987, 1988, and 1989, passim.

BIBLIOGRAPHY

Ahl, F. 1991. *Sophocles' Oedipus: Evidence and Self-Conviction.* Ithaca: Cornell University Press.

Alexiou, M. 1974. *The Ritual Lament in Greek Tradition.* Cambridge: Cambridge University Press.

Allen, A. 1986. "Electra's Hair." *AJP.* 107: 246–48.

Althusser, L. 1971. "Ideology and Ideological State Apparatuses (Notes Towards an Investigation)." In *Lenin and Philosophy,* trans. B. Brewster, 127–186. New York: Monthly Review Press.

———. 1977. "Contradiction and Overdetermination." In *For Marx,* trans. B. Brewster, 89–128. London: Gresham Press.

Armstrong, D. 1986. "Sophocles' *Trachiniae* 559 ff." *BICS* 33: 101–2.

Armstrong, D., and E. A. Ratchford. 1985. "Iphigenia's Veil: Aeschylus, *Agamemnon* 228–48." *BICS* 32: 1–12.

Arthur (Katz), M. 1977. "Politics and Pomegranates: An Interpretation of the Homeric Hymn to Demeter." *Arethusa* 10: 7–47.

———. 1982. "Cultural Strategies in Hesiod's *Theogony*: Law, Family, Society." *Arethusa* 15: 63–82.

Bal, M. 1984. "The Rhetoric of Subjectivity." *Poetics Today* 5: 337–76.

Barrett, W. S. 1964. *Euripides' Hippolytos.* Oxford: Oxford University Press.

Benardete, S. 1966. "Sophocles' *Oedipus Tyrannus.*" In *Sophocles,* ed. T. Woodard, 105–21. Englewood Cliffs, N.J.: Prentice-Hall.

Bergren, A. 1983. "Language and the Female in Early Greek Thought." *Arethusa* 16: 69–95.

————. 1992. "Architecture Gender Philosophy." In Hexter and Selden 1992, 253–305.

Boegehold, A. 1994. "Perikles' Citizenship Law of 451/50 B.C." In Boegehold and Scafuro 1994, 57–66.

Boegehold, A., and A. Scafuro, eds. 1994. *Athenian Identity and Civic Ideology.* Baltimore: The Johns Hopkins University Press.

Bowman, L. 1996. "Sex, Drugs and Prophecy: The Creation of Patriarchy in the *Trachiniai.*" Unpublished paper delivered at the Kentucky Foreign Languages Conference, 1996.

————. 1997. "Klytaimnestra's Dream: Prophecy in Sophokles' *Elektra.*" *Phoenix* 51: 131–51.

Bremer, J. M. 1991. "Exit Electra." *Gymnasium* 98: 325–42.

Broadbent, M. 1968. *Studies in Greek Genealogy.* Leiden: E. J. Brill.

Brown, A., ed. 1986. *Sophocles' Antigone.* Warminster, Wilts, England: Aris and Phillips.

Brown, S. G. 1977. "A Contextual Analysis of Tragic Meter: The Anapest." In *Ancient and Modern: Essays in Honor of Gerald F. Else,* ed. J. H. D'Arms and J. W. Eadie, 45–79. Ann Arbor, Mich.: Center for Coordination of Ancient and Modern Studies.

Burian, P. 1972. "Supplication and Hero Cult in Sophocles' *Ajax.*" *GRBS* 13: 151–56.

Burkert, W. 1966. "Kekropidensage und Arrhephoria: Vom Initiationsritus zum Panathenäenfest." *Hermes* 94: 1–25.

————. 1983. *Homo Necans.* Translated by P. Bing. Berkeley: University of California Press.

————. 1985. *Greek Religion.* Translated by J. Raffan. Cambridge, Mass.: Harvard University Press.

Calder, W. M., III. 1962. "*Oedipus Tyrannus,* 1515–1530." *CPhil.* 57: 219–29.

————. 1963. "The End of Sophocles' *Electra.*" *GRBS* 4: 213–16.

————. 1968. "Sophocles' Political Tragedy: *Antigone.*" *GRBS* 9: 389–407.

Cameron, A., and A. Kuhrt, eds. 1983. *Images of Women in Antiquity.* Detroit, Mich.: Wayne State University Press.

Campbell, D., ed. 1967. *Greek Lyric Poetry.* New York: Macmillan.

Case, S.-E. 1988. *Feminism and Theater.* New York: Methuen.

Chase, C. 1979. "Oedipal Textuality: Reading Freud's Reading of Oedipus." *Diacritics* 9.4: 54–68.

Clay, D. 1982. "Unspeakable Words in Greek Tragedy." *AJP.* 103: 277–98.

Cole, S. G. 1984. "The Social Function of Rituals of Maturation: The Koureion and the Arkteia." *ZPE* 55: 233–44.

Collier, J. F. 1974. "Women in Politics." In *Women, Culture, and Society,* ed. M. Z. Rosaldo and L. Lamphere, 89–96. Stanford, Calif.: Stanford University Press.

Crane, G. 1990. "Ajax, the Unexpected, and the Deception Speech." *CPhil.* 85: 89–101.

Cunningham, M. L. 1984. "Aeschylus, *Agamemnon* 231–47." *BICS* 31: 9–12.

Davies, M. 1973. "Ajax and Tekmessa." *Antike Kunst* 16: 60–70.

Dawe, R. D. 1973. *Studies on the Text of Sophocles.* Vols. 1 and 3. Leiden: E. J. Brill.

———, ed. 1979. *Sophoclis Tragoediae.* Leipzig: B. G. Teubner.

———, ed. 1982. *Sophocles' Oedipus Rex.* Cambridge: Cambridge University Press.

———, ed. 1984. *Sophoclis Tragoediae.* 2d ed. Leipzig: B. G. Teubner.

Dean-Jones, L. 1992. "The Politics of Pleasure: Female Sexual Appetite in the Hippocratic Corpus." *Helios* 19: 72–91.

de Lauretis, T. 1987. *Technologies of Gender.* Bloomington: Indiana University Press.

———. 1990. "Eccentric Subjects: Feminist Theory and Historical Consciousness." *Feminist Studies* 12: 115–50.

Detienne, M. 1988. "Les Danaides entre elles ou La Violence Fondatrice du Mariage." *Arethusa* 21: 159–75.

Devereux, G. 1976. *Dreams in Greek Tragedy.* London: Oxford University Press.

Diggle, J., ed. 1981. *Euripidis Fabulae.* Vol. 2. New York: Oxford University Press.

———. 1984. *Euripidis Fabulae.* Vol. 1. New York: Oxford University Press.

Dougherty, C. 1993. *The Poetics of Colonization: From City to Text in Archaic Greece.* Oxford: Oxford University Press.

duBois, P. 1979. "On Horse/Men, Amazons, and Endogamy." *Arethusa* 12: 35–49.

———. 1988. *Sowing the Body.* Chicago: University of Chicago Press.

Earle, M. L. 1902. "Studies in Sophocles' *Trachiniae.*" *TAPA* 33: 5–29.

Easterling, P. E., ed. 1982. *Sophocles' Trachiniae.* Cambridge: Cambridge University Press.

———. 1984. "The Tragic Homer." *BICS* 31: 1–8.

Evans-Grubbs, J. 1989. "Abduction Marriage in Antiquity: A Law of Constantine and Its Social Context." *JRS* 79: 59–83.

Faludi, S. 1991. *Backlash: The Undeclared War against American Women.* New York: Crown.

Faraone, C. A. 1990. "Aphrodite's κεστός and Apples for Atalanta: Aphrodisiacs in Early Greek Myth and Ritual." *Phoenix* 44: 219–43.

Flaceliere, R. 1959. *La Vie quotidienne en Grèce.* Paris: Hachette.

Foley, H. 1981. "The Concept of Women in Athenian Drama." In *Reflections of Women in Antiquity,* ed. H. Foley, 127–68. New York: Gordon and Break.

———. 1982a. "Marriage and Sacrifice in Euripides' *Iphigenia at Aulis.*" *Arethusa* 15: 159–80.

———. 1982b. "The Female Intruder Reconsidered." *CPhil.* 77: 1–22.

———. 1992. "*Anodos* Dramas: Euripides' *Alcestis* and *Helen.*" In Hexter and Selden 1992, 133–60.

———. 1993. "The Politics of Tragic Lamentation." In *Tragedy, Comedy, and the Polis,* ed. A. Sommerstein, 101–43. Bari: Levante Editori.

———. 1994. *The Homeric Hymn to Demeter: Translation, Commentary, and Interpretive Essays.* Princeton: Princeton University Press.

———. 1995. "Tragedy and Democratic Ideology: The Case of Sophocles' *Antigone.*" In *History, Tragedy, Theory,* ed. B. Goff, 131–50. Austin: University of Texas Press.

Forster, E. S., ed. 1927. *Isaeus*. Loeb Classical Library. Cambridge, Mass.: Harvard University Press.

Fowler, B. H. 1969. "Plot and Prosody in Sophocles' *Antigone*." *C&M* 28: 143–71.

———. 1981. "Thought and Underthought in Three Sophoclean Plays." *Eranos* 79: 1–22.

Foxhall, L. 1989. "Household, Gender and Property in Classical Athens." *CQ* 39: 22–44.

Freud, S. 1935. *A General Introduction to Psychoanalysis*. Translated by J. Riviere. New York: Liveright Publishing Co. Relevant excerpts reprinted in M. J. O'Brien, ed., *Twentieth Century Interpretations of* Oedipus Rex, 104–5 (Englewood Cliffs, N.J.: Prentice Hall, 1968).

———. 1938. *The Interpretation of Dreams*. New York: Modern Library.

Gardner, J. F. 1986. *Women in Roman Law and Society*. Bloomington: Indiana University Press.

Garland, R. 1990. *The Greek Way of Life*. Ithaca: Cornell University Press.

Girard, R. 1972. *Deceit, Desire, and the Novel: Self and Other in Literary Structure*. Translated by Yvonne Freccero. Baltimore: The Johns Hopkins University Press.

———. 1990. "Do You Love Him Because I Do! Mimetic Interaction in Shakespeare's Comedies." *Helios* 17: 89–108.

Goheen, R. 1951. *The Imagery of Sophocles' Antigone*. Princeton: Princeton University Press.

Goldhill, S. 1986. *Reading Greek Tragedy*. New York: Cambridge University Press.

Gomme, A. 1925. "The Position of Women in Athens in the Fifth and Fourth Centuries." *CPhil.* 20: 1–25.

Goodhart, S. 1978. "Ληστὰς Ἔφασκε: Oedipus and Laius' Many Murderers." *Diacritics* 8: 55–71.

Gould, J. P. 1978. "Dramatic Character and 'Human Intelligibility' in Greek Tragedy." *PCPS* 24: 43–67.

———. 1980. "Law, Custom, and Myth: Aspects of the Social Position of Women in Classical Athens." *JHS* 100: 38–59.

Grene, D., trans. 1991. *Oedipus the King*. In *The Complete Greek Tragedies*, Vol. 2, ed. D. Grene and R. Lattimore. University of Chicago Press.

Halleran, M. 1986. "Lichas' Lies and Sophoclean Innovation." *GRBS* 27: 239–47.

Halliburton, D. 1988. "Concealing Revealing: A Perspective on Greek Tragedy." In *Post-Structuralist Classics*, ed. A. Benjamin, 245–67. London: Routledge.

Harris, E. 1990. "Did Athenians Regard Seduction as a Worse Crime than Rape?" *CQ* 40: 370–77.

Hathorn, R. Y. 1958. "Sophocles' *Antigone*: Eros in Politics." *CJ* 54: 109–15.

Heinrichs, A. 1993. "The Tomb of Aias and the Prospect of Hero Cult in Sophocles." *Cl. Ant.* 12: 165–80.

Henderson, J. 1975. *The Maculate Muse*. New Haven: Yale University Press.

Hester, D. A. 1971. "Sophocles the Unphilosophical." *Mnemosyne* 24: 11–59.

Hexter, R., and D. Selden, eds. 1992. *Innovations of Antiquity*. New York: Routledge.

Hoey, T. F. 1970. "The *Trachiniae* and Unity of Hero." *Arethusa* 3: 1–22.

———. 1979. "The Date of the *Trachiniae*." *Phoenix* 33: 210–32.

Holst-Warhaft, G. 1992. *Dangerous Voices: Women's Lament and Greek Literature*. New York: Routledge.

Holt, P. 1987. "Light in Sophocles' *Trachiniae*." *Cl. Ant.* 6: 205–17.

———. 1989. "The End of the *Trachiniae* and the Fate of Herakles." *JHS* 109: 69–80.

Hoppin, M. C. 1990. "Metrical Effects, Dramatic Illusion, and the Two Endings of Sophocles' *Philoctetes*." *Arethusa* 23: 141–82.

Humphreys, S. A. 1978. "Public and Private in Classical Athens." *CJ* 73: 97–104.

———. 1986. "Kinship Patterns in the Athenian Courts." *GRBS* 27: 57–91.

Irigaray, L. 1985a. "Any Theory of the 'Subject' Has Always Been Appropriated by the Masculine." In *Speculum of the Other Woman*, trans. Gillian C. Gill, 133–46. Ithaca: Cornell University Press.

———. 1985b. "Women on the Market." In *This Sex Which Is Not One*, trans. Catherine Porter, 170–91. Ithaca: Cornell University Press.

Jameson, M. 1990. "Domestic Space in the Greek City-State." In *Domestic Architecture and the Use of Space*, ed. Susan Kent, 92–113. Cambridge: Cambridge University Press.

Jay, N. 1985. "Sacrifice as Remedy for Having Been Born of Woman." In *Immaculate and Powerful*, ed. C. Atkinson, C. Buchanan, and M. Miles, 283–309. Boston: Gordon Press.

Jebb, R. C., ed. 1887–96. *Sophocles, the Plays and Fragments.* 7 vols. Cambridge: Cambridge University Press.

Jenkins, I. 1983. "Is There Life after Marriage? A Study of the Abduction Motif in Vase Paintings of the Athenian Wedding Ceremony." *BICS* 30: 137–45.

Jost, L. J. 1983. "Antigone's Engagement: A Theme Delayed." *LCM* 8–9: 134–36.

Juffras, D. M. 1991. "Sophocles' *Electra* 973–85 and Tyrannicide." *TAPA* 121: 99–108.

Just, R. 1989. *Women in Athenian Law and Life*. London: Routledge.

Kamerbeek, J. C. 1953. *The Plays of Sophocles*. Vol. 1, *Ajax*. Leiden: E. J. Brill.

———. 1967. *The Plays of Sophocles*. Vol. 4, *Oedipus Tyrannus*. Leiden: E. J. Brill.

———. 1970. *The Plays of Sophocles*. Vol. 2, *Trachiniae*. Leiden: E. J. Brill.

———. 1974. *The Plays of Sophocles*. Vol. 5, *Electra*. Leiden: E. J. Brill.

———. 1978. *The Plays of Sophocles*. Vol. 3, *Antigone*. Leiden: E. J. Brill.

Katz (Arthur), M. 1994. "The Character of Tragedy: Women and the Greek Imagination." *Arethusa* 27: 81–103. Response by D. Sider, pp. 105–9.

Kells, J. H., ed. 1973. Sophocles' *Electra*. Cambridge: Cambridge University Press.

Keuls, E. 1984. "Male-Female Interaction in Fifth-Century Dionysiac Ritual as Shown in Attic Vase Painting." *ZPE* 55: 287–97.

King, H. 1983. "Bound to Bleed: Artemis and Greek Women." In Cameron and Kuhrt 1983, 109–27.

Kirkwood, G. 1965. "Homer and Sophocles' *Ajax*." In *Classical Drama and Its Influence: Essays Presented to H.D.F. Kitto*, ed. M. J. Anderson, 53–70. New York: Barnes & Noble.

Kitzinger, R. 1991. "Why Mourning Becomes Electra." *Cl. Ant.* 10: 298–327.

Knox, B. M. W. 1957. *Oedipus at Thebes.* New Haven: Yale University Press.

———. 1964. *The Heroic Temper.* Berkeley: University of California Press.

———. 1966. "The *Ajax* of Sophocles." In *Sophocles,* ed. T. Woodard, 29–61. Englewood Cliffs, N.J.: Prentice Hall.

Konstan, D. 1994. "Oedipus and His Parents: The Biological Family from Sophocles to Dryden." *Scholia* 3: 3–23.

———. 1996. "Greek Friendship." *AJP* 117: 71–94.

Kraus, C. S. 1991. "Λόγος μέν ἐστ' ἀρχαῖος: Stories and Story-telling in Sophocles' *Trachiniae.*" *TAPA* 121: 75–98.

Lacey, W. K. 1968. *The Family in Classical Greece.* Ithaca: Cornell University Press.

Lattimore, R. 1942. *Themes in Greek and Latin Epitaphs.* Urbana-Champaign: University of Illinois Press.

Lawrence, S. 1978. "The Dramatic Epistemology of Sophocles' *Trachiniae.*" *Phoenix* 32: 288–304.

Ledbetter, G. M. 1991. "Sophocles' *Antigone* 1226–30." *CQ* 41: 26–29.

Lefkowitz, M. 1986. *Women in Greek Myth.* Baltimore: The Johns Hopkins University Press.

Lefkowitz, M., and M. Fant. 1992. *Women's Life in Greece and Rome.* 2d ed. Baltimore: The Johns Hopkins University Press.

Lévi-Strauss, C. 1969. *The Elementary Structures of Kinship.* Boston: Beacon.

Linforth, I. M. 1961. "Antigone and Creon." University of California Publications in Classical Philology 15: 183–260.

———. 1963. "Electra's Day in the Tragedy of Sophocles." *University of California Publications in Classical Philology* 19: 89–126.

Lloyd-Jones, H., and N. G. Wilson, eds. 1990a. *Sophoclis Fabulae.* Oxford: Oxford University Press.

———. 1990b. *Sophoclea.* Oxford: Oxford University Press.

Loraux, N. 1986. "L'Empreinte de Jocaste." *Écrit du temps* 12: 35–54.

———. 1987. *Tragic Ways of Killing a Woman.* Translated by A. Forster. Cambridge, Mass.: Harvard University Press. Originally *Façons tragiques de tuer une femme* (Hachette, 1985).

———. 1993. *The Children of Athena: Athenian Ideas about Citizenship and the Division between the Sexes.* Translated by C. Levine. Princeton: Princeton University Press. Originally *Les Enfants d'Athéna: Idés athéniennes sur la citoyenneté et la division des sexes* (Paris: Editions La Découverte, 1984).

McCall, M. 1972. "*The Trachiniae:* Structure, Focus, and Heracles." *AJP* 93: 142–63.

McDevitt, A. S. 1982. "The First Kommos of Sophocles' *Antigone* (806–822)." *Ramus* 11:134–44.

MacDowell, D. M. 1978. *The Law in Classical Athens.* London: Thames and Hudson.

———. 1989. "The *Oikos* in Athenian Law." *CQ* 39: 10–21.

Macherey, P. 1978. *A Theory of Literary Production.* Translated by G. Wall. London: Routledge and Kegan Paul.

MacKinnon, J. K. 1971. "Heracles' Intention in His Second Request of Hyllus: *Trachiniae* 1216–51." *CQ* 21: 33–41.

McManus, B. F. 1990. "Multicentering: The Case of the Athenian Bride." *Helios* 17: 225–35.

March, J. 1993. "Sophocles' *Ajax*: The Death and Burial of a Hero." *BICS* 38: 1–36.

Mason, H. A. 1963. "The Women of Trachis." *Arion* 2.1: 59–81; 2.2: 105–21.

Miles, G. 1992. "The First Roman Marriage and the Theft of the Sabine Women." In Hexter and Selden 1992, 161–96.

Moore, J. 1977. "The Dissembling-Speech of Ajax." *YClS* 25: 47–66.

Murnaghan, S. 1986. "Antigone 904–20 and the Institution of Marriage." *AJP* 107: 192–207.

Neuberg, M. 1990. "How Like a Woman: Antigone's 'Inconsistency.'" *CQ* 40: 54–76.

Nisetich, F. 1986. "The Silencing of Pylades (*Orestes* 1591–92)." *AJP* 107: 46–54.

North, H. 1977. "The Mare, the Vixen, and the Bee: *Sophrosyne* as the Virtue of Women in Antiquity." *ICS* 2: 35–48.

Nussbaum, M. 1986. *The Fragility of Goodness*. Cambridge: Cambridge University Press.

———. 1994. "Platonic Love and Colorado Law: The Relevance of Ancient Greek Norms to Modern Sexual Controversies." *Virginia Law Review* 80.7: 1515–1651.

Oakley, J., and R. Sinos, 1993. *The Wedding in Ancient Athens*. Madison: University of Wisconsin Press.

O'Brien, M. J., ed. 1968. *Twentieth-Century Interpretations of Oedipus Rex*. Englewood Cliffs, N.J.: Prentice Hall.

Ogden, D. 1996. *Greek Bastardy in the Classical and Hellenistic Periods*. New York: Oxford University Press.

O'Higgins, D. 1993. "Above Rubies: Admetus' Perfect Wife." *Arethusa* 26: 77–97.

Ormand, K. 1993. "*Trachiniae* 1055ff.: More Wedding Imagery." *Mnemosyne* 67: 224–27.

———. 1996a. "Silent by Convention? Sophocles' Tekmessa." *AJP* 117: 37–64.

———. 1996b. Review of J. Oakley and R. Sinos, *The Wedding in Ancient Athens* (Madison: University of Wisconsin Press, 1993). *CPhil.* 91: 80–84.

Ortner, S. B. 1974. "Is Female to Male as Nature Is to Culture?" In *Women, Culture, and Society*, ed. M. Z. Rosaldo and L. Lamphere, pp. 67–88. Stanford, Calif.: Stanford University Press.

Oudemans, T.C.W., and A.P.M.H. Lardinois. 1987. *Tragic Ambiguity*. New York: E. J. Brill.

Padel, R. 1990. "Making Space Speak." In Winkler and Zeitlin 1990, 336–65.

Page, D., ed. 1972. *Aeschyli Tragoediae*. Oxford: Oxford University Press.

Parlavantaza-Friederich, U. 1969. *Täuschungsszenen in den Tragödien des Sophocles*. Berlin.

Patterson, C. 1981. *Pericles' Citizenship Law of 451–50 B.C.* Salem, N.H.: Ayer.

———. 1987. "*Hai Attikai*: The Other Athenians." *Helios* 13: 49–67.

———. 1990. "Those Athenian Bastards." *Cl. Ant.* 9: 40–73.

————. 1991. "Marriage and the Married Woman in Athenian Law." In *Ancient History/Ancient Women*, ed. S. B. Pomeroy, 48–72. Chapel Hill: University of North Carolina Press.

————. 1994. "The Case against Neaira and the Public Ideology of the Athenian Family." In Boegehold and Scafuro 1994, 199–216.

Peek, W. 1988. *Greek Verse Inscriptions*. Chicago: Ares. (An exact reprint of *Griechische Vers-Inschriften* [Berlin, 1955].)

Pelling, C. 1996. "The Urine and the Vine: Astyages' Dreams at Herodotus 1.107–8." *CQ* 46: 68–77.

Peradotto, J. 1977. "Oedipus and Erichthonius: some Observations on Paradigmatic and Syntagmatic Order." *Arethusa* 10: 85–101.

Perkins, C. A. 1996. "Persephone's Lie in the *Homeric Hymn to Demeter*." *Helios* 23: 135–42.

Perrin, B., ed. 1914. *Plutarch's Lives*. Loeb Classical Library. Cambridge, Mass: Harvard University Press.

Petersen, L. H. 1997. "Divided Consciousness and Female Companionship: Reconstructing Female Subjectivity on Greek Vases." *Arethusa* 30: 35–74.

Pickard-Cambridge, A. 1968. *The Dramatic Festivals of Athens*. 2d ed. Revised by J. Gould and D. M. Lewis. Oxford: Oxford University Press.

Poe, J. P. 1986. *Genre and Meaning in Sophocles' Ajax*. Hain Verlag: Athenäum.

Pomeroy, S. 1975. *Goddesses, Whores, Wives, and Slaves: Women in Classical Antiquity*. New York: Dorset.

————. 1990. "The Persian King and the Queen Bee." *AJAH* 1990: 98–108.

Powell, A., ed. 1990. *Euripides, Women and Sexuality*. New York: Routledge.

Pozzi, D. C. 1994. "Deianeira's Robe: Diction in Sophocles' *Trachiniae*." *Mnemosyne* 47: 577–85.

Pucci, P. 1977. *Hesiod and the Language of Poetry*. Baltimore and London: The Johns Hopkins University Press.

————. 1992. *Oedipus and the Fabrication of the Father*. Baltimore and London: The Johns Hopkins University Press.

Rabinowitz, N. S. 1986. "Aphrodite and the Audience: Engendering the Reader." *Arethusa* 19: 171–86.

————. 1987. "Female Speech and Female Sexuality: Euripides' *Hippolytos* as a Model." *Helios* 13: 127–40.

————. 1992. "Tragedy and the Politics of Containment." In *Pornography and Representation in Greece and Rome*, ed. A. Richlin, 36–52. New York: Oxford University Press.

————. 1993. *Anxiety Veiled: Euripides and the Traffic in Women*. Ithaca: Cornell University Press.

Radt, S., ed. 1977. *Tragicorum graecorum fragmenta*. Vol. 4. Göttingen: Vandenhoek und Ruprecht.

————. 1985. *Tragicorum graecorum fragmenta*. Vol. 3. Göttingen: Vandenhoek und Ruprecht.

Redfield, J. 1982. "Notes on the Greek Wedding." *Arethusa* 15: 181–201.

Reed, J. 1995. "The Sexuality of Adonis." *Cl. Ant.* 14: 317–47.

Rehm, R. 1994. *Marriage to Death.* Princeton: Princeton University Press.

Reinhardt, K. 1979. *Sophocles.* Translated by H. Harvey and D. Harvey. New York: Barnes and Noble.

Rennie, W., ed. 1921. *Demosthenes' Orationes.* Vol. 2. Oxford: Oxford University Press.

———, ed. 1931. *Demosthenes' Orationes.* Vol. 3. Oxford: Oxford University Press.

Richardson, N., ed. 1974. *The Homeric Hymn to Demeter.* Oxford: Oxford University Press.

Roberts, D. H. 1987. "Parting Words: Final Lines in Sophocles and Euripides." *CQ* 37: 51–64.

———. 1988. "Sophoclean Endings: Another Story." *Arethusa* 21: 177–96.

———. 1989. "Different Stories: Sophoclean Narrative(s) in the *Philoctetes.*" *TAPA* 119: 161–76.

Rosaldo, M. Z. 1974. "Women, Culture, and Society: A Theoretical Overview." In *Women, Culture, and Society,* ed. M. Z. Rosaldo and L. Lamphere, 17–42. Stanford, Calif.: Stanford University Press.

Rose, P. 1992. *Sons of the Gods, Children of Earth: Ideology and Literary Form in Ancient Greece.* Ithaca: Cornell University Press.

———. 1995. "Historicizing Sophocles' *Ajax.*" In *History, Tragedy, Theory,* ed. B. Goff, 59–90. Austin: University of Texas Press.

Roussel, P. 1922. "Les fiançailles d'Haimon et d'Antigone." *Rev. Ét. Grec.* 25: 63–81.

Rubin, G. 1975. "The Traffic in Women: Notes on the 'Political Economy' of Sex." In *Towards an Anthropology of Women,* ed. R. Reiter, 157–210. New York: Monthly Review Press.

Scafuro, A. 1994. "Witnessing and False Witnessing: Proving Citizenship and Kin Identity in Fourth-Century Athens." In Boegehold and Scafuro 1994, 156–98.

Scaife, R. 1995. "Ritual and Persuasion in the House of Ischomachus." *CJ* 90: 225–32.

Schaps, D. M. 1977. "The Woman Least Mentioned: Etiquette and Women's Names." *CQ* 27: 323–30.

———. 1979. *Economic Rights of Women in Ancient Greece.* Edinburgh: Edinburgh University Press.

Scodel, R. 1984. *Sophocles.* Boston: Twayne.

Seaford, R. 1981. "Dionysiac Drama and Dionysiac Mysteries." *CQ* 31: 252–75.

———. 1985. "The Destruction of Limits in Sophocles' *Electra.*" *CQ* 32: 315–23.

———. 1986. "Wedding Ritual and Textual Criticism in Sophocles' 'Women of Trachis.'" *Hermes* 114: 50–59.

———. 1987. "The Tragic Wedding." *JHS* 107: 106–30.

———. 1990a. "The Imprisonment of Women in Greek Tragedy." *JHS* 100: 76–90.

———. 1990b. "The Structural Problems of Marriage in Euripides." In Powell 1990, 151–76.

———. 1994. *Reciprocity and Ritual: Homer and Tragedy in the Developing Greek City-State.* New York: Oxford University Press.

Sealey, R. 1990. *Women and Law in Classical Greece.* Chapel Hill: University of North Carolina Press.

Sedgwick, E. Kosofsky. 1985. *Between Men: English Literature and Male Homosocial Desire*. New York: Columbia University Press.

Segal, C. 1964. "Sophocles' Praise of Man and the Conflicts of the *Antigone*." *Arion* 3: 46–66.

———. 1966. "The *Electra* of Sophocles." *TAPA* 97: 473–545.

———. 1975. "Mariage et sacrifice dans les Trachiniennes de Sophocle." *L'Antiquité classique* 44: 30–53.

———. 1977. "Sophocles' *Trachiniae*: Myth, Poetry and Heroic Values." *YClS* 25: 99–158.

———. 1978. "Sophocles' *Antigone*: The House and the Cave." In *Miscellanea di Studi in Memoria di Marino Barchiesi*, 1171–88. Rome: Edizioni dell' Ateneo & Bizzarri.

———. 1981. *Tragedy and Civilization: An Interpretation of Sophocles*. Cambridge, Mass.: Harvard University Press.

———. 1992. "Time, Oracles, and Marriage in the *Trachiniae*." *Lexis* 9–10: 63–91. Reprinted in Segal 1995, 69–94.

———. 1995. *Sophocles' Tragic World*. Cambridge, Mass.: Harvard University Press.

Sicherl, M. 1977. "The Tragic Issue in Sophocles' *Ajax*." *YClS* 25: 67–98.

Sider, D. 1994. Response to M. Katz 1994. *Arethusa* 27: 105–9.

Smith, P. 1988. *Discerning the Subject*. Minneapolis: University of Minnesota Press.

Solmsen, F., ed. 1990. *Hesiodi Theogonia, Opera et dies, Scutum*. Oxford: Oxford University Press.

Sorum, C. E. 1978. "Monsters and the Family: The Exodos of Sophocles' *Trachiniae*." *GRBS* 19: 59–73.

———. 1982. "The Family in Sophocles' *Antigone* and *Electra*." *Classical World* 75: 201–11.

Sourvinou-Inwood, C. 1983. "The Young Abductor of the Locrian Pinakes." *BICS* 20: 12–21.

———. 1987. "A Series of Erotic Pursuits: Images and Meanings." *JHS* 107: 131–54.

———. 1989a. "Assumptions and the Creation of Meaning: Reading Sophocles' *Antigone*." *JHS* 109: 134–48.

———. 1989b. "The Fourth Stasimon of Sophocles' *Antigone*." *BICS* 36: 141–65.

Stanford, W. B. 1965. *The Odyssey of Homer*. 2d ed. New York: St. Martin's Press.

———. 1981. *Sophocles' Ajax*. Bristol: Bristol Classical Press.

Steiner, G. 1984. *Antigones*. Oxford: Oxford University Press.

Stevens, P. T. 1986. "Ajax in the *Trugrede*." *CQ* 36: 327–36.

Stigers (Stehle), E. 1981. "Sappho's Private World." In *Reflections of Women in Antiquity*, ed. H. Foley, 45–62. New York: Gordon and Break.

Stinton, T.C.W. 1976. "Notes on Greek Tragedy, I." *JHS* 96: 121–45.

Sutton Jr., R. 1981. *"The Interaction between Men and Women Portrayed on Attic Red-Figure Pottery."* Diss., University of North Carolina.

Suzuki, M. 1989. *Metamorphoses of Helen: Authority, Difference, and the Epic*. Ithaca: Cornell University Press.

Taplin, O. 1977. *The Stagecraft of Aeschylus: The Dramatic Use of Exits and Entrances in Greek Tragedy.* Oxford: Oxford University Press.

———. 1978. *Greek Tragedy in Action.* Berkeley: University of California Press.

———. 1979. "Yielding to Forethought: Sophocles' *Ajax.*" In *Arktouros: Hellenic Studies Presented to Bernard M. W. Knox,* 122–30. Berlin: de Gruyter.

———. 1984. "The Place of Antigone." *Omnibus* 7: 13–16.

Tyrrell, W. 1984. *Amazons: A Study in Athenian Mythmaking.* Baltimore: The Johns Hopkins University Press.

Tyrrell, W., and F. Brown, 1991. *Athenian Myths and Institutions: Words in Action.* New York: Oxford University Press.

Vernant, J. P. 1980. "Marriage." In *Myth and Society in Ancient Greece,* trans. J. Lloyd, 45–70. Princeton, N.J.: Humanities Press. Originally published as *Mythe et société en Grèce ancienne* (Paris: Editions Maspero, 1974).

———. 1981. (With P. Vidal-Naquet.) *Tragedy and Myth in Ancient Greece.* Translated by J. Lloyd. Princeton, N.J.: Humanities Press. Originally published as *Mythe et tragoedie en Grèce ancienne* (Paris: Editions Maspero, 1972).

———. 1982. "From Oedipus to Periander: Lameness, Tyranny, Incest in Legend and History." Translated by P. duBois. *Arethusa* 15: 19–38.

———. 1983. "Hestia-Hermes: The Religious Expression of Space and Movement in Ancient Greece." In *Myth and Thought among the Greeks,* trans. J. Lloyd, 127–75. London: Routledge and Kegan Paul. Originally published as *Mythe et pensée chez les Grecs* (Paris: Editions Maspero, 1965).

von Fritz, K. 1934. "Haimons Liebe zu Antigone." *Philologus* 89: 19–33.

Walker, S. 1983. "Women and Housing in Classical Greece: The Archaeological Evidence." In Cameron and Kuhrt 1983, 81–90.

Wender, D. 1974. "The Will of Beast: Sexual Imagery in the *Trachiniae.*" *Ramus* 3: 1–17.

West, M. L. 1963. "The Oxyrhynchus Papyri 28 ed. Lobel." *Gnomon* 35: 752–59.

West, M. L., and R. Merkelbach, eds. 1967. *Fragmenta Hesiodea.* London: Oxford University Press.

———, eds. 1990. *Hesiodi opera.* New York: Oxford University Press.

Whitlock-Blundell, M. 1992. Review of Ahl 1991. *CJ* 87: 299–301.

Whitman, C. 1951. *Sophocles: A Study of Heroic Humanism.* Cambridge, Mass.: Harvard University Press.

Wiersma, S. 1984. "Women in Sophocles." *Mnemosyne* 37: 25–55.

Wigodsky, M. 1962. "The 'Salvation' of Ajax." *Hermes* 90: 149–58.

Williams, R. 1978. *Marxism and Literature.* Oxford: Oxford University Press.

Wiltshire, S. F. 1976. "Antigone's Disobedience." *Arethusa* 9: 29–36.

Winkler, J. 1990a. *The Constraints of Desire.* New York: Routledge.

———. 1990b. "The Ephebes' Song: *Tragôidia* and *Polis.*" In Winkler and Zeitlin 1990, 20–62. Originally published in *Representations* 11 (1985): 26–62.

Winkler, J., and F. Zeitlin, eds. 1990. *Nothing to Do with Dionysus?* Princeton, N.J.: Princeton University Press.

Winnington-Ingram, R. P. 1980. *Sophocles: An Interpretation*. New York: Cambridge University Press.

———. 1982. "Sophocles and Women." *Fondation Hardt Entretiens* 29: 233–49.

Wohl, V. 1998. *Intimate Commerce: Exchange, Gender, and Subjectivity in Greek Tragedy*. Austin: University of Texas Press.

Wolff, H. J. 1944. "Marriage Law and Family Organization in Ancient Athens: A Study of the Interrelation of Public and Private Law in the Greek City." *Traditio* 2: 43–95.

Woodard, T. 1966. "The *Electra* of Sophocles." In *Sophocles*, ed. T. Woodard, 125–45. Englewood Cliffs, N.J.: Prentice-Hall.

Wyckoff, E., trans. 1954. *Antigone*. In *Sophocles I*, ed. D. Grene and R. Lattimore. Chicago: University of Chicago Press.

Zeitlin, F. 1978. "The Dynamics of Misogyny: Myth and Mythmaking in the *Oresteia*." *Arethusa* 11: 149–84.

———. 1981. "Travesties of Gender and Genre in Aristophanes' *Thesmophoriazusae*." In *Reflections of Women in Antiquity*, ed. H. Foley, 169–218. New York: Gordon and Break.

———. 1982. "Cultic Modes of the Female: Rites of Dionysus and Demeter." *Arethusa* 15: 129–57.

———. 1990a. "Playing the Other: Theater, Theatricality, and the Feminine in Greek Drama." In Winkler and Zeitlin 1990, 63–96. Originally published in *Representations* 11 (1985): 63–94.

———. 1990b. "Thebes: Theater of Self and Society in Athenian Drama." In Winkler and Zeitlin 1990: 130–67.

———. 1992. "The Politics of Eros in the Danaid Trilogy of Aeschylus." In Hexter and Selden 1992, 203–52.

Zizek, S. 1989. *The Sublime Object of Ideology*. London: Verso.

INDEX

abduction in marriage, 31, 36, 45
accessibility of wives, 4, 20. *See also*
  seclusion
Achelous, 15, 37, 38, 39, 40, 42, 44,
  45, 56
Achilles, 113, 186 n.18
adelphos, meaning "from womb," 85,
  86. *See also autadelphos*
Admetus, 19
Aegisthus, 34, 61, 65, 67, 69, 72, 73, 74,
  75, 76, 77, 153; as stepfather, 63, 64
Aelianus, 62
Aeschylus, 18, 63; marriage in, 6, 7, 33,
  34, 148, 149; version of Oedipus, 130
Agamemnon, 27, 28, 64, 75, 169 n.65,
  176 n.55
Agamemnon, in *Agamemnon*, 28; in
  Ajax, 105, 106, 108, 109, 119, 121–123;
  in Euripides' *Electra*, 18; in *Iphigenia at Aulis*, 53; in Sophocles' *Electra*, 63, 65, 66, 67, 70, 71, 73, 74, 76,
  77, 158
agriculture, beginning of, 88; as image

of marriage, 21, 49, 138–140, 148,
  164 n.24. *See also* fields, cultivated;
  furrows
Ahl, F., 191 n.12
Ajax, 14; date of, 7
Ajax, 104–123 *passim*, 149, 158–159; as
  Athenian, 104–105; burial of, 121–123;
  as father, 111, 115–116; as *gnesios*, 105–
  108; as husband, 110–119
Alcestis, 19, 119, 170 n.100, 171 n.102,
  189 n.53, 190 n.70
Alcestis, 25, 119, 171 n.102
Alcibiades, 22
Alcmene, 177 n.76
alektros, 62, 68, 69, 70. *See also*
  nonmarriage
Alexiou, M., 118, 121
alienation, bride's in marriage, 24, 42,
  59, 114, 154; of Antigone, 93–95, 102;
  of Deianeira, 39, 41, 42, 44, 55, 59; of
  Electra, 72, 77
Althusser, L., 1, 129, 130, 135, 163 n.1,
  172 n.125

Anacreon, 90
anakalupteria, 9, 59, 149. *See also* wedding ritual
anchisteia, 73, 85, 92. *See also* inheritance, laws regarding
Andromache, 189 n.54
Andromache, 113–116
Antigone, 4, 25, 79–103 *passim*, 117
Antigone, 79–103 *passim*; as bride of death, 25, 65, 79, 90–98; as bride of Haemon, 81–86, 89–90; as daughter, 18, 95–98; as disruptive, 34, 90–98, 121; as *epikleros*, 92, 96–98, 102, 183 n.46; as subversive, 14, 16, 85–86, 102; as unfulfilled, 90–98, 154–155, 158–159
anumpheia, 67
anumpheutos, 101
anumphos, 69
Aphrodite, 33, 34, 40, 45, 148, 149
Apollo, 144
Apollodorus, 10–12, 134, 166 n.7
Ares, 100
aristocratic ideology, 104, 106, 108, 109, 112, 122–123, 190 n.69. *See also* class, production of
Aristotle, 187 n.25
arkteia, 19
Armstrong, D., 41
arranged marriages, 19
Artemidorus, 145, 176 n.61, 193 n.73
Artemis, 65, 66, 67, 113, 178 n.18, 179 n.22
Astyages, 71, 180 n.42
Astyanax, 116
Athena, compared to Artemis, 66
Athenaion Politeia of Aristotle, 109
autadelphos, 86. *See also adelphos*
autochthony, 88, 104, 105, 166 n.9

bedmate, opposed to bride, 82, 113
biological relationships. *See* identity, biological
birth, aristocratic. *See* aristocratic ideology

birth without women, 57
blindness of bride at marriage, 44
bloodline, women's threat to, 21–22. *See also epikleros*; fidelity; loyalty
Boegehold, A., 164 n.17, 165 n.3
Bowman, L., 179 n.35
bride-price, 170 n.85
Briseis, 112, 113, 186 n.18
Burkert, W., 66

Calder, W., III, 77, 182 n.13
cargo, bride as, 175 n.52. *See also* object of exchange, bride as
Cassandra, 25
chastity. *See* fidelity
cheir' epi karpo, 29
chera, 117. *See also* widows
Choephoroi, 63, 70–71
Chrysothemis, 61, 63, 64, 73, 74
Cithaeron, 132, 139, 140
citizenship, Athenian, 181 n.8, 190 n.7; production of, 105, 192 n.41; proof of, 12, 137; requirements for, 104, 132; of Tecmessa, 110; threats to, 33; in tragedy, 13; of women, 4, 11, 12, 14, 74, 82, 152, 166 n.13, 166 n.16. *See also* Pericles' citizenship law
civilization, bride as threat to, 90; foundation of, 86–89; marriage and, 138, 139; marriage as, 20, 21; women's role in, 89
class, production of, 113, 122, 123, 133, 134, 187 n.29. *See also* aristocratic ideology
Cleopatra (of Greek myth), 98, 100–102, 185 n.84
closure, lack of, 78, 152, 156–157, 160, 161
Clytemnestra, 14; as active, 27–28; in *Agamemnon*, 27–28, 75, 176 n.55; in Sophocles' *Electra*, 60–78 *passim*, 148; as threat to men, 16, 50, 69, 74, 75, 78; as unmarried, 61, 68–72, 78
Cole, S., 166 n.16
contract, marriage as, 14–15

Creon, in *Antigone* 35, 79–98, 100, 102, 159; as father, 80–86, 159; as king, 147–152; in *Oedipus tyrannus*, 142, 147–152; relation to Oedipus, 142–143, 146–152
Creusa, 101

Danae in *Antigone*, 98–100
Danaids, 18, 25, 33, 34, 170 n.92
Dean-Jones, L., 168 n.64, 171 n.105, 172 n.125
death, of heroes, 159; as marriage, 25, 79, 80, 94, 97, 102, 153, 154, 171 n.104; in marriage, 111; marriage as, 98, 154; marriage to, 25, 26, 91–98; of wives, 159
Deianeira, 25, 27, 36–59 *passim*, 174 n.25; as object of exchange, 15, 16, 37, 41–43, 49, 51–53, 56, 57, 59; as seducible, 14, 51–55; as subject, 2, 35, 36, 44–45, 46, 50, 54–55, 59, 174 n.39, 175 n.51, 175 n.52, 176 n.54; as tablet, 7, 52–54; wedding of, 38–42
deltos, 52, 53. *See also* tablets
Demeter, 26, 31, 32, 34, 148
Demosthenes, 82
Demosthenes' *Against Neaira*, 10–12, 14, 134; *De falsa legatione*, 182 n.13
Derridean theory, 190 n.6
desire, bride's, 29, 32, 34; Deianeira's, 50, 57; feminine, 168 n.64; Heracles', 45–49; heterosexual, 37, 44, 45, 47, 49, 51, 54, 90; male homosocial, 14–18, 37, 40, 45, 48, 49, 55; for marriage, 34; masculine, 168 n.64; mutual, 4, 30; women's, 6, 15, 16, 28, 30, 34, 175 n.53
Detienne, M., 33
Devereux, G., 71, 179 n.36, 180 n.42
difference, 88, 134, 135, 138, 144
Diodorus, 100
Dionysus, 99
displacement, 125, 127, 131, 132, 133, 135, 136, 138, 142, 147, 149, 150

Dougherty, C., 168 n.63
dowry, 17, 22, 23, 30, 34, 169 n.79, 170 n.85
dramatic conventions, 121, 158, 188 n.53. *See also* three-actor rule
dreams, 72, 144, 145, 179 n.35; Clytemnestra's, 70–72, 74; modes of interpreting, 145–146
duBois, P., 4, 6, 7, 50–51, 53, 57, 124, 141

Easterling, P., 54
economic transaction, marriage as, 5, 17, 18, 22, 23, 46, 49. *See also* exchange, marriage as; male homosocial economy
economy, male homosocial. *See* male homosocial economy
Electra, desiring marriage, 73–75, 153, 157–158; as disruptive, 14, 16, 34, 75–78; as *epikleros*, 72–75, 76, 77, 78; in Euripides' *Electra*, 18; in Sophocles' *Electra*, 60–78 *passim*, 148; as unmarried, 18, 62–68, 92, 94, 157–158
endogamy, 3, 13, 58, 59, 67, 69, 72, 75, 76, 78, 96, 98, 104, 183 n.54, 184 n.76, 186 n.17
engyesis, 165 n.1
ephebe, 168 n.57
epikleros, 3, 17, 18, 32, 101, 151, 167 n.42, 167 n.43, 168 n.49; Antigone as, 92, 96–98, 102, 183 n.46; Electra as, 62, 72–75, 76, 77, 78, 180 n.46; Jocasta analogous to, 143
Erechtheids, 186 n.6
Erechtheus, 101, 105
Eriboia, 116
Eros, 48, 120–121; in marriage, 90–91
esthlos, 123. *See also* aristocratic ideology; class, production of
Eumenides, 70
Euripides, 6, 16, 18, 33, 53, 164 n.25; marriage in, 7
Europa, 26
Eurydice, 25, 153, 159–161, 182 n.12

Eurysakes, 107, 115, 116, 118, 119, 120, 122, 123

Eurystheus, 56

Eurytus, 47, 48, 52

Evans-Grubbs, J., 29, 31

excess, women as, 193 n.66

exchange, marriage as, 13, 23, 27, 28, 30, 37, 46, 48, 49, 51, 59, 84, 116, 119, 174 n.39. *See also* economic transaction, marriage as; male homosocial economy

exogamy, 69, 98, 184 n.76, 186 n.17

Faraone, Chris, 32

father–daughter relation, 18, 60, 61, 66, 67, 69, 150, 158

fatherland, husband as, 114

father's name, 129

father–son relation, 57, 81, 82, 83, 84, 92, 102, 115, 116, 177 n.86

fear of marriage, bride's 38, 39–40, 42

feet, Oedipus's, 146

fertility, 138; cosmic, 148–149, 152; of land, 139; women's, 71–72, 76, 138–141

fidelity, of bride, 29, 30, 31, 53, 57; of husband, 66; of wife after marriage, 4, 62, 66, 134

fields, cultivated as image of bride, 20, 21, 26, 42, 43, 89, 139, 140, 141; uncultivated as image of bride, 6, 20, 34. *See also* agriculture; furrows

Finkelstein, N., 179 n.34

flowers, as image of bride, 26, 43

Foley, H., 58, 171 n.102, 184 n.66, 186 n.17

foreigners, women as, 20, 95, 103

foreign women, as brides, 19; as threat, 11, 102

Fowler, B., 97

Foxhall, L., 18, 22

Freud, S., 124–126, 144, 146

funerary ritual, 121, 123

Furies, 68, 70

furrows, as image of bride, 4, 6, 7, 141. *See also* agriculture; fields

Garland, R., 169 n.76

gender reversal, 56, 59, 96, 149, 177 n.89, 177 n.90

Girard, R., 173 n.5

gnesios, 14, 108, 117, 134, 188 n.41. *See also* legitimacy; *nothos*

Goheen, R., 89

golden age, end of, 88–89

Goodhart, S., 126–127, 131

Gould, J. P., 75

Grene, D., 144

guardian, 63, 68, 78. *See also kurios*

gune, meaning "wife," 10, 19, 26, 65, 113, 118, 119, 187 n.24, 188 n.48

Hades, 26, 31, 92, 95. *See also* death

Haemon, as bridegroom, 79, 80, 90, 102; death of, 101, 159–160; marriage of, 18, 19, 92, 98, 154–155; as son, 80, 81, 84, 85, 97, 159–160

hailing. *See* interpellation

harbor, as image of bride, 139–141

Harmodius and Aristogeiton, 75

hearth, 71, 72, 74, 166 n.22. *See also* Hestia

Hector, 113–116

hedna. See bride-price

Helen, 18, 106

Helen of Euripides, 168 n.55

Helios, 159

Henderson, Jeffrey, 52

Hera, 56, 177 n.76

Heracles, in *Alcestis*, 19; as bride, 36, 58–59, 147, 149; as father, 57–58; relations with men, 15, 39–41, 44–49, 51, 54; in *Trachiniae*, 2, 15, 25, 35, 36–59 *passim*, 82, 85, 89, 155, 156, 174 n.25, 174 n.39, 175 n.52, 176 n.54, 177 n.76; view of marriage, 43, 44–49, 82, 85

Herodotus, 71, 97, 145, 146, 175 n.45, 180 n.42

Hesiod, 82–83, 88, 89, 134, 182 n.28, 182 n.29

Hesione, 107, 109, 113, 187 n.29

Hester, D. A., 181 n.3

Hestia, 12, 13, 14, 17, 67, 69, 78, 96, 97, 166 n.22, 178 n.21, 180 n.43. *See also* hearth

Hippias, dream of, 145–146, 193 n.73

Hippolytus, 7, 15–16, 53, 164 n.25

Hippolytus, 7, 15–16

Homeric Hymn to Demeter, 31–32, 186 n.17

homeunetis, 113. *See also* bedmate

horses, as image of bride, 89, 90

hubris, 132

Humphreys, S., 167 n.31

hunting as image of marriage, 91

Hyllus, 2, 15, 25, 36, 38, 54, 56, 57, 58, 155, 177 n.79

Hypermestra, 33, 34

identity, biological, 124, 125, 126, 128, 131, 132, 133, 135, 138, 141, 142, 150, 151; legal, 133, 137; political, 143; production of, 2, 127–132, 135, 136, 137, 138, 140, 142–146, 149; social, 132, 142, 150, 151, 152; women's change of, 19

ideological state apparatus, 1

ideology, of citizenship, 104; definition of, 1–2, 163 n.1, 163 n.7; of marriage, 13, 17, 29, 34, 59, 61, 125, 141; marriage as, 1, 2, 138–139; of subjects, 129, 130, 131, 152, 172 n.125; in tragedy, 25, 80, 191 n.23; tragedy as, 5, 59, 62, 126, 138

Iliad, 113–116, 186 n.18

illegitimacy, 133, 134. *See also* legitimacy; *nothos*

incest, 58, 125, 129, 131, 134, 135, 136, 138, 141, 145, 146

infidelity, 21; of Clytemnestra, 69

inheritance, disputes about, 12, 192 n.41; laws regarding, 17, 85, 107, 118, 149, 168 n.43; as sign of legitimacy, 132; in tragedies, 69, 73–74, 76, 143, 158. *See also anchisteia*

Intaphernes' wife, 97

interpellation, 1–2, 110, 129

Io, 26

Iole, 36, 37, 38, 44, 45–49, 58, 174 n.39, 175 n.51

Ion, 101, 189 n.54

Iphigenia, 25, 26, 53, 64, 65, 84

Iphigenia among the Taurians, 189 n.53, 189 n.54

Iphigenia at Aulis, 53, 173 n.13

Iphitus, 48, 49

Isaeus, 17, 82, 92, 192 n.41

Ismene, 79, 82, 84

isolation of bride, 43, 56, 95, 98. *See also* alienation

Jameson, M., 166 n.22

Jebb, R. C., 114, 144

Jocasta, 85; analogous to *epikleros*, 143; death of, 155–156, 157, 158, 159; embodying excess, 142–146, 157; as furrow, 141; as harbor, 140, 141; in *Oedipus tyrannus*, 124, 125, 126, 134, 140, 141, 142–146, 155–156, 157, 158, 159, 193 n.61

Juffras, D. M., 73

Just, R., 168 n.49

Kamerbeek, J. C., 54, 85, 144, 183 n.36

King, H., 168 n.64

Kitzinger, R., 61, 77, 178 n.1, 180 n.62

Knox, B. M. W., 133, 190 n.10

Konstan, D., 169 n.80, 181 n.9, 182 n.15

kore, 10, 19, 65

Kore, as name for Persephone, 183 n.54

koureion, 19

Kraus, C. S., 194 n.6

kurios, 10, 17, 19, 96, 150, 163 n.9, 168 n.60, 181 n.11, 194 n.86. *See also* guardian

labor pangs, 45

Lacan, J., 124

Lacanian theory, 190 n.6, 191 n.30

Laertes, 105

Laius, 124, 125, 126, 127, 130, 133, 142, 151, 156; relation to Oedipus, 137, 143, 144, 146

lament, Antigone's, 91, 93–95; Electra's, 60, 61, 64, 67, 76, 77, 158, 178 n.1, 179 n.24; Eurydice's, 159, 161; Tecmessa's, 117–118, 121; women's right to, 118, 120, 123

law of the father, 58, 192 n.39

lechos, 91, 160. See also marriage bed

legitimacy, as citizen, 11, 13, 14, 109; of marriage, 12, 13, 116–119, 122; Oedipus', 133–135, 137, 138; of child, 104, 105, 109, 116, 133–135, 137, 138; political, 143. See also *gnesios*; *nothos*

Levi-Strauss, C., 173 n.4; 190 n.5

Lichas, 45, 47, 48, 174 n.39, 174 n.40, 175 n.44

Linforth, I. M., 77

Lloyd-Jones, H., 139, 159–160, 183 n.36

Loraux, N., 25, 42, 105, 153, 166 n.9, 171 n.104, 193 n.59, 193 n.61

loyalty, bride's divided, 16, 17, 24, 75, 92; bride's to father, 18, 64, 65, 75, 95, 98; bride's to husband, 35; daughter's to father, 70, 76; son's to father, 79–80

Lycurgus, 98, 100

Lysistrata, 172 n.142

MacDowell, D., 168 n.49

male homosocial economy, 16, 18, 48, 49, 52, 54, 55, 56, 57, 59, 84, 85, 111, 116, 119, 177 n.74. See also economic transaction, marriage as; exchange, marriage as; male–male relations

male–male relations, 46, 47, 49, 50–51, 55, 58, 110, 123, 144. See also male homosocial economy

marriage bed, 38, 42, 55, 63, 91, 140, 143, 155, 157, 160, 161, 194 n.9. See also *lechos*

Marxist theory, 1, 190 n.6. See also ideology; interpellation

matricide, 70, 76, 178 n.2

matrikin, 167 n.31

matrilineage, 72, 84, 85, 86, 92, 97, 98, 102, 143

McManus, B., 28, 30, 171 n.123

Medea, 42

Medea, 16, 19, 24, 50; as bride, 23

Megareus, 159–160

Menelaos, in *Ajax*, 105, 106, 120, 122; in Sophocles' *Electra*, 65

men's role in marriage, 19, 21

Merope, 132, 136

metoikos, 94–95, 101, 102

mimetic desire, 173 n.5

Murnaghan, S., 96–97

naming, function of, 130, 131, 135, 137

Neaira, 10–12, 14, 134, 166 n.7

Nessus, 38, 41, 45, 50, 51–54, 56, 57

Neuberg, M., 95

Niobe, 75, 154

Nisetich, F., 189 n.54

nonmarriage, 101; Clytemnestra's, 68–72, 74; death as, 93, 95, 96; Electra's, 62–68, 77. See also *alektros*

nothos, 25, 107–110, 112, 117, 122, 123, 134, 135, 186 n.12, 188 n.41, 188 n.44. See also *gnesios*; legitimacy

Oakley, J., 165 n.2

Ode on Man, 86–90

Odysseus, 105, 119, 122, 123

Odyssey, 129, 188 n.44

Oedipus, 64, 124–152 *passim*, 153, 155–156, 157, 178 n.12; birth of, 132–138; as bride, 147–152; as father, 150–152; identity of, 127–138; as interpellated subject, 129–131; as polluted, 147–152; relation to Laius, 143–144, 146

Oedipus at Colonus, 189 n.54, 194 n.2, 194 n.84

Oedipus complex, 124–126

O'Higgins, D., 190 n.70

Oikonomikos of Xenophon, 169 n.72, 170 n.100
Oineus, 15, 37, 55
Omphale, 48, 49, 174 n.40, 175 n.44
oracles, 52, 54, 130, 131, 133, 135, 137, 138, 144, 145
Orestes, 189 n.54
Orestes, in Clytemnestra's dream, 70–72; death of, 72–75; in Euripides' *Electra*, 18; return of, 63, 75–78; in Sophocles' *Electra*, 60, 63, 69, 70–78 *passim*
ostentation, restrictions on, 121
outsiders, women as, 10, 12, 16, 19. *See also* foreigners, women as

Pandora, 88, 89
parankalisma (embrace), 82
parody of wedding, 36, 56, 59, 149, 150
parricide, 129, 134, 136, 146, 151
parthenos, 10, 19, 21, 26, 27, 59, 64, 65, 90, 91–95, 99, 139, 147, 148, 149, 185 n.88
patrilineage, 69, 70, 71, 73, 74, 75, 76, 84, 85, 92, 96, 116, 151, 168 n.46, 182 n.21
patrouchos, 167 n.42
Patterson, C., 4, 10, 11, 12, 24–25, 107, 109, 164 n.17, 166 n.5, 166 n.7, 166 n.9, 168 n.43, 181 n.8
Peleus, 26
Penelope, 26
Peradotto, J., 175 n.42
Pericles, ancestry of, 107, 186 n.17
Pericles' citizenship law, 4, 7, 10, 11, 13, 20, 24–25, 102, 107, 109, 164 n.17, 165 n.3, 166 n.5, 170 n.86, 181 n.8. *See also* citizenship
Pericles' funeral oration, 180 n.51
Persephone, 25, 26, 31, 32, 94, 95
Petersen, L. H., 171 n.109
Phaedra, 7, 15–16, 33, 53
Phano, 166 n.7

philia, 81, 148, 181 n.9. *See also philos*
Philoctetes, 180 n.69
Philomela, 46
philos, 81, 83, 92, 118, 122. *See also philia*
Phineidos, 100
phratry, 9, 11, 12, 19, 137, 166 n.7, 166 n.10, 166 n.16, 192 n.41
Pickard-Cambridge, A., 189 n.54
plague, in *Oedipus tyrannus*, 127, 138
plastos, 135
Plutarch, 32; *Alcibiades* of, 22
Poe, J. P., 111
poisoning of Heracles, 36, 38, 50, 54, 57, 175 n.52
Politics of Aristotle, 187 n.25
pollution, Oedipus as, 147, 149, 152
Polybus, 132, 136
Polyneices, 84, 86, 90, 92, 96
Pozzi, D., 177 n.89
Procne, 46, 75
Prometheus, 88
proteleia, 26. *See also* sacrifice
psychoanalytic criticism, 124–126
Pucci, P., 88, 190 n.6, 190 n.7, 191 n.30, 193 n.59

Rabinowitz, N. S., 15, 170 n.99, 174 n.32
rape, 15, 45, 51, 52, 66, 68; as marriage, 29, 30; during marriage, 38
Redfield, J., 30, 170 n.94, 179 n.28
Reed, J., 165 n.38, 171 n.109
Rehm, R., 170 n.99, 177 n.91, 181 n.11, 184 n.70
Reinhardt, K., 57, 95
replaceability in marriage, 97, 102
resistance to marriage, bride's, 26, 27, 30, 32, 34, 37, 42
riddle, 126–127, 128, 136, 137; of sphinx, 127, 190 n.10; structure of, 191 n.11
rites of passage, 19, 164 n.27
Rose, P., 163 n.1, 177 n.76, 185 n.5, 186 n.14, 190 n.69
Rubin, G., 37, 173 n.4

sacrifice, 182 n.21; as marriage, 170 n.89; marriage as, 84; self-, 170 n.99; wife's death as, 159. *See also proteleia*
sailing, images of, 139–140
Salamis, 105
Scafuro, A., 12, 166 n.5
scepter, of Agamemnon, 70–72
Scodel, Ruth, 47
Seaford, R., 3, 34, 41, 42, 43, 61, 98, 170 n.87, 178 n.16, 179 n.22, 179 n.24, 184 n.76, 192 n.50
Sealey, R., 12
seclusion of brides, 22, 99, 159, 169 n.76. *See also* accessibility
Sedgwick, E., 15, 37
Segal, C., 50, 58, 60, 69, 75, 77, 84, 87, 94, 172 n.2, 174 n.25, 174 n.32, 177 n.75, 181 n.67, 189 n.61
self-recognition, 129, 140, 141
sexuality, ancient, 149; bride's, 74–75; women's, 73, 84, 92, 98, 99, 100
sexual reproduction, beginning of, 88
sharp stick, poke in eye with, 58
signification, modes of, 145
silence, bride's, 58, 111; Tecmessa's, 119–123; women's in tragedy, 119–123, 147, 153–161
Sinos, R., 165 n.2
Sisyphos, 105
slavery, as erotic, 46, 48, 84; Heracles', 48; tied to birth, 108
slaves, female, 112, 115, 188 n.44
Socrates, 176 n.65
Solon's laws, 32, 118
Sorum, C., 58, 76, 175 n.49, 178 n.7, 181 n.8
Sourvinou-Inwood, C., 86, 91, 171 n.111, 182 n.13
spear-captive, 109, 112, 114, 115, 116, 117
Stanford, W. B., 114
Stephanus, 10–12, 14
stepmother, 100
Stigers, E., 169 n.69, 175 n.48
subjectivity, 1, 5, 130, 152, 163 n.1; An-

tigone's, 80, 95; bride's 5, 15, 27, 61; civic, 33; Deianeira's, 36, 44, 55, 174 n.31, 175 n.51, 175 n.52, 176 n.54; as male, 59; Marxist definition of, 125, 129; men's, 16, 34, 97, 123, 124; Oedipus', 130, 137, 138; Tecmessa's, 110, 122; women's, 6, 12, 16, 18, 26, 33, 57, 59, 109, 119, 160, 173 n.12, 174 n.28; women's erotic, 27, 31, 32, 33, 50, 68, 72, 82, 102; women's in marriage, 6, 28, 34, 37, 62, 72; women's in tragedy, 6, 50; women's legal, 92. *See also* ideology
suggenes, 142
suicide, of women, 153; of wives, 159
suneunos, 82
sunoikein, 10, 165 n.1
Sutton, R., 30, 171 n.111

tablets, as image of bride, 7, 52–54
taming, as marriage, 21, 80, 90, 169 n.69
Taplin, O., 188 n.53
Tecmessa, 14, 110–123 *passim*, 159; legitimacy as wife, 110–119; parallel to Andromache, 113–115; silence of, 119–123
Telamon, 107, 108, 116
telos, marriage as, 153, 155, 158, 159, 161, 173 n.14
Tereus of Sophocles, 33, 42
Teucer, 105–110, 112, 113, 118–123, 159; as *kurios*, 116; as *nothos*, 106–110
thalamos, 9, 64, 65, 66, 67, 93, 154; Antigone's, 94, 97, 102; Danae's, 99
Theogony of Hesiod, 169 n.65
Theseus in *Hippolytus*, 15–16
Thetis, 26
three-actor rule, 119, 189 n.54. *See also* dramatic convention
Tiresias, 132, 134, 137, 139, 140
tooth, as semen, 146
tragic marriages, features of, 5, 23, 24, 26, 29, 30, 34, 38
trophe, 116

Troy, 114
tuche, 132

vases depicting marriage, 29, 30, 34,
171 n.109, 188 n.49, 194 n.82
Vernant, J.-P., 12, 13, 72, 126–127, 163 n.9,
183 n.46
virtue, female, 100
von Fritz, K., 183 n.42

Walker, S., 169 n.76
wedding ritual, 9–10, 14, 41, 84, 166 n.16
Wender, D., 45, 173 n.10
Whitman, C., 142, 193 n.60
widows, 119, 159. *See also chera*
Wilson, N. G., 139, 159–160, 183 n.36
Winkler, J., 171 n.108
Winnington-Ingram, R. P., 67, 70,
185 n.85, 193 n.59
Wohl, V., 55, 173 n.7, 173 n.12, 174 n.28,
174 n.31, 174 n.39, 175 n.51, 175 n.52,
176 n.54, 177 n.79

woman as other, 142, 144, 157
womb, 85, 98, 140
women's experience of marriage, 25–27,
29–31, 34, 41, 142, 147, 153–161
women's role in tragedy, 3, 5, 8
Woodard, T., 61, 76, 178 n.1
Works and Days, 83, 88

Xanthus, 62
xenia (guest privilege), 47
xenia (marriage to a foreigner), trials for,
10–12

yoking, as image of marriage, 46, 89, 99,
169 n.69

Zeitlin, F., 3, 34, 177 n.90
Zeus, 88, 99, 159, 177 n.76
Zizek, S., 2
zoma (girdle), 65

PASSAGE INDEX

Line numbers are in *italics*.

Aeschylus, *Agamemnon*
11, 50
243–245, 64
1387–1392, 27–28

Aeschylus, *fragment 44*
33–34, 148

Anacreon, *fragment 417*
1–3, 90

Artemidorus, *Oneirocritica*
2.45, 176 n.61

[Demosthenes] *Against Neiara (59)*
108, 11
110ff., 33

Euripides, *Hippolytus*
976–978, 16

Euripides, *Medea*
238–240, 11–12
252–258, 23

Hesiod, *Works and Days*
42–46, 88
235, 134
699–703, 83

Homer, *Odyssey*
1.215–216, 137

Homeric Hymn to Demeter
411–413, 23

Isaeus 3
3.17, 32–33

Plato, *Phaedrus*
275d–e, 176 n.65

Plutarch, *Life of Solon*
20.3, 32

Sophocles, *Ajax*
145–146, 112
201–202, 105
211, 112
285–289, 110
292–294, 111
392–393, 111
395–397, 111
489–491, 112
530, 115
550–559, 115
562–563, 116
652, 117
678–682, 122
684–686, 117
861, 105
894–895, 117
903, 117
917–919, 118
923–924, 120
940–941, 117
942, 118
985–987, 119
1012–1016, 108
1093–1096, 106
1168–1169, 120
1169, 119
1199–1205, 120–121
1223–1225, 121
1228, 112
1259–1263, 108
1304, 109
1393, 106

Sophocles, *Antigone*
1, 84
73–75, 92
173–174, 85
192–195, 85
209–210, 86
248, 89
332–352, 86–87
365, 88
376–378, 90

423–425, 91
477–478, 90
511, 85
568, 79
569, 84
571, 82
632–634, 81
635–638, 81
641–647, 83
648–651, 81
755–756, 84
793–797, 91
810–816, 93–94
830, 154
832–833, 154
850–853, 94
866–868, 101
867–868, 95
876–878, 94
891, 93
909–912, 96
917–920, 154
940–941, 85
946–950, 99
970–980, 100
981–982, 101
983–984, 101
1240–1241, 18–19, 97, 154
1251–1252, 160
1303–1305, 159–160

Sophocles, *Electra*
164–166, 63
187–192, 63
190, 64
275–276, 68
352–356, 67
365–367, 72
417–423, 70
459–460, 71
489–494, 68,
516–518, 67, 148
544–545, 65
560–562, 66

563–565, 65
587–590, 69
593–594, 66
959–966, 72–73
970–972, 74
975–983, 74
1105, 73
1143–1145, 66
1183, 64
1209–1211, 76
1448–1449, 76
1508–1510, 77

Sophocles, *Oedipus tyrannus*
25–27, 138
258–263, 143
260, 140
420–423, 139
438, 132
457–460, 134–135
577, 142
742–743, 134
791–793, 135–136
842–845, 127
978, 145
981–982, 144–145
982–983, 146
1016–1021, 136
1025, 133
1031–1036, 130–131
1058–1059, 137
1062–1063, 133
1071–1072, 147, 155–156
1078–1079, 133
1207–1213, 140–141
1242–1247, 156
1249, 156
1255–1257, 140
1403–1404, 138
1424–1429, 147
1436–1437, 129
1492–1502, 150
1503–1507, 150–151

1505–1506, 153
1522, 151
1522–1523, 151

Sophocles, *fragment 583 (from Tereus)*
24, 27, 46

Sophocles, *Trachiniae*
7–8, 38
9–10, 15
20–25, 39, 44, 46
28, 42
31–33, 43, 155
41–42, 45
142–150, 43
252–255, 48
256–257, 48
262–269, 47
325–327, 45
359–362, 47
402–407, 2
465, 46
507–530, 39–40
536–538, 46
548–551, 49
560–563, 41
575–577, 50
682–683, 52
707–710, 51
791, 55
792, 55
911, 54, 155
920–922, 155
924–928, 157
1058–1063, 56
1064–1065, 21, 57
1078, 59
1109–1111, 56
1170–1172, 52
1204–1205, 57
1230–1231, 58
1238–1239, 58